WITHDRAWN

NOTHING IS TRUE AND EVERYTHING IS POSSIBLE

NOTHING IS TRUE AND EVERYTHING IS POSSIBLE

THE SURREAL HEART OF THE NEW RUSSIA

PETER POMERANTSEV

PUBLICAFFAIRS
New York

LONDON PUBLIC LIBRARY

Copyright © 2014 by Peter Pomerantsev.

Published in the United States by PublicAffairs™,
a Member of the Perseus Books Group

All rights reserved.
Printed in the United States of America.

No part of this book may be reproduced in any manner whatsoever without written permission
except in the case of brief quotations embodied in critical articles and reviews. For information,
address PublicAffairs, 250 West 57th Street, 15th Floor, New York, NY 10107.

PublicAffairs books are available at special discounts for bulk purchases in the U.S. by
corporations, institutions, and other organizations. For more information, please contact the
Special Markets Department at the Perseus Books Group, 2300 Chestnut Street, Suite 200,
Philadelphia, PA 19103, call (800) 810-4145, ext. 5000, or e-mail special.markets@
perseusbooks.com.

Many names have been changed throughout the book to protect people.

Book Design by Brent Wilcox

Library of Congress Cataloging-in-Publication Data
Pomerantsev, Peter.
    Nothing is true and everything is possible : the surreal heart of the new Russia / Peter
Pomerantsev.—First edition.
      pages cm
    ISBN 978-1-61039-455-0 (hardcover)—ISBN 978-1-61039-456-7 (electronic)
    1. Russia (Federation)—Social conditions—1991–   2. Russia (Federation)—
History—1991—Biography.   3. Interviews—Russia (Federation) 4. Social change—Russia
(Federation)   5. Social problems—Russia (Federation)   6. Power (Social sciences)—Russia
(Federation)   7. Corruption—Russia (Federation)   8. Authoritarianism—Social aspects—
Russia (Federation)   9. Russia (Federation)—Economic conditions—1991-   I. Title.
    HN530.2.A8P665 2014
    306.0947—dc23
                                                                                      2014018638

First Edition
10 9 8 7 6 5 4 3

For my wife, parents, children, Aunt Sasha, and Paul

CONTENTS

ACT I

REALITY SHOW RUSSIA

Flying in at night over Moscow you can see how the shape of the city is a series of concentric ring-roads with the small ring of the Kremlin at the center. At the end of the twentieth century the light from the rings glowed a dim, dirty yellow. Moscow was a sad satellite at the edge of Europe, emitting the dying embers of the Soviet Empire. Then, in the twenty-first century, something happened: money. Never had so much money flowed into so small a place in so short a time. The orbital system shifted. Up above the city the concentric rings began to shine with the lights of new skyscrapers, neon, and speeding Maybachs on the roads, swirling faster and faster in high-pitched, hypnotic fairground brilliance. The Russians were the new jet set: the richest, the most energetic, the most dangerous. They had the most oil, the most beautiful women, the best parties. From being ready to sell anything, they became ready to buy anything: football clubs in London and basketball clubs in New York; art collections, English newspapers, and European energy companies. No one could understand them. They were both lewd and refined, cunning and naive. Only in Moscow did they make sense, a city living in fast-forward, changing so fast it breaks all sense of reality, where boys become billionaires in the blink of an eye.

"Performance" was the city's buzzword, a world where gangsters become artists, gold diggers quote Pushkin, Hells Angels hallucinate themselves as saints. Russia had seen so many worlds flick through in such blistering progression—from communism to perestroika to shock therapy to penury to oligarchy to mafia state to mega-rich—that its new heroes were left with the sense that life is just one glittering masquerade, where every role and any position or belief is mutable. "I want to try on every persona the world has ever known," Vladik Mamyshev-Monroe would tell me. He was a performance artist and the city's mascot, the inevitable guest at parties attended by the inevitable tycoons and supermodels, arriving dressed as Gorbachev, a fakir, Tutankhamen, the Russian President. When I first landed in Moscow I thought these infinite transformations the expression of a country liberated, pulling on different costumes in a frenzy of freedom, pushing the limits of personality as far as it could possibly go to what the President's vizier would call "the heights of creation." It was only years later that I came to see these endless mutations not as freedom but as forms of delirium, in which scare-puppets and nightmare mystics become convinced they're almost real and march toward what the President's vizier would go on to call the "the fifth world war, the first non-linear war of all against all."

But I am getting ahead of myself.

I work in television. Factual television. Factual entertainment, to be exact. I was flying into Moscow in 2006 because the television industry, like everything else, was booming. I knew the country already: since 2001, the year after I graduated from university, I had been living there most of my time, jumping jobs between think tanks and as a very minor consultant on European Union projects meant to be aiding Russian "development," then at film school, and lately as an assistant on documentaries for Western networks. My parents had emigrated from the Soviet Union to England in the 1970s as political exiles, and I grew up speaking some sort of demotic émigré Russian. But I had always been an observer looking in at Russia. I wanted to get closer: London seemed so measured, so predictable; the America the rest of my émigré family lived in seemed so content; while the real Russians seemed truly alive, had the sense that anything was possible. What I really wanted to do was film. To press "record" and just point and shoot. I took my camera, the battered metal Sony Z1 small enough to always drop in my bag, everywhere. A lot of the time I just filmed so as not to let this world escape; I shot blindly, knowing I would never have a cast like this again. And I was in demand in the new Moscow for the simple reason that I could say the magic words "I am from London." They worked like "open sesame." Russians are convinced Londoners know the alchemical secret of successful television, can distill the next hit reality or talent show. No matter that I had never been more than a third-rate assistant on other people's projects; just by whispering "I come from London" could get me any meeting I wanted. I was a stowaway on the great armada of Western civilization, the bankers, lawyers, international development consultants, accountants, and architects who have sailed out to seek their fortune in the adventures of globalization.

But in Russia, working in television is about more than being a camera, an observer. In a country covering nine time zones, one-sixth of the world's land mass, stretching from the Pacific to the Baltic, from the Arctic to the Central Asian deserts, from near-medieval villages where people still draw water from wooden wells by hand, through single-factory towns and back to the blue glass and steel skyscrapers of the new Moscow—TV is the only force that can unify and rule and bind this country. It's the central mechanism of a new type of authoritarianism, one far subtler than twentieth-century strains. And as a TV producer I would be directed right into the center of its workings.

My first meeting took me to the top floor of Ostankino, the television center the size of five football fields that is the battering ram of Kremlin propaganda. On the top floor, down a series of matt-black corridors, is a long conference room. Here Moscow's flashiest minds met for the weekly brainstorming session to decide what Ostankino would broadcast. I was taken along by a friendly Russian publisher. Due to my Russian surname no one had yet noticed I was British; I kept my mouth shut. There were more than twenty of us in the room: tanned broadcasters in white silk shirts and politics professors with sweaty beards and heavy breath and ad execs in trainers. There were no women. Everyone was smoking. There was so much smoke it made my skin itch.

At the end of the table sat one of the country's most famous political TV presenters. He is small and speaks fast, with a smoky voice:

> We all know there will be no real politics. But we still have to give our viewers the sense something is happening. They need to be kept entertained. So what should we play with? Shall we attack oligarchs? [He continued,] Who's the enemy this week? Politics has got to feel like . . . like a movie!

The first thing the President had done when he came to power in 2000 was to seize control of television. It was television through which the Kremlin decided which politicians it would "allow" as its puppet-opposition, what the country's history and fears and consciousness should be. And the new Kremlin won't make the same mistake the old Soviet Union did: it will never let TV become dull. The task is to synthesize Soviet control with Western entertainment. Twenty-first-century Ostankino mixes show business and propaganda, ratings with authoritarianism. And at the center of the great show is the President himself, created from a no one, a gray fuzz via the power of television, so that he morphs as rapidly as a performance artist among his roles of soldier, lover, bare-chested hunter, businessman, spy, tsar, superman. "The news is the incense by which we bless Putin's actions, make him the President," TV producers and political technologists liked to say. Sitting in that smoky room, I had the sense that reality was somehow malleable, that I was with Prosperos who could project any existence they wanted onto post-Soviet Russia. But with every year I worked in Russia, and as the Kremlin became ever more paranoid, Ostankino's strategies became ever more twisted, the need to incite panic and fear ever more urgent; rationality was tuned out, and Kremlin-friendly cults and hate-mongers were put on prime time to keep the nation en-tranced, distracted, as ever more foreign hirelings would arrive to help the Kremlin and spread its vision to the world.

But though my road would eventually lead back to Ostankino, my initial role in the vast scripted reality show of the new Russia was to help make it look and sound and feel Western. The network I initially worked with was TNT, which is housed in a new office center called Byzantium. On the ground floor is a spa done up in faux Roman style with Doric plaster columns and ruins, frequented by languid, leggy girls here to deepen already deep tans and have endless manicures and pedicures. The manicures are elaborate: rainbow-colored, multilayered, glitter-dusted designs of little hearts and flowers, so much brighter than the girls' bored eyes, as if they pour all their utopias into the tiny spaces of their nails.

The network occupies several floors higher up in the building. When the elevator door opens you're greeted by TNT's logo, designed in blindingly bright, squealingly happy pinks, bright blues, and gold. Over the logo is written the network's catchphrase, "Feel our Love!" This is the new, desperately happy Russia, and this is the image of Russia TNT projects: a youthful, bouncy, glossy country. The network sends a beam of hyperactive yellows and pinks into people's darkling apartments.

The offices are open plan, full of shiny, happy young things hurrying about, sprinkling their Russian with Anglicisms, whistling the tunes of Brit-pop hits. TNT makes hooligan television, and the young staff buzz with the excitement of cultural revolution. For them TNT is a piece of subversive pop art, a way to climb into the nation's psyche and rewire it from inside. The network introduced the reality show to Russia: one raunchy show is—joy of TV producer joys—censured as immoral by aging Communists. TNT pioneered the Russian sitcom and the Russian trashy talk show à la Jerry Springer. The network gobbles up Western concepts one after the other, going through more formats in a year than the West can come up with in a decade. Many of the city's brightest are defecting to entertainment channels and glossy magazines; here they won't be forced to make propaganda, are encouraged to be rebellious. They just can't do real politics here; it's a news-free zone. Most are happy with the trade-off: complete freedom for complete silence.

"We want to find out what the new generation are really thinking. Piiitrrr."

"What excites them, Piiitrrr."

"We want to see real people on screen. The real heroes, Piiitrrr."

"Piiitrrr." That's what the producers at TNT call me. Three women, all in their twenties. One raven haired, one curly haired, and one straight-haired, each picking up the ends of the other's sentences. They could call me by the Russian version of my name, "Piotr." But they prefer Piiitrrr, which makes me sound more English. I am their window-dressing westerner, helping them create a pretend Western society. And I, in turn, pretend to be a much greater producer than I am. We start by launching TNT's first documentary strand. It takes me just thirty minutes to get my first commission: *How to Marry a Millionaire (A Gold Digger's Guide)*. I reckon I could have got three films if I had made the effort. In London or New York you would spend months trying to get a project off the ground. But TNT is sponsored by the world's largest gas company. Actually, scratch that; it's the world's largest company, full stop.

NO COMPLEXES

"Business theory teaches us one important lesson," says the instructress. "Always thoroughly research the desires of the consumer. Apply this principle when you search for a rich man. On a first date there's one key rule: never talk about yourself. Listen to him. Find him fascinating. Find out his desires. Study his hobbies; then change yourself accordingly."

Gold Digger Academy. A pool of serious blonde girls taking careful notes. Finding a sugar daddy is a craft, a profession. The academy has faux-marble halls, long mirrors, and gold-color-painted details. Next door is a spa and beauty salon. You go for your gold-digger lessons, then you go get waxed and tanned. The teacher is a forty-something redhead with a psychology degree, an MBA, and a shrill smile, her voice high and prim, a Miss Jean Brodie in short skirts: "Never wear jewelry on a first date, the man should think you're poor. Make him want to buy you jewelry. Arrive in a broken-down car: make him want to buy you a smarter one."

The students take notes in neat writing. They have paid a thousand dollars for each week of the course. There are dozens of such "academies" in Moscow and St. Petersburg, with names such as "Geisha School" or "How to Be a Real Woman."

"Go to an expensive area of town," continues the instructress. "Stand with a map and pretend you are lost. A wealthy man might approach to help."

"I want a man who can stand strong on [his] own two feet. Who will make me feel as safe as behind a wall of stone," says Oliona, a recent graduate, employing the parallel language of the gold digger (what she means is she wants a man with money). Usually Oliona wouldn't even think of talking to me, one of those impossible-to-access girls who would bat me away with a flick of her eyelashes. But I'm going to put her on television, and that changes everything. The show is going to be called *How to Marry a Millionaire*. I had thought it would be tough to get Oliona to talk, that she would be shy about her life. Quite the opposite: she can't wait to tell the world; the way of the gold digger has become one of the country's favorite myths. Bookstores are stocked with self-help books telling girls how to bag a millionaire. A roly-poly pimp, Peter Listerman, is a TV celebrity. He doesn't call himself a pimp (that would be illegal), but a "matchmaker." Girls pay him to introduce them to rich men. Rich men pay him to introduce them to girls. His agents, gay teenage boys, search at the train stations, looking for long-legged, lithe young things who have come to Moscow for some sort of life. Listerman calls the girls his "chickens"; he poses for photos with kebab sticks of grilled poussins: "Come to me if you're after chicken," his advertisements say.

Oliona lives in a small, sparkly new apartment with her nervous little dog. The apartment is on one of the main roads that leads to billionaire's row, Rublevka. Rich men put their mistresses there so they can nip in and visit them on the way home. She first came to Moscow from Donbas, a Ukrainian mining region taken over by mafia bosses in the 1990s. Her mother was a hairdresser. Oliona studied the same profession, but her mother's little boutique went bust. Oliona came to Moscow with next to nothing when she was twenty and started as a stripper at one of the casinos, Golden Girls. She danced well, which is how she met her sugar daddy. Now she earns the basic Moscow mistress rate: the apartment, $4,000 a month, a car, and a weeklong holiday in Turkey or Egypt twice a year. In return the sugar daddy gets her supple and tanned body any time he wants, day or night, always rainbow happy, always ready to perform.

"You should see the eyes of the girls back home. They're deadly jealous," says Oliona. "'Oh, so your accent's changed, you speak like a Muscovite now,' they say. Well, fuck them: that just makes me proud."

"Could you ever go back there?"

"Never. That would mean I'd failed. Gone back to mummy."

But her sugar daddy promised her a new car three months ago, and he still hasn't delivered; she's worried he's going off her.

"Everything you see in this flat is his; I don't own anything," says Oliona, peering at her own apartment as if it's just a stage set, as if it's someone else who lives there.

And the minute the sugar daddy gets bored with her, she's out. Back on the street with her nervous little dog and a dozen sequined dresses. So Oliona's looking for a new sugar daddy (they're not called "sugar daddies" here but "sponsors"). Thus the Gold Digger Academy, a sort of adult education.

"But how can you meet with others guys?" I ask. "Doesn't your present sponsor keep tabs on you?"

"Oh yeah, I have to be careful; he has one of his bodyguards check up on me. But he does it in a nice way; the bodyguard turns up with shopping. But I know he's checking there've been no guys here. He tries to be subtle. I think that's sweet. Other girls have it much worse. Cameras. Private eyes."

Oliona's playing fields are a constellation of clubs and restaurants designed almost exclusively for the purpose of sponsors looking for girls and girls looking for sponsors. The guys are known as "Forbeses" (as in *Forbes* rich list); the girls as "tiolki," cattle. It's a buyer's market: there are dozens, no, hundreds, of "cattle" for every "Forbes."

We start the evening at Galeria. Opposite is a red-brick monastery leaning like an ocean liner in the snow. Outside the restaurant black cars are quadruple parked up the narrow pavement and onto the boulevard; scowling, smoking bodyguards wait for their masters, who sit inside. Galeria was created by Arkady Novikov: his restaurants are *the* place to go in Moscow (he also does the Kremlin's catering). Each restaurant has a new theme: the Middle East, Asia. Not so much imitative pastiche as knowing hints at someone else's style. Galeria is a collage of quotations: columns, chrome black tables, panels with English paisley fabric. The tables are lit up with cinema spotlights. The seating plan is such that you can see people in other corners. And the main subjects on display are women. They sit by the bar, careful to just order Voss water and thus provoke a Forbes to invite them for a drink.

"Ha, they're so naïve," says Oliona. "Everyone knows that trick by now."

She orders a cocktail and sushi: "I always pretend I don't need anything from a man. That gets them in."

At midnight Oliona heads for the latest club. Worming cavalcades of black (always black), bullet-proof Bentleys and Mercedeses move slowly toward the entrance. Near the door thousands of stilettos slide and shuffle on black ice, somehow always keeping their immaculate balance. (Oh nation of ballet dancers!) Thousands of platinum-blonde manes brush against bare, perma-tanned backs moist with snow. The winter air is rent with cries from thousands of puffed up lips, begging to be let in. This is not about fashion, about cool; this is about work. Tonight is the one chance for the girls to dance and glance their way over the usually impossible barriers of money, private armies, security fences. For one evening a week the most divided city in the northern hemisphere, where the mega-rich live fenced off in a separate, silky civilization, opens a little, narrow sluice into paradise. And the girls pile and push and crawl into that little sluice, knowing full well that it will be open for one night only before it shuts them back out in a mean Moscow.

Oliona walks lightly to the front of the line. She's on the VIP list. At the beginning of every year she pays the bouncer several thousand dollars to make sure she can always be let in, a necessary tax for her profession.

Inside, the club is built like a baroque theater, with a dance floor in the center and rows of loggias up the walls. The Forbeses sit in the darkened loggias (they pay tens of thousands for the pleasure), while Oliona and hundreds of other girls dance below, throwing practiced glances up at the loggias, hoping to be invited up. The loggias are in darkness. The girls have no idea who exactly is sitting there; they're flirting with shadows.

"So many eighteen-year-old girls," says Oliona, "breathing down my neck." She's only twenty-two, but that's already near the end of a Moscow mistress's career. "I know I'll have to start lowering my standards soon," she tells me, amused rather than appalled. Now that Oliona has taken me into her confidence, I find that she's nothing like I thought she would be. Not hard, but soft-drink bubbly. Everything's just play with her. This must be the secret to her success: the room feels fizzier when she's there. "Of course I'm still hoping for a real Forbes," she says, "but if the worst comes to the worst I'll settle for some millionaire dunce who's come up from the provinces, or one of those dull ex-pats. Or some vile old man." But no one knows what a gold digger's future really holds; this is the first generation to have treated this sort of life as a career. Oliona has a mafia mining town behind her and god-knows-what in front of her; she's giggling and dancing over an abyss.

Back at the academy the lessons continue.

"Today we will learn the algorithm for receiving presents," the instructor tells her students. "When you desire a present from a man, place yourself at his left, irrational, emotional side. His right is his rational side: you stand to his right if you're discussing business projects. But if you desire a present, position yourself by his left. If he is sitting in a chair crouch down, so he feels taller, like you're a child. Squeeze your vaginal muscles. Yes, your vaginal muscles. This will make your pupils dilate, making you more attractive. When he says something, nod; this nodding will induce him to agree with you. And finally, when you ask for your car, your dress, whatever it is you want, stroke his hand. Gently. Now repeat: Look! Nod! Stroke!"

The girls chant back in unison: "Look. Nod. Stroke. . . . Look, Nod, Stroke."

("They think they've won something when they get a dress out of us," one millionaire acquaintance tells me when I tell him about the lessons at the academy. "I let them win sometimes. But come on: What could they ever, ever take from us we didn't actually let them?" "You know what my word for them is?," asks another. "I call them gulls, like sea-gulls, circling over garbage dumps. And they sound like gulls, you know, when they sit and gossip in a bar together. Kar-Kar! Kar-Kar! Gulls! Funny: isn't it?")

As I research the show I get to know more graduates from the academies. Natasha speaks decent German. She works as a translator for visiting businessmen. The translation agency only advertises for girls with "no complexes": code for being prepared to bed the client. Everywhere you see advertisements for secretaries or PAs with "no complexes" added in small print at the bottom. The phrase somehow transforms humiliation into an act of personal liberation. Natasha is working for a German energy boss. She hopes he'll take her back to Munich.

"Russian men are completely spoilt for choice; Western men are much easier," she says earnestly, like one carrying out market research. "But the problem with westerners is they don't buy you presents, never pay for dinner. My German guy will need some work."

Lena wants to be a pop star. In Moscow they're known as "singing knickers": girls with no talent but rich sponsors. Lena knows perfectly well she can't sing, but she also knows that doesn't matter.

"I don't understand the whole thing of working 24–7 in some office. It's humiliating having to work like that. A man is a lift to the top, and I intend to take it."

The red-haired instructress with the MBA agrees: "Feminism is wrong. Why should a woman kill herself at a job? That's a man's role. It's up to us to perfect ourselves as women."

"But what about you?" I ask her when the students are out of the room. "You work; the academy makes you money."

The instructress gives a little smile and changes the subject: "Next I'm opening up a clinic that will help stop aging: Would you like to come and film that, too?"

The class continues. The instructress draws a pie chart on a white board. She divides it into three.

"There are three types of men," she tells her students. "The creatives. The analysts. We're not interested in those. The ones we want are 'the possessors'," and she repeats the tell-all, prison-intimating phrase, "a man behind whom you feel like behind a wall of stone. We all know how to spot them. The strong, silent men. They wear dark suits. They have deep voices. They mean what they say. These men are interested in control. They don't want a forceful woman. They have enough of that already. They want a girl who'll be a pretty flower."

Do I even need to mention that Oliona grew up fatherless? As did Lena, Natasha, and all the gold diggers I met. All fatherless. A generation of orphaned, high-heeled girls, looking for a daddy as much as a sugar daddy. And that's the funny thing about Oliona and the other students: her cunning comes with fairy-tale fantasies about the tsar who, today or tomorrow or the day after, will jet her off to his majestic Maybach kingdom. And of course it's the President who encapsulates that image. All the shirtless photos hunting tigers and harpooning whales are love letters to the endless queues of fatherless girls. The President as the ultimate sugar daddy, the ultimate protector with whom you can be as "behind a stone wall."

When I see Oliona back at her flat she brings out a tome of Pushkin. She met a Forbes at the club the other night who is fond of literature. She's learning whole stanzas of "Eugene Onegin" by heart:

Whom to love, whom to believe in,
On whom alone shall we depend?

Who will fit their speech and on,
To our measure, in the end?
. . . Never pursue a phantom,
Or waste your efforts on the air
Love yourself, your only care. . . .

"I'll slip them in, just when he's least expecting it." She winks, keen to show off her cunning.

The Forbes has already taken her on a ride in his private jet. "Can you imagine: you can smoke in there, drink in there, throw your feet up on the seat. No seat belts! Freedom! It's all true, you can really have the life; it's not just in the movies!"

She met the Forbes when she went up to the VIP room.

"He's handsome as a God," Oliona tells me, whispering with excitement. "He was giving out hundred dollar bills to girls for blow jobs. Kept going all night. Imagine his stamina! And those poor girls, they don't just do it for the money you know; every one of them thinks he'll remember them, that they're special, so they try extra hard. Of course I refused when he offered: I'm not like THEM. . . . Now we're seeing each other. Wish me luck!"

The one thing Oliona will never, ever think of herself as is a prostitute. There's a clear distinction: prostitutes have to have sex with whomever a pimp tells them to. She does her own hunting.

"Once, when I was working as a dancing girl, my boss said I had to go home with one of the clients. He was a regular. Influential. Fat. Not too young either. 'Do I really have to go home with him?' I asked my boss. 'Yes.' I went back to his hotel. When he wasn't looking I slipped some Ruffinol in his drink and ran off."

Oliona tells this proudly. It's a badge of distinction.

"But what about love?" I ask Oliona. It's late; we're taping an interview in her apartment. We're drinking sticky, sweet Prosecco. Her favorite. The nervous little dog snores by the couch.

"My first boyfriend. Back home in Donbas. That was love. He was a local authority."

Authority is a nice word for gangster.

"Why didn't you stay together?"

"He was at war with another gang—they used me to get to him. I was standing on the corner. I think I was waiting for a tram. Then these two guys, big guys, grab me and start putting me in a car. I kicked and screamed. But they just told passersby I was a drunk friend. No one was going to mess with guys like that. They took me to an apartment. Tied my hands to a chair. Kept me there for a week."

"Did they rape you?"

Oliona keeps on sipping the sweet Prosecco. Keeps on smiling. She's still wearing a sparkly dress. She's taken off her high heels and wears pink, fluffy slippers. She smokes thin, perfumed cigarettes. She talks about everything matter-of-factly, even with amusement: the story of a very bad, but somehow slightly funny, working day.

"They took turns. Over a week. Occasionally one would go out for pickled fish and vodka. The whole room smelt of pickled fish and vodka. I can still remember that room. It was bare. A wooden table. Dumbbells. A workout bench: they would lift weights in between sessions. I remember there was a Soviet flag on the wall. I would stare at that flag during the sessions. In the end one of them took pity on me. When the other went for more vodka he let me go."

"And your authority?"

"When I told him what happened he raged, promised to kill them. But then he made peace with the other gang. And that was that, he never did anything. I would see those men often. One, the one who let me go, even apologized. He turned out to be a nice guy. The other would always smirk when I saw him. I left town."

As we pack up Oliona is as thoughtful as I've ever seen her: "Actually could you avoid what happened in that room in your program?"

"Of course. It could be dangerous."

"Dangerous? No, it's not that. But it would make me seem, well, sad. Depressing. I wouldn't want people to see me that way. People think of me as bubbly. That's good."

I feel bad for making her talk about what happened. "Look, I'm sorry I raised all that. I didn't mean to. It must be awful to bring it all up again."

Oliona shrugs. "Listen. It's normal. Happens to all the girls. No biggie."

Oliona's relationship with the Pushkin-loving Forbes didn't last long. "I thought at first he wanted a bitch. So I played that role. Now I'm not sure, maybe he doesn't want a bitch. Maybe he wants a nice girl. You know, sometimes I get confused, I can't even tell which one I am, the nice girl or the bitch." This isn't said dejectedly but as always softly detached, like she thinks about herself in the third person. Whenever I look for a vein of sadness in Oliona it melts away. As a director it's my job to catch her out, find a chink, pull the emotional lever where her façade crumbles and she breaks and cries. But she just turns and twists and smiles and shimmers with every color. She's not scared of poverty, humiliation. If she loses her sponsor she'll just start again, reinvent herself, and press reload.

At 5:00 A.M. the clubs get going properly; the Forbes stumble down from their loggias, grinning and swaying tipsily. They are all dressed the same, in expensive striped silk shirts tucked into designer jeans, all tanned and plump and glistening with money and self-satisfaction. They join the cattle on the dance floor. Everyone is wrecked by now and bounces around sweating, so fast it's almost in slow motion. They exchange these sweet, simple glances of mutual recognition, as if the masks have come off and they're all in on one big joke. And then you realize how equal the Forbes and the girls really are. They all clambered out of one Soviet world. The oil geyser has shot them to different financial universes, but they still understand each other perfectly. And their sweet, simple glances seem to say how amusing this whole masquerade is, that yesterday we were all living in communal flats and singing Soviet anthems and thinking Levis and powdered milk were the height of luxury, and now we're surrounded by luxury cars and jets and sticky Prosecco. And though many westerners tell me they think Russians are obsessed with money, I think they're wrong: the cash has come so fast, like glitter shaken in a snow globe, that it feels totally unreal, not something to hoard and save but to twirl and dance in like feathers in a pillow fight and cut like papier-mâché into different, quickly changing masks. At 5:00 A.M. the music goes faster and faster, and in the throbbing, snowing night the cattle become Forbeses and the Forbeses cattle, moving so fast now they can see the traces of themselves caught in the strobe across the dance floor. The guys and girls look at themselves and think: "Did that really happen to me? Is that *me* there? With all the Maybachs and rapes and gangsters and mass graves and penthouses and sparkly dresses?"

A HERO FOR OUR TIMES

I am in a meeting at TNT when my phone goes off. The display says "undisclosed," which could mean it's something important from home. I apologize and move to the corridor, under the neon sign "Feel our Love!" When I answer at first there's a long silence. Breathing. Then a hoarse, whistling laugh.

"Piiitrrr. You recognize me? It's Vitaly Djomochka. I need you to do me a favor. Will you do me a favor? Just a small favor?"

Vitaly has a way of asking that makes it uncomfortable to say "no."

"Sure."

"Come to D— station. Bring a camera. And not a little one. A real one. Deal?"

"Sure. . . ."

In the evening I make my way down to D—. The journey will take an hour on one of the slow, suburban trains. These trains are among the most miserable rides in Russia: full of the angry poor of satellite towns, the shop assistants and cops and cleaners, who come every day to the big city to be within breathing distance of all the platinum watches and Porsches, only to be blown back again each evening to their dark peripheries, carrying their shift clothes crumpled in plastic bags, drinking lukewarm beer in a cold train. The benches are wooden and impossible to sit on comfortably. I fidget and wonder what Vitaly could possibly be doing in D—, it doesn't strike me as his sort of place. But it has been a while since I last heard from him.

Once upon a time Vitaly Djomochka had been a gangster. In the 1990s the words "Russian" and "gangster" became almost synonymous, but when the President ascended to the Kremlin the era of the gangster ended. The secret services took over organized crime themselves; there was no way hoodlums could compete. Some became Duma deputies to make their money safe, while others retired to become regular businessmen. But in Siberia Vitaly Djomochka had other plans: he wanted to direct movies. He gathered his crew. No more grand theft auto and extorting businessmen, he told them; they were going to make films about themselves, starring themselves.

None of them knew anything about filmmaking. They had never heard of montage, storyboards, or camera movements. There was no film school they could go to, no famous director to guide them. Vitaly worked out how to make movies himself. He watched and rewatched the classics, breaking down every shot, every cut, every twist and turn in the plot. There was no script on paper; scripts were for saps. Everyone knew the scenes from memory. They didn't use makeup or stuntmen; they jumped from tall buildings themselves and crashed their own cars. All the blood you saw on screen was real; when there wasn't enough from the wound, Vitaly would stab a syringe in his own vein and spray the contents all over himself. The guns and bullets were all real, too; when they filmed a shoot-'em-up in a bar the place was wasted.

The result was an epic, six-hour miniseries, *The Spets* (literally "The Specialist"), and when it was ready the gangster auteurs had their own ideas about managing distribution. They would walk into local TV stations with a copy of the series and tell the managers to show it—or else. No one argued. The sound was all over the place, and some of the shots didn't match. But overall Vitaly had cracked it. There was plot, action, drive. It was a sensation. He became a Siberian star.

When I first met Vitaly he was at the height of his fame and had come to Moscow to appear on talk shows and look for money for his next big film. I was working as an assistant to an American documentary director, and we were trying to persuade Vitaly to let us make a documentary about him. We set a date in one of the new Moscow cafés. Pastel lights diffused through a gentle indoor fountain. Muzak played softly in the background. Tall and lean and shaven headed, Vitaly looked uncannily like the President's meaner, taller twin. He wore a designer tracksuit, pressed flat. He drank cappuccinos, dabbing his lip with a tightly folded napkin, careful that no trace of froth remained. "Capp-ooo-she-knows," he called them, enjoying the word. He told the waitress off for giving him a dirty spoon.

"Did you always want to be a gangster?" we asked.

"I always knew I could be *more* than other people. Run faster, jump higher, shoot better. Just more."

He talked in a way that was ever so statuesque, with silences between each short sentence. Everything about him seemed so contained. He didn't drink, didn't smoke, and told me off for swearing. He used to be a junkie, but he quit. He laughed in a hoarse, slow way, and at the oddest things (the word "latte" he found hilarious). It had taken weeks to set up this little meeting; he first arranged dates, then broke them off at the last moment, leaving us fretting and exhausted. With time I learned this was his way, a little tactic to wrap you around him.

"What made you want to make movies?"

"I'd spent eight years in jail. You watch a lot of TV in jail. There were all these cops and robbers shows. They were showing my life, my world. But it was all fake. The fights were fake. The guns were fake. The crimes were fake. What can an actor know about being a gangster? Nothing. Only I could tell my story."

Vitaly's TV miniseries showed his life of crime in scrupulous detail. In his violent pomp he had been a modern Dick Turpin, a real highwayman. He would hide in the bushes by the side of the motorway, waiting for a coach-load of brand new Mitsubishis or Toyotas just brought in from Japan. Then he would pull a kerchief over his face, draw out his sawn-off shotgun, and walk out into the middle of the highway. He would stand legs apart, gun pointed out from his hips, alone in the middle of the road, facing down the oncoming truck. They always stopped, and the cars were all his. If the driver struggled, Vitaly would beat him. The TV series reveled in these moments of violence. The dialogue was sometimes stilted (Vitaly wouldn't let his crew swear on screen), but when it came to kicking, stomping on, and humiliating, the gangster actors were in their element, their faces lighting up with joy and anger.

"But what about your victims—did you ever feel sorry for them?" asked the American.

Vitaly looked nonplussed. He turned to me:

"Of course not. No one who does what I do feels sorry for the victim. You're either a dope or a real man, and dopes deserve all they get."

The central scene of *Spets* involved Vitaly killing another mob boss. In the film he calmly walks up and shoots his rival, then calmly walks away again. The whole thing happens so fast I had to rewind and replay to double check what had happened.

"How many have you killed?" I asked when the waitress left.

"I can only talk about one time. That was revenge for my brother. I served time for the killing, but after that no one messed with me."

"Can anyone be a killer?" asked the American.

"No. When I was in prison there were men who regretted what they'd done. They wept, went to church. Not everyone has the inner strength to do it. But I do."

"And would you ever return to crime?

Vitaly smiled: "Nowadays my life is all about art."

We persuaded him to take us down to his hometown and let us film him shooting a scene for his next project. We'd have an exclusive with the gangster director at work, and he'd have a promo to help raise money.

"Usually you'd be one of my victims," he said matter-of-factly. "But in this case we'll be partners."

The flight to Ussuriysk, Vitaly's hometown, took all day. Vitaly just lay back, smiled, and slept the whole journey. I chatted to another former gangster friend of his, Sergey, who wrote the music for *The Spets*. A former power-lifting champion, Sergey took up two seats on the flight. He had quit being a gangster when he found God: a bullet that should have killed him miraculously passed through his body. Afterward he had seen the light (with the help of an American evangelical sect that helped nurse him back to health after the shooting). He was a laughing, jolly, blonde bear of a man, with questioning, kind, light blue eyes. Previously he had dealt heroin and smuggled girls from Ukraine to Europe.

"How does the new, religious you make sense of the past?" I asked.

"When I was baptized all my sins were washed away," answered Sergey.

"But do you feel guilt for what you used to do?"

"I was a demon, but I was still fulfilling God's will. All my victims must have deserved it. God only punishes bad people."

On the flight Sergey was trying to write a film script. It was to be a modern spin on the old Russian fairy tale of the "three bogatyri," huge knights of unnatural strength who traveled old Russia taming dragons and invaders. In Sergey's version the "bogatyri" were former gangsters.

When we finally landed in Vladivostok (the nearest airport to Ussuriysk) I expected to see the orient; we were, after all, 1,000 km east of Beijing, where Russia meets the Pacific. Apart from Vitaly this region is famous for its tigers. But instead it looked like more of the same Russia, the same green-brown blur of hills and thin, unhappy trees. We might as well have been in suburban Moscow. Vitaly's crew were at the hanger of an airport to meet us: young, polite men with darting eyes, shell suits, gold medallions, tidy haircuts, and neat nails. One brought Vitaly a new Jeep, a vassal fetching his lord a new, stolen steed. No plates. We drove in a spread-eagled cortege across both lanes of the highway, so fast it made me first scared and then ecstatic. Vitaly ignored the first traffic cop who waved at him, then stopped for the second one. When the cop saw who it was, he waved him on.

"They know better than to mess with me," said Vitaly.

Vitaly didn't need to stop. It was all just demonstration, just to let everyone know: he's back.

We sped into Ussuriysk itself, past the oversized, windy central square, designed with military parades and not human beings in mind. The cinema, town hall, and swimming pool were all in the same stiff Soviet classicism. Wide avenues led to nowhere, stopping abruptly at the endless taiga. You find the same towns throughout the old Soviet Empire, all designed in some Moscow Ministry for Urbanism, awkward and ill at ease.

The town was clean. Quiet.

"Us gangsters keep this town disciplined," said Vitaly. "There used to be druggies, prostitutes. Teens with long hair. They wouldn't dare show their faces now. We showed them who's boss. I don't even let anyone in my crew smoke cigarettes. If anyone of my boys were to get drunk in public, I'd give them such a beating."

Vitaly was a celebrity here. When we walked down the streets teenage girls with large shoulders and short skirts stopped to have their pictures taken with him. When we paused by a school the kids saw him through the window and came running out, mobbing Vitaly and thrusting forward their math books and homework pads for him to sign, the teachers smiling benignly.

His new film was to be about his teenage years, in the late 1980s, when the first gangsters emerged together with the first businessmen. The next day Vitaly was casting teens to play his younger self. A crowd gathered in front of the Palace of Culture and Leisure, the old Soviet theater. Fathers had taken their sons out of school and brought them to try out for the parts of the Young Vitaly and his first gang.

"I want my son to learn about our history," said one of the dads. "The gangsters hold this town together, keep it disciplined."

Vitaly did his casting in a rehearsal room. On the walls were pictures of Chekhov and Stanislavsky, the great Russian inventor of method acting. Vitaly had the boys walk up and down the room:

"You need to walk like gangsters, like you mean it. Don't look to the sides. Don't look tense. Imagine everyone's looking at you. Slowly. Walk slowly. This is your territory."

He picked out a few of the boys. They were thrilled. He lined them up against the wall, scanning the line, choosing which one would play him.

"Too short. Too fat. Too loud. You. You'll do. But you'll have to cut off that forelock."

The kid he chose was the quiet one (and the best looking). His name was Mitya. He studied history at the local college. He seemed entirely emotionless at the idea of acting out Vitaly—or maybe he was just in the role already.

Vitaly drove him to the local park for a lesson on how to play him.

"See those kids over there? The ones drinking beer over by those benches? I want you to go over and tell them to leave. And get them to pick up their litter, too. Act like you own the place. Talk quietly. Firmly. Instruct. Let them feel you've got numbers behind you. Imagine that you're me."

The kid did well. His menace came in the pauses between the words. He told the drinking boys to pack up. Just as they were leaving, he threw in the little humiliation: "Don't forget your rubbish." That touch was pure Vitaly: always looking to jab you with a put-down. ("That camera you use is so small Peter, don't you have a real camera?" he liked to ask me, or "you don't know how to interview; am I going to have to teach you?")

Mitya seemed a good boy, who would finish university and probably go on to a career in a state corporation. But his behavior, his style, was already pure gangster.

"Do you think Mitya could be as good a gangster as you?" we asked.

"He has potential," said Vitaly, "but he would need to toughen up a bit. By his age I was already serving my first term in prison for racketeering."

We went to see Vitaly's parents. I had hoped they would help explain the way he is, but I was disappointed. Vitaly's father was a hard-working factory man, used to soldering parts on tanks. He was small and shy and talked about fishing. Vitaly's mother, slightly tipsy but polite, kept a neat home. They seemed frightened of Vitaly themselves, and he was so disdainful of them he wouldn't even enter the apartment.

"He had been a tear-away at school," said the dad. "We so hoped prison would help calm him down. That he would come out and get a normal job at the armaments factory. But when he came out of prison you could tell he was a big boss already."

Prison was Vitaly's alma mater. This part of Siberia was full of them. Everywhere you looked were barbed wire, watchtowers, and concrete walls. We shot an interview with Vitaly as he gazed toward where he had first served time.

"Everything I learned was there," he said. It was the first time I'd seen him even vaguely sentimental. "You have to prove you're a real man and not a chicken straight away. You don't cry, you don't blabber, you don't let anyone tell you what to do. Only say what you mean, speak slowly, and if you promise something, keep it."

Vitaly had served five years that first time. He had first gone inside in 1988. When he came out in 1993 the whole universe he had grown up in was transformed. The Soviet Union had disappeared. Everyone who had previously been someone was suddenly a nobody. The teachers and cops and judges went unpaid. The factory workers were making fridges and train parts no one needed. The war heroes were penniless pensioners. When he had been first put away, men like Vitaly had been destined for a life on the margins; they were *shpana*, scum. Now, suddenly, he sensed this was his era.

"Why would I work for pennies in a factory like my dad? That would be crazy."

The only values in this new Ussuriysk were cars and cash. The gangsters could access these things the fastest, with the most direct methods. But they didn't just extort and steal. Businessmen called them in to guarantee deals (if one partner reneged, the gangsters would sort him out); people turned to them instead of the uninterested police to catch rapists and thieves. They became the establishment, the glue that holds everything together. In this new world no one knew quite how to behave: all the old Soviet role models had been made redundant, and the "West" was just a story far away. But the gangsters had their own prison code, which had survived perestroika. And this made the gangsters more than just feared bullies. They were the only people in this lost, new Russia who knew who on earth they were and what they stood for. And now in the twenty-first century, although many gangsters were out of a job, their way of behaving has become ubiquitous.

As he prepared for his shoot Vitaly would often disappear, his usual trick of keeping us on tenterhooks. He designated a friend of his, Stas, to look after us. Stas had a Jeep with a little shovel screwed on at the front: the gangster's sign. He had a girlfriend with him. She was a tall, pale, bored blonde who only lit up when she talked about her collection of hosiery: "I even have a pair of snakeskin tights at home," she told me.

Stas took us on a tour of Ussuriysk.

The town was famous for its car market, one of the biggest in the whole of Russia. We were near the sea with Japan, and all the new Mitsubishis and Toyotas were traded here. The market was on a hill at the entrance to the town. As we approached, it gleamed silver like a magic mountain. Only when we got closer did we realize it was the sun glinting off the new Jeeps and other four-by-fours. Everyone here drove the latest models. They might have their toilets in wooden outhouses, and their apartments might be yellowing, but the big, black cars were always shining with a TV commercial sparkle. Stas took us to a meet at which locals showed off how they'd upgraded their automobiles. One guy had installed a Jacuzzi in the back; another had a movie theater. There was tenderness in how they showed off their prized possessions. These heavy men touched their cars so delicately. Stas took out a little toothbrush to clean the headlights on his Land Cruiser: he scrubbed it softly, patiently, like he was washing a toddler.

Stas took us to the hills above the town so we could get the best view. The corroding factories still chugged smoke. Among the hills were the cemeteries with their black marble headstones. On them were engravings for young gangsters: "Buba the boxer," "Boris Mercedes." Their portraits were engraved into the headstones, depicting them in gangster pomp—one dangled the keys to his Mercedes, another posed with his mobile phone—like Egyptian pharaohs sent to the next world with their most vital possessions. Dates on the headstones often coincided; the young men had died on the same days in the 1990s. These were the dates of gang battles, a whole generation decimated.

"You have many friends here?" I asked Stas.

"Most of my class," he answered, matter-of-factly. "Not just gangsters. Many were just caught in the cross fire."

In the evening we headed to a restaurant, The Miami. Outside was a twelve-foot, plastic palm tree. The plastic palm trees were everywhere around town; they were considered fashionable. The Miami had a parking garage out front and a massage parlor in the basement.

"It's compact," explained Stas, "all you might want in one place." The restaurant itself was done up with plush burgundy walls and black lacquer chairs. All the clientele wore ironed shell suits. The restaurant was Chinese owned; we were just fifty miles from the Chinese border, and rumor had it that a third of the population was illegal Chinese immigrants.

"The Chinks used to just walk anywhere," said Stas, "but the gangsters sorted that out. Now they just keep themselves to the market and the suburbs. They need to know this is Russian territory. . . . But they do have the best restaurants."

With the meal there was karaoke. As the Chinese waiters brought the food, everyone at the restaurant sang "shanson," the gravelly, syrupy gangster ballads that have become some of Russia's favorite pop music. Shanson reflect the gangsters' journeys to the center of Russian culture. These used to be underground, prison songs, full of gangster slang, tales of Siberian labor camps and missing your mother. Now every taxi driver and grocery plays them. "Vladimirsky Tsentral" is a wedding classic. Tipsy brides across the country in cream-puff wedding dresses and high, thin heels slow-dance with their drunker grooms: "The thaw is thinning underneath the bars of my cell / but the Spring of my life has passed so fast." At the Chinese restaurant Miami Stas sang along too, but he seemed too meek, too obliging to be a gangster.

"Me? A gangster? God no," he seemed surprised when asked. "I'm just a businessman. The shovel, well that's just for show. I like hanging around with Vitaly."

I asked him what their relationship was. He changed the subject fast.

We asked Vitaly the next time we saw him.

"Stas? Stas is one of the businessmen we used to extort money from."

"And now you're friends?"

"He does what I tell him to."

It turned out Vitaly had once beaten Stas to a pulp, and now Stas half worshiped, half lived in fear of him, helping Vitaly put on his coat and holding his phone for him. And everyone we met in the town seemed somehow crumpled, mumbling, black and white. Only the gangsters strode tall in glorious Technicolor. This was Vitaly's town, the representative, cross-section town of Russia, the country where a third of males have been to prison, the sort of town spin doctors and TV men look at when they design politicians.

The day of his big shoot Vitaly took over a whole market. The scene had the young Vitaly and his gang being busted as they extorted money from the market traders. The traders played themselves, and cops had been hired to play cops.

"Isn't there a problem that you're working for a gangster today?" we asked the cops.

They laughed. "Who do you think we work for anyway?" (The new mayor of Vladivostok was a man nicknamed Winnie-the-Pooh, a mob boss who had previously served time for threatening to kill a businessman.)

Vitaly's set had a cast of hundreds, and it should have been chaos, but I'd never seen a film set so slickly run. His gangster crew was the production team. Who would dare to be late on set when professional killers are running the show? Vitaly was a natural. Cap pulled low, long finger tapping against his mouth, he set up every camera position unerringly. Though there was no script on paper, he never got lost, giving terse, tight instructions to all the players.

"It's just like setting up a heist," he told me. "Everything's got to be exact. Not like one of your little documentaries."

Every detail of the clothes, the guns, and the items the market trad-ers were selling had been reproduced just as they were in the late 1980s. But for all its detailed accuracy, the way Vitaly shot his films was more like a cheesy B-movie than documentary-style realism. Every shot of Vitaly was a glamorous close-up. He wiped his sweaty brow, sighed like a pantomime hero, looked intently into the distance, and escaped death to the sound of the *Star Wars* sound track. This was how he saw himself, his life, his crimes. All the pain and death he had caused and suffered were viewed by him through the corny music and cloud-machine smoke of a bad action movie.

"What sort of films inspire you?" we asked.

Vitaly paused.

"*Titanic*. That's a real film. With DiCaprio. That's real life. That's the sort of thing I aim to make if I get my budget. . . ."

That was the last time I had seen him, three years before. But I was still reminded of him often. There's a little scene that gets played out on the Ostankino channels every week. The president sits at the head of a long table. Along each side sit the governors of every region: the western, central, northeastern, and so on. The president points to each one, who tells him what's going on in his patch. "Rogue terrorists, pen-sions unpaid, fuel shortages. . . ." The governors looked petrified. The president toys with them, pure Vitaly. "Well, if you can't sort out the mess in your backyard, we can always find a different governor. . . ." For a long time I couldn't remember what the scene reminded me of. Then I realized: it's straight out of *The Godfather*, when Marlon Brando gathers the mafia bosses from the five boroughs. Quentin Tarantino used a similar scene when Lucy Liu meets with the heads of the Tokyo Yakuza clans in *Kill Bill*—it's a mafia movie trope. And it fits the image the Kremlin has for the President: he is dressed like a mob boss (the black polo top underneath the black suit), and his sound bites come straight out of gangster flicks ("we'll shoot the enemy while he's on the shitter . . ."). I can see the spin doctors' logic: Whom do the people respect the most? Gangsters. So let's make our leader look like a gangster; let's make him act like Vitaly.

But while the country's leaders were imitating gangsters, word went out from the Ministry of Culture and Ostankino that the Kremlin wanted positive, upbeat films. Russian gangster movies, which should theoretically have rivaled the greatest in the world, were phased out. Actors who had primed themselves to be the Russian De Niros suddenly had to revamp their images and star in rom-coms. It's the reverse of the situation in the West, where politicians try to act like upstanding citizens while films and TV shows are obsessed with the underworld; here the politicians imitate mobsters but the films are rosy. Whenever I pitch a gangster program to TNT, they stare, aghast: "We make happy things, Peter. Happy!" I supposed Vitaly never found money for his blockbuster. I was a little worried for him.

• • •

Vitaly was at the station to meet me. He was wearing his usual ironed tracksuit; it had been a while since I'd seen anybody wear one. He greeted me warmly. I sensed he was genuinely glad to see someone from the "old days."

"Thanks for coming."

"You live in D— now?"

"I'm lying low. I avoid Moscow: too many cops wanting to check your documents. Everyone back home has been put away, the last of my crew. I wouldn't have anyone to film with even if I could raise the money."

I sensed Vitaly was flirting with his old profession, but I thought it best not to pry. We walked over to his car: a brand new four-by-four (of course). No plates. Vitaly had a freshly pressed shell suit hanging in the back.

"I'm living in the car while I lie low. I've always preferred it to apartments anyway."

"Whatever happened to your film project?" I ask.

"I met some Moscow producers. They wanted me to show them a script. Do they think I'm stupid? I know they'll just steal it."

"But Vitaly, that's how it works here. You'd have a copyright, guarantees."

"That means nothing. You can't trust producers, they're all crooks. I tried to get money from my own people, mob bosses. People you can trust. But none of them wanted to invest in gangster movies. 'Not the future,' they told me."

It turned out Vitaly wanted me to shoot a short interview with him. He was planning a documentary about himself.

"None of you TV people could capture me right in your films. Did you bring a big camera? Good."

We shot the interview in the car. Vitaly put on his most statuesque look, part reptilian, part Romantic, speaking ever so slowly.

"Ever since I was a child I knew I could be more than other people. Run faster. Jump higher—" Suddenly, mid-sentence, he broke off and burst out of the car. He started screaming, spitting at a crumpled bum with wildly swollen eyes drinking from a bottle in a plastic bag behind the car. The bum crawled away. Vitaly got back in, still breathing hard, but the anger switched off like a light.

"You wouldn't want him in the same shot as me. He'd make it ugly."

Then Vitaly shot an interview with me. He had all my words written out already; I just had to memorize the script.

"The first time I met Vitaly he struck me as the most talented dangerous man, and the most dangerous talented man, I had ever encountered. . . ."

It was a long speech, and I kept fluffing my lines. But Vitaly was a patient director, and by the fifth take we got it right.

After the shoot Vitaly leaned into the back and brought out a pile of hardcover books.

"These are for you."

They were novels, written by Vitaly.

"I've taken to writing books. They're selling pretty well. I'll be honest, the first one was ghostwritten. But since then I've learned how to write myself."

Most of the early books were based on Vitaly's life of crime. But in the last book he had changed genres. It was a satire of Russian politics, about a bully, gangster state that uses its giant reserves of fart gases to manipulate the countries around it into submission (at the time Russia was threatening Ukraine with shutting off its gas supply).

"I often think now I should have gone into politics," said Vitaly. "I just thought it boring, I didn't realize they used the same methods as us. It's too late now, though. I've dedicated myself to art. If I can't film, I'll write. And you know what the future is, Peter? Comedy. Set up a meeting for me at TNT; they might want to televise my fart-book."

I told Vitaly I'd do my best. He insisted I take a stack of thick, black glossy books to show people. I couldn't say no and carried them in two plastic bags back to town, the sharp edges of the books tearing through the plastic and spiking against my legs with every step.

At TNT I went through the motions of helping Vitaly and gave the scripted comedy department a copy of the book.

"No idea whether it's any good, but I promised," I explained, almost apologizing. And thought that would be the end of it.

But a few weeks later I walked into TNT and there was Vitaly, sitting in one of the little glass meeting rooms with a couple of producers, wearing his shell suit and cap. He noticed me when I came in, stood up, took off his cap, and waved. "Hi, brother," I could hear him calling, the words low and distorted through the glass. Suddenly I wanted to turn away, ignore him, pretend I'd never met him and didn't know him. 'Brother!' he called again, waving his cap in ever larger motions. And the only way I could override the sudden desire to run away was to play up and call out even louder: 'Brother! Brother!' until everyone in the office could hear and was looking at me.

"Is he for real?" the women in the drama department asked me afterward. "It all seems a bit of an act."

"Oh, he's quite real. You actually interested in his book?"

"It's well written. We need to think about it."

One of the areas TNT specializes in is satire. If the USSR drove humor underground and thus made it an enemy of the state, the new Kremlin actively encourages people to have a laugh at its expense: one TNT sketch show is about corrupt Duma deputies who are always whoring and partying while praising each other's patriotism; another is about the only traffic cop in Russia who doesn't take bribes—his family is starving and his wife is always nagging him to become "normal" and more corrupt. As long as no real government officials are named, then why not let the audience blow off some steam? Vitaly's sense that his satire would work inside the Kremlin's rules was right.

When I tried to follow up on the meeting with Vitaly, he had disappeared. Sergey told me that another warrant had been issued for his arrest, and he was lying low again, sleeping in his Jeep, and keeping well out of any cities. But I guess he's okay; every year I see a new novel of his on the pulp fiction shelves in bookstores, most of them comedies.

RUSSIA TODAY

Western ex-pats first arrived in Russia as emissaries of the victorious party in the Cold War. They were superior and came to teach Russia how to be civilized. Now all that is changing. Russia is resurgent, the teachers have become the servants, and I'm not even sure who won the Cold War after all.

I first got to know Benedict in Scandinavia, a favorite restaurant of those ex-pats come to school Russia in the ways of the West in the decades of glorious afterglow after the end of the Cold War: "magic circle" lawyers, "big five" accountants, investment bankers. It's just off

Tverskaya, Moscow's central drag, in a little courtyard of large green trees. It's owned by Swedes, and when it first opened everything was imported from Stockholm: the waiters, cooks, burgers, fries—all flown in. In the early 2000s the guests largely spoke English; it wasn't opulent enough for Russian oligarchs and was too expensive for "ordinary" Russians. The westerners would come here like to an oasis, before they got drunk and courageous enough to explore the Moscow night. It felt like the descendant of an old colonial club in an age that prided itself on being past all that.

The Scandinavia set were tanned and spoke earnest schoolbook English. They discussed compliance, corporate governance, and work-outs. Finding somewhere to go jogging, the consensus went, was a nightmare in Moscow. As was the smoking. And the traffic. When they got tipsy they made jokes about Russian girls, unless they were with their wives, in which case they discussed holiday plans. They had white teeth. Benedict had yellow teeth, drank wine at lunch, and smoked long, thick Dunhills. He was slight and moved like a cricket, waving his smoke away from others in mock apology. He was Irish, but of the Shaw or Wilde variety.

"I'm a lapsed economist," he liked to tell people when they asked what he did.

Benedict was an international development consultant. "International development consultants" are the missionaries of democratic capitalism. They emerged en masse at the end of the Cold War, at the end of history, marching out of America and Europe to teach the rest of the world to be like them. They work on projects for the EU, WB, OECD, IMF, OSCE, IMF, DIFD, SIDA, and other national and multinational bodies that represent the "developed world" (the donor) and advise governments, central and local, of the "developing world" (the beneficiary). They wear Marks and Spencer (or Zara or Brooks Brothers) suits, and under their arms they carry wide binders that contain the Terms of Reference (known as TORA) for their projects, which have names like "building a market economy in the Russian Federation" or "achieving gender equality in the post-Soviet space." The TORA lay out "logical framework matrices" to achieve "objectively verifiable indicators of democratization." Western civilization condensed into bullet points:

"Elections? Check."
"Freedom of Expression? Check."
"Private Property? Check."

Underlying the projects is a clear vision of history, taught in the new "international development" departments of universities and taken as gospel in ministries and multinational bodies: postcommunism, the former Soviet states would pass through the temptations of "transition" to the plateaus of liberal democracy and the market economy.

Benedict was still an economics lecturer in a small-town Irish university when he went to Russia for the first time. He gave a lecture on principles of "business and effective management" at St. Petersburg University. It was 1992. The students listened carefully, lapping up the new language: "SME," "IPO," "cash flow." In the evening after the lecture Benedict walked back to his hotel. He took a wrong turn at reception and found himself in the middle of a wedding party. He tried to ask the way in English. The bride and groom were delighted a westerner had joined them and insisted he stay. He was a piece of exotica, a present in himself. They drank his health, and he stayed on drinking with them. At one point he went to his room and brought back a carton of Marlboros and some Imperial Leather soap as presents. The bride and groom were thrilled. They drank more, and everyone danced. Benedict felt that Russia would be like the West very soon.

He left his job at the Irish university a few years later, swapping $50,000 a year in a provincial college for the tax-free, six-figure sums of the strutting new development industry. Benedict was offered a position as team leader on a project called Technical Assistance for the Economic Development of the Kaliningrad Free Economic Zone. He had no idea where Kaliningrad was; he had to look it up on a map.

Kaliningrad used to be known as Koenigsberg, the capital of Eastern Prussia, the home of Kant. It lies on the Baltic Sea, between Lithuania and Poland, opposite Sweden. At the end of World War II it was captured by the Soviets, renamed, repopulated with imported Soviets from across the empire, and made into a high-security, closed-off military port. It was the most western point of the USSR. After the Cold War the Russians held onto it, though Kaliningrad has no border with Russia proper. It is now an exclave of Russia inside the European Union, a geopolitical freak. The EU recognized "the special position of Kaliningrad" but had "concerns regarding soft security issues"; that is to say, it was leaking heroin, weapons, AIDS, and a mutant strain of tuberculosis into the EU. Kaliningrad either had to change or risk having a wall built around it. There were no direct flights from Europe. Benedict had to fly all the way to Moscow, then double back and fly west to Kaliningrad. He was in his late forties and divorced, and he wanted a new start.

It was almost painful to see the difference between the tired, elegant nineteenth-century houses of the old Koenigsberg and the postwar Soviet new-builds. The red gothic cathedral, home to Kant's grave, was surrounded, on one side by shabby hordes of aggressive, concrete apartment blocks and on the other by a harbor full of rusting, resting warships. In the evening sailors would go drinking in the bars along the waterfront. I remember finding myself in such a bar on a brief visit to Kaliningrad. The light in the bar was a murky, Baltic Sea green. I ordered a cognac.

"A local one?" asked the waitress.

"What sort of grapes grow in Kaliningrad?" I asked, not disingenuously.

"Why would you need grapes for cognac?" asked the waitress.

The shot was poured. One gulp took me through thirty seconds of pure euphoria straight through to the worst hangover I have ever known.

The Kaliningrad Ministry for Economic Development was a weighty Soviet palace on a central square. Benedict and his translator, Marina, passed through the low, heavy doors and into the world of Russian bureaucracy. Wide, dusty, empty corridors where everything happens as if under water. Telephones, installed in the mid-1970s, rang patiently without being answered. Stopped. Then rang again. Velvet curtains sagged. In all the offices hung photos of the President, smiling almost apologetically, with his head tilted to the side. The officials were mainly strong, stern women in their forties and fifties, the real foundations of the Russian state. There were fewer men, and they all seemed to be stooping. All called each other by their patronymics: "Igor Arkadievich" and "Lydia Alexandrovna."

Benedict's opposite number was P, a midlevel official. He wore sagging suits and had a paunch that seemed to pull him downward.

"You the man with the European technical assistance? We need computers," said P when they met.

Technical assistance, Benedict explained, did not mean technology. It meant schooling from Western consultants. Benedict's interpreter tried to get the point across.

"We need computers," answered P.

Benedict arranged for some $200,000 worth of computers to be delivered; he explained to P that he would need to sign some paperwork when they arrived to confirm receipt.

He got on with the development strategy for Kaliningrad. He was given an office in the Institute of Cybernetics. He asked the dean of the institute whether he cared to advise on IT development in the region. Sorry, said the dean, though the Institute of Cybernetics was still officially a university, the salaries were so low all the staff were now involved in trading fish. It was every man for himself in Kaliningrad. The old armaments factories were making macaroni. Soldiers demobbed from East Germany sold off stockpiles of Kalashnikovs and RPGs. One of the saddest places was the zoo, once the city's pride: the fox ran round its cage chasing its own tale; the wolf stumbled around stunned in an open pit, the polar bears grinned wildly and stared into the distance, the wild squirrel would run and slam itself against the bars of its cage again and again and again.

Benedict had the beige walls of his office painted white and replaced the velvet curtains with venetian blinds. He brought in top managers from EU blue chip companies to inspect the telecommunications, aviation, agrarian, financial, and tourism sectors. Over the next four years they produced SWOT analyses and intervention plans and knowledge trees and gender mainstreaming strategies. Benedict would then send the reports on to P. But when he phoned afterward he could only ever get through to the assistant, Elena.

"P will get back to you next week," Elena, would say. And giggle. P never did. Elena had been a singer at the Crystal Nightclub on Karl Marx Street before she joined the ministry. Some time later, even Elena disappeared, running off to live in Turkey with a Scandinavian ambassador who had left his wife, children, and diplomatic career for her.

The local government had its own ideas about development. The governor also ran the commercial port, and now his economics minister was busy setting up a network of banks to launder money from the proceeds. The governor himself was large and bald and always sweating. "I went to Poland recently," he told Benedict the only time they met. "I saw them making ketchup in cement mixers. That's the sort of innovation we need here."

At the end of the project Benedict asked P for the paperwork to confirm that the $200,000 worth of computers had arrived. P refused to give it to him; the computers had never made it, he claimed. Benedict suspected the computers had been sold out the back door, but he couldn't prove anything.

Benedict put his lack of progress down to the provincial nature of Kaliningrad local government. He was given a new job, in Moscow, working with a federal-level ministry, where he hoped the bureaucrats would be of a different class. And there was much he was enjoying about life in Russia. He had married his translator, Marina, a friendly, unpretentious lady the same age and with the same sense of humor as him. He enjoyed the relative wealth: no longer the down-at-heel academic, he was now a consultant with a driver, and he always bought the drinks. And another good thing had come out of the project: Benedict had allocated $136,000 for Danish experts to fix the zoo. The animals were acting normally again. Even the squirrel had calmed down.

In Moscow Benedict worked opposite the federal Ministry for Economic Development to guide the EU's strategy in Russia. The minister for economic development was considered the most enlightened minister in Russia. He was an academic and a personal friend of the President, wore sharp suits and pink shirts, and was beloved at Davos. He had fifteen deputy ministers, many of them bright young things with MBAs (or at least studying for MBAs). The ministry was in the middle of reconstruction: some floors were bright and new, many more an extension of what Benedict had seen in Kaliningrad: the same darkling corridors and ever-ringing phones and heavy curtains and photos of the President—now the new one, but still smiling apologetically.

"Can you bring paper?" a woman who was Benedict's liaison at the ministry asked him. "Always bring paper. A4. Every department is allowed a quota, and we can never get the amount of paper we need."

Every time Benedict went for a meeting at the ministry he would load himself up with stacks of A4, sheltering them with his overcoat from the snowstorm.

"I'm not sure the ministry understand what we're here for," he told me one evening in Scandinavia. "The other day they asked us to organize and pay for a New Year's party for the whole department."

Meanwhile the country around us was changing. Every day Benedict would evaluate the hundreds-of-millions-of-dollars' worth of EU projects in Russia. They all ticked their boxes:

> "Democracy? Check: Russia is a presidential democracy with elections every four years."
> "Civil Society Development? Check. Russia has many new NGOs."
> "Private Property? Check."

Now, Russia does have elections, but the "opposition," with its almost comical leaders, is designed and funded in such a way as to actually strengthen the Kremlin: when the beetroot-faced communists and the spitting nationalists row on TV political debating shows, the viewer is left with the feeling that, compared to this lot, the President is the only sane candidate. And Russia does have nongovernmental organizations, representing everyone from bikers to beekeepers, but they are often created by the Kremlin, which uses them to create a "civil society" that is ever loyal to it. And though Russia does officially have a free market, with mega-corporations floating their record-breaking IPOs on the global stock exchanges, most of the owners are friends of the President. Or else they are oligarchs who officially pledge that everything that belongs to them is also the President's when he needs it: "All that I have belongs to the state," says Oleg Deripaska, one of the country's richest men. This isn't a country in transition but some sort of postmodern dictatorship that uses the language and institutions of democratic capitalism for authoritarian ends.

I would rarely see Benedict angry, but when he talked about this he would start to stutter and grow red in the face. He was just a bugler in the grand march of international bureaucracy, but he felt frustrated and unheard. The West was condoning this, agreeing to this perversion of meaning. Benedict was never a moralist, but there was something about fakery that dismayed him.

"If you start saying one thing is another, then, well, then the whole thing will come tumbling down, . . ." he would say, slapping his lighter on the table. And then, when he would calm down: "It's like the West reflected in a crooked mirror."

I told Benedict I had learned how Russian TV channels were structured. On the surface most Russian TV channels are organized like any Western TV station. Independent production companies pitch program ideas at the network in what looks like open competition. But there is a twist. Most of the production companies, I soon realized, were either owned or part-owned by the heads of the network and senior execs. They were commissioning for themselves. But as they had a genuine interest in making good shows and gaining ratings, they would create a plethora of companies, each competing against the other and thus improving the quality of ideas. And while the channels themselves pay their taxes and are housed in new office buildings, the production companies, where the real money is made, operate in a quite different world.

Recently I had been cutting a show at one such production company, Potemkin. It was based far away from Moscow's blue-glass-and-steel center, in a quiet road on an industrial estate. No graduates in horn-rimmed glasses snorting coke and eating organic sandwiches here, just the blotchy faces and twinkle-drunk eyes of factory workers and the tattooed bellies of the long-distance lorry drivers who ferry goods across one-sixth of the world's mud, ice, and bogs. The gray warehouse building where Potemkin was based had no sign, no number on the black metal door. Behind the door was a dirty, draughty, prison-like room where I was met by a bored, unsober guard who would look at me each day as if I were a stranger encroaching on his living space. To get to the office I walked down an unlit concrete corridor and turned sharp right, up two flights of narrow stairs, at the top of which was another black, unmarked metal door. There I rang the bell and an unfriendly voice asked through the intercom: "Who are you?" I waved my passport at where I guessed the spy camera to be. Then came the beep-beep-beep of the door being opened, and I was inside Potemkin Productions.

Suddenly I was back in a Western office, with Ikea furniture and lots of twentysomethings in jeans and bright T-shirts running around with coffees, cameras, and props. It could be any television production office anywhere in the world. But going past the reception desk, the conference room, coffee bar, and casting department, you reach a closed white door. Many turn back at this point, thinking they have seen the whole office. But tap in a code and you enter a much larger set of rooms: here the producers and their assistants sit and argue; here the accountants glide around with spreadsheets and solemnity; and here are the loggers, rows of young girls staring at screens as their hyperactive fingers type out interviews and dialogue from rushes. At the end of this office is another door. Tap in another code and you enter the editing suites, little cells where directors and video editors sweat and swear at one another. And beyond that is the final, most important, and least conspicuous of all the inconspicuous doors, with a code that few people know. It leads to the office of the head of the company, Ivan, and the room where the real accounts are kept. This whole elaborate setup is intended to foil the tax police. That's who the guards are there to keep out, or keep out long enough for the back office to be cleared and the hidden back entrance put to good use.

Whatever measures were taken, the tax police would occasionally turn up anyway, tipped off by someone. When they did we knew the drill: pick up your things and leave quietly. If anyone asks, say you've just come in for a meeting or casting. The first time it happened I was convinced we were about to be handcuffed and sent down for fraud.

But for my Russian colleagues the raids were a reason to celebrate: the rest of the day was invariably a holiday (deadlines be damned) as Ivan haggled with the tax police to keep down the size of the payoff. "Only a dozen people work here," he would say with a wink as they looked around at the many dozens of desks, chairs, and computers still warm from use. Then, I imagine, Ivan would bring out the fake accounts from the front office to support his case, and they would sit down to negotiate, with tea and biscuits, as if this were the most normal of business deals. And in Russia it was. The officials would look at the fake books, which they knew perfectly well to be fake, and extract fines in line with legislation they knew Ivan did not need to comply with. So everything would be settled, and every role, pose, and line of dialogue would reproduce the ritual of legality. It was a ritual played out every day in every medium-sized businesses, every restaurant, modeling agency, and PR firm across the country.

I once asked Ivan whether all this was necessary. Couldn't he just pay his taxes? He laughed. If he did that, he said, there would be no profit at all. No entrepreneurs paid their taxes in full; it wouldn't occur to them. It wasn't about morality; Ivan was a religious man and paid a tithe in voluntary charity. But no one thought taxes would ever be spent on schools or roads. And the tax police were much happier taking bribes than going to the trouble of stealing money that had been paid in the orthodox fashion. In any case, Ivan's profits were already squeezed by the broadcasters. Around 15 percent of any budget went to the guy at the channel who commissioned the programs and part-owned the company. When a British TV producer I knew tried opening a production company and didn't agree to let the head of the channel in on the deal, he was out of the country in a flash. You had to play by these rules.

Benedict's problem was that he couldn't, and his career suffered for it. People at the ministry kept asking him for "favors": a study tour to Sweden, a plasma TV for an office. Benedict refused. The ministry complained about him to Brussels; as the "beneficiary" it was up to the Russian side to approve Western consultants. Any new projects for Benedict were put on hold until the whole thing was cleared up. In the meantime he needed money to support himself and Marina.

The Moscow movie business was booming, and I helped him get bit parts as the token English man in Russian action movies. He got to know some Russian actors and would give them lessons to get their English accents right. The work was irregular. He moved into a smaller apartment. When we saw each other again it was in Sbarro; Scandinavia was a little pricy.

Benedict didn't look glum. There was always much of the chirpy, bright public school boy about him.

"I've joined the media," he told me. "I'm at Russia Today."

Russia Today is Russia's answer to BBC World and Al-Jazeera, a rolling 24/7 news channel broadcasting in English (and Arabic and Spanish) across every hotel and living room in the world, set up by presidential decree with an annual budget over $300 million and with a mission to "give Russia's point of view on world events." Wasn't Benedict worried he might end up doing the Kremlin's PR work?

"I'll leave if they censor me on anything. And it's only fair Russia should have the chance of expressing its point of view."

Benedict had been asked to put together a strategy for the business news section. He wrote papers to the head of the channel advising what sectors business news should cover, questions journalists should ask Russian CEOs so City analysts would watch the channel. He wasn't censored or leaned on in any way. Russia Today began to look and sound like any 24/7 news channel: the thumping music before the news flash, the earnest, pretty newscasters, the jock-like sports broadcasters. British and American twentysomethings straight out of university would be offered generous compensation packages, whereas in London or Washington they would have been expected to work for free. Of course they all wondered whether RT would turn out to be a propaganda channel. The twenty-three-year-olds would sit in Scandinavia after work and talk about it: "Well, it's all about expressing the Russian point of view," they would say, a little uncertain.

Since the war in Iraq many were skeptical about the virtue of the West. And then the financial crash undermined any superiority they felt the West might have. All the words that had been used to win the Cold War—"freedom," "democracy"—seemed to have swelled and mutated and changed their meaning, to become redundant. If during the Cold War Russia gave the West the opposition it needed to unify its various freedoms (cultural and economic and political) into one narrative, now that the opposition has disappeared, the unity of the Western story seems unwound. And in such a new world, what could be wrong with a "Russian point of view?"

"There is no such thing as objective reporting," the managing editor of Russia Today once told me when I asked him about the philosophy of his channel. He had been kind enough to meet me in his large, bright office. He speaks near-perfect English.

"But what is a Russian point of view? What does Russia Today stand for?"

"Oh, there is always a Russian point of view," he answered. "Take a banana. For someone it's food. For someone else it's a weapon. For a racist it's something to tease a black person with."

As I left the office I noticed a bag of golf clubs and a Kalashnikov leaning by the door.

"Does it scare you?" asked the managing editor.

It took a while for those working at RT to sense something was not quite right, that the "Russian point of view" could easily mean "the Kremlin point of view," and that "there is no such thing as objective reporting" meant the Kremlin had complete control over the truth. Once things had settled down it turned out that only about two hundred of the two-thousand-or-so employees were native English speakers. They were the on-screen window dressing and spell-checkers of the operation. Behind the scene the real decisions were made by a small band of Russian producers. In between the bland sports reports came the soft interviews with the President. ("Why is the opposition to you so small, Mr. President?" was one legendary question.) When K, a twenty-three-year-old straight out of Oxford, wrote a news story in which he stated that Estonia had been occupied by the USSR in 1945, he received a bollocking from the head of news: "We saved Estonia," he was told and was ordered to change the copy. When T, straight out of Bristol, was covering forest fires in Russia and wrote that the President wasn't coping, he was told: "You have to say the President is at the forefront of fighting against the fires." During the Russian war with Georgia, Russia Today ran a banner across its screen nonstop, screaming: "Georgians commit genocide in Ossetia." Nothing of the kind had been, or would ever be, proven. And when the President will go on to annex Crimea and launch his new war with the West, RT will be in the vanguard, fabricating startling fictions about fascists taking over Ukraine.

But the first-time viewer would not necessarily register these stories, for such obvious pro-Kremlin messaging is only one part of RT's output. Its popularity stems from coverage of what it calls "other," or "unreported," news. Julian Assange, head of WikiLeaks, had a talk show on RT. American academics who fight the American World Order, 9/11 conspiracy theorists, antiglobalists, and the European Far Right are given generous space. Nigel Farage, leader of the nonparliamentary anti-immigration UKIP party, is a frequent guest; Far Left supporter of Saddam Hussein George Galloway hosts a program about Western media bias. The channel has been nominated for an Emmy for its reporting on the Occupy movement in the United States and is described as "antihegemonic" by its fans; it is the most watched channel on YouTube, with one billion viewers, and the third most watched news channel in the United Kingdom, and its Washington office is expanding. But the channel is not uniformly "antihegemonic": when it suits, RT shows establishment stalwarts like Larry King, who hosts his own show on the network. So the Kremlin's message reaches a much wider audience than it would on its own: the President is spliced together with Assange and Larry King. This is a new type of Kremlin propaganda, less about arguing against the West with a counter-model as in the Cold War, more about slipping inside its language to play and taunt it from inside. In the ad for Larry King's show, keywords associated with the journalist flash up on-screen: "reputation," "intelligence," "respect," more and more of them until they merge into a fuzz, finishing with the jokey "suspenders." Then King, sitting in a studio, turns to the camera and says: "I would rather ask questions to people in positions of power instead of speaking on their behalf. That's why you can find my new show, *Larry King Now*, right here on RT. Question more." The little ad seems to be bundling the clichés of CNN and the BBC into a few seconds, pushing them to absurdity. There is a sense of giving two fingers to the Western media tradition: anyone can speak your language; it's meaningless!

The journalists who cotton on to what is happening leave quickly, often keen to scrub RT out of their résumés. Some even resign or complain on air, saying they no longer want to be "Putin's pawns." But most stay: those who are so ideologically driven by their hatred of the West they don't notice (or don't care) how they are being used, those so keen to be on TV they would work anywhere, or those who simply think "well, all news is fake, it's all just a bit of a game—isn't it?" At any time the turnover at RT is high, as those who make a fuss are sifted out, but there is no shortage of newcomers. In the evenings they hang out at Scandinavia, joined by the other new ex-pats, the communications experts and marketing consultants. An easy relativism ambles through the conversation. A Western journalist who has just taken up a Kremlin PR portfolio is asked how he squares it with his old job. "It's a challenge," he explains. There's nothing unusual in his career trajectory. Why, even the head of the BBC in Moscow moved to work in

Kremlin PR. "It would be an interesting job," everyone at Scandinavia agrees. "Russia might be naughty—but the West is bad, too," one often hears.

I would still see the old ex-pats at Scandinavia, the investment bankers and consultants. They still have tans and white teeth and talk about jogging. Many left their wives for Russian girls; many left to work for Russian companies.

Benedict spent six months at RT. He worked mainly from home, e-mailing his reports to the head of the channel. They were all ignored. The business news section on RT is slim; deep reporting on Russian companies would mean analyzing their corruption.

On his last day, as Benedict left the RT offices, the managing editor stepped into the corridor to greet him. He was, as ever, wearing a tweed suit.

"Would you like to pop into my office for a second?" he asked in his near-perfect English. Inside the office the managing editor brought out a bag of golf clubs.

"I'm a great fan of golf," he said to Benedict. "Would you care to come share a round with me some time?"

"I don't play golf," said Benedict.

"Pity. But we should become friends anyway. Look me up."

Benedict walked out, confused. The incident stayed with him. This strange Russian, dressed like an Edwardian gentleman, in the bland corridors of RT, speaking in a faintly plummy accent, offering to play golf.

"What was he thinking? Dressed that way? What did he want from me?" Benedict wondered.

If he had stayed longer at RT, Benedict would have found out the managing editor was thought by all to be the (alleged) secret service guy in the office.

When Benedict's blacklisting was lifted, he was given another EU job: first in Montenegro and then back in Kaliningrad. The ex-clave has changed. There are Lexuses and Mercedeses everywhere, shopping malls and sushi bars. P is now a minister. He wears Italian tailored suits and a Rolex; rumor has it he asks $10,000 for his signature to greenlight local deals. Kaliningrad is sealed off from the EU states around it, but local bureaucrats have made that into an advantage: there is great business to be made from bribes at border crossings. From their point of view it's more profitable for Kaliningrad to be sealed off. The border-bribes business is carefully organized on principles of effective management and cash flow, with every layer of bureaucrat taking an agreed upon cut, all the way up to the customs headquarters in Moscow. Russia has taken on the business lessons that development consultants like Benedict had come to teach, but applies them like gross carbuncles to state corruption.

Benedict has stayed on in Kaliningrad after his last project. It is Marina's home, and there is little to connect him any more to Ireland. He is in his sixties now. He has spent well over a decade in Russia. He teaches a little English on the side.

In the evening he walks his dog through the new Kaliningrad. New-builds are coming up everywhere. The old waterfront with its sailor bars has been replaced with a replica of a seventeenth-century gingerbread German town, all merrily colored in pastels. At night the new houses are largely dark and empty. As he strolls along the waterfront, Benedict raps his knuckles on the pastel houses. They are hollow to the touch, painted Perspex and plaster imitating stone, timber, and iron.

HELLO-GOODBYE

I met Dinara in a bar near one of Moscow's train stations. Girls would come from all over the country to be in that one bar. They would take the train into town, go straight to the bar, and hope to pick up a client. There were all types of girls: students looking for a few hundred bucks,

Botox-and-silicone hookers, old and sagging divorcees, provincial teens just out for a good time. It could be hard to tell between the girls who were working and those who were just hanging out. Once you get in it is basically an old, dark shed with one long bar running the whole length. The girls sit in one interminable row along the dark bar, staring hard at every man who comes in. Above the row of girls is a row of televisions, which if you come early in the evening might be tuned to the hysterical neon pinks and yellows, the hyperactive bursts of color, the canned laughter, the swelling, swirling logo "Feel our Love!" of my entertainment channel, TNT (later in the evening it's tuned to sports). The girls at the bar are TNT's target audience: eighteen- to thirty-five-year-old females with basic education, approximately $2,000 a month salary, and a thirst for bright colors. When I tell the girls I work for TNT, they drop their stares and become excited groupies. They crowd around me asking for autographs from our stars. Their favorite show is a sitcom called *Happy Together*, a Russian remake of the US show *Married with Children*, in which a wife with bright red hair and bright high heels dominates her slow, weak husband. It's the first show in Russia in which women are stronger than men, and the girls in the bar love it. They're less crazy about the show I'm working on: a reality series called *Hello-Goodbye*, about passengers meeting and parting in the Moscow airport. It's an emotional affair with lots of tears.

"There are so many lovers saying good-bye in your show. You should have more happy stories," advised one of the girls.

"Are all the people in your show real?" asked another.

The question was fair. Russian reality shows are all scripted—just like the politicians in the Duma are managed by the Kremlin ("the Duma is not a place for debate," the Speaker of the House once famously said), just like election results are all preordained—so Russian TV producers are paranoid about surrendering even a smidgen of control. *Hello-Goodbye* was an experiment in a real reality format in prime time (single documentary films don't count; they could never fill a prime-time slot).

Dinara stood modestly in the corner and smiled at me, her large black eyes behind the bangs of her bobbed black hair: the girls who looked least like prostitutes, I noticed, were often the most successful. I bought her whisky and colas, and we were still drinking the next morning. I offered to buy pizza. She said sure—but no pepperoni, she didn't eat pork. "I'm still a Muslim. Even though I'm a pro-sti-tute." She let each syllable of the word pop through her mouth, as if she were saying it for the first time in a strange language: "a pro-sti-tute."

And so it was that talk turned to matters of God.

Dinara said she believed in God but was afraid to touch the Koran since she became a prostitute. Would Allah forgive her? She liked being a prostitute—or at least she didn't mind. But what of Allah? He hated whoring. She could feel his rebuke. It kept her awake at night.

I told her that I'm sure Allah keeps things in perspective.

She told me her real name; up until then she'd called herself Tanya. Then she told me her story.

Dinara's parents were schoolteachers in Dagestan, a republic in the North Caucasus next to Chechnya. Her parents, and most people they knew, were out of work. She had come to Moscow to study but had failed all her entrance exams. She couldn't go back and tell them. She couldn't move forward and get a good job. So she hung out in bars and waited for people like me. She would do this for a while, then she would stop.

In her hometown things had started to get very religious. Her parents were secular Soviets, but the younger ones were all enthralled by the Wahhabi preachers who had come to the Caucasus from Saudi Arabia. Dinara couldn't stand the Wahhabis. But her younger sister was hooked. She had started to wear a head scarf and talked incessantly about jihad, about freeing the Caucasus from Moscow's yoke, about a caliphate stretching from Afghanistan to Turkey. Dinara was worried they would make her into a suicide bomber, a "Black Widow." All her sister's friends wanted to become Black Widows, to come to Moscow and blow themselves up.

Two sisters. One a prostitute. The other on jihad.

• • •

It was the Black Widows who had given me my first break in television. On October 23, 2002, between forty and fifty Chechen men and women drove in a blacked-out van through the evening Moscow traffic and out to a suburb once home to the world's largest ball-bearing factory. Having pulled balaclavas or scarves over their heads and belts of dynamite across their bodies, the terrorists walked briskly into the main entrance of a concrete, brutalist theater known as Palace of Culture Number 10.

The theater that evening was showing a performance of *Nord Ost*, a musical set in Stalin's Russia. It was Russia's first musical, a sign that Russian entertainment was becoming as good as the West's, and the show was sold out. The terrorists came onto the stage during a love aria. They fired into the air. At first many in the audience thought the terrorists were part of the play. When they realized they weren't, there were screams and a charge for the doors. The doors were blocked off already by Black Widows with explosives wired between their bodies and the doors. The men on the stage ordered the audience back into their seats; anyone who moved would be executed. The Moscow theater siege had begun; it would last four nights. By the time I arrived the next morning, as a fixer to a tabloid journalist (later I would assist on a documentary), the theater was surrounded by soldiers, medics, TV cameras, cops, and crowds of the curious. Hacks high-fived; police sucked on cigarettes with teenage girls playing hooky from school. Baked potato and hot dog vendors had come from across town and were having a field day. "Get your sausages here," they called to the crowd. A hundred yards between jolliness and terror, between hot dog stalls and hostages. At first I couldn't understand: Why is everyone acting like they're in a comedy, when this is a tragedy? Weren't we all meant to sit in silence? Bite our nails? Pray?

Back in the theater the orchestra pit was being used as a toilet; the people in the front row were sweating from the stench. Rows of seats were rattling as the hostages shook with fear. "When we die, how will I recognize you in paradise?" a seven-year-old girl asked her mother.

The hostages were losing hope. The terrorists demanded the President pull all federal forces out of the North Caucasus. The Kremlin had said there was no way it would negotiate: the President's credibility was based on quelling the rebellion in Chechnya. In the late 1990s, when he was still prime minister, he had been transformed from gray nobody to warrior by the Second Chechen War, suddenly appearing in camouflage sharing toasts with soldiers on the front. The war had been launched after a series of apartment buildings had been bombed in mainland Russia, killing 293 people in their homes. Nowhere, nowhere at all, had seemed safe. The perpetrators were announced on TV to be Chechen terrorists—though many still suspect they were working with the Kremlin's connivance to give the gray nobody who was meant to become president a reason to start a war. Many in the Russian public, cynical after living among Soviet lies so long, often assume the Kremlin's reality is scripted. There were indeed some grounds for skepticism: the Russian security services had been caught planting a bomb in an apartment block (they claimed it was a training accident); the speaker of the Duma had publicly announced one of the explosions before it had taken place.

While they held the *Nord Ost* theater the Chechen terrorists welcomed TV crews inside to give interviews live for Russian TV. The men spoke in heavily accented Russian, the southern accents usually used in Russian comedies.

"We've come to die here for Allah. We'll take hundreds of unbelievers with us," they announced.

One of the Black Widows spoke on camera. Through her head scarf you could see the most elegant, almond eyes. She said she was from a secular family and had joined a sect when her father, husband, and cousin were killed during the war with Russia.

"If we die it's not the end," she told the television audience, quite calmly. "There are many more of us."

It was my job to stay outside and wait to see if anything happened while my bosses went back to their hotel. It drizzled. The cold rain tasted salty. I drank warm beer, listening for an explosion or gunfire. There wouldn't be any. At 5:00 A.M. on the fourth night of the siege, special forces slipped a fizzing, mystery anesthetic blended with an aerosol spray gas into the ventilation system of the theater. A gray mist rose through the auditorium. The Black Widows were knocked out instantly, slouching over and sliding onto the floor. The hostages and hostage-takers all snored. Barely a shot was fired as special forces, safe from the fumes in gas masks, entered. All the Chechens were quickly killed. The soldiers celebrated the perfect operation. The darkness around me was lit up with the spotlights of news crews reporting a miracle of military brilliance.

The medics moved in to resuscitate the audience. They hadn't been warned about the gas. There weren't enough stretchers or medics. No one knew what the gas was, so they couldn't give the right antidotes. The sleeping hostages, fighting for breath, were carried out, placed face up on the steps of the theater, choking on their tongues, on their own vomit. I, and a thousand TV cameras, saw the still-sleeping hostages dragged through cold puddles to city buses standing nearby, thrown inside any which way and on top of each other. The buses pulled past me, the hostages slumped and sagging across the seats and on the wooden floor, like wasted bums on the last night bus. Some 129 hostages died: in the seats of the auditorium, on the steps of the theater, in buses.

The news crews reported a self-inflicted catastrophe.

The *Nord Ost* theater siege, this terror-reality show—in which the whole country saw its own sicknesses in close-up, broadcast on live TV; saw its smirking cops, its lost politicians desperate for guidance not knowing how to behave; saw Black Widows, somehow pitiable despite their actions, elevated to prime-time TV stars; saw victories turn to disasters within one news flash—was when television in Russia changed. No longer would there be anything uncontrolled, unvetted, un-thought-through. The conflict in the Caucasus disappeared from TV, only to be mentioned when the President announced the war there was over, that billions were being invested, that everything was just fine, that Chechnya had been rebuilt, that tourism was booming, that 98 percent of Chechens voted for the President in elections, and that the terrorists had been forced out to refuges in the hills and forests. When someone from the Caucasus appears on television now, it's usually as entertainment, the butt of jokes like the Irish are for the English.

But despite all the good news from the Caucasus, Black Widows still make it up to Moscow with rhythmic regularity. Over time their profile has changed: they are less likely to be the wives or daughters of those killed in the war in Chechnya. Instead they are from middle-class families in Makhachkala or Nalchik: the Salafi and Wahhabi preachers are doing their work. My journey to TNT in the mornings is on the subway. My line stops by the coach station, where long-haul coaches finish their fifty-hour journey from the Caucasus. On the morning of March 29, 2010, two Black Widows arrived there, descended into the subway, and blew themselves up a few stops into town, killing forty and injuring a hundred. This was done before 9:00 A.M. By the time I got on the subway a few hours later, the blood and glass and flesh entwined with metal had been cleaned away, and when I arrived at Byzantium and ascended the elevator to TNT, the whole thing, if not forgotten, was then out of mind.

There are no Black Widows in this neon-colored land.

. . .

When I went down to the Caucasus four years after *Nord Ost*, it was to work on a documentary about a local celebrity.

I landed in the capital of Balkaria, Nalchik, toward evening. Balkaria is right next to Chechnya, the other side from Dagestan. The suburbs were dark; streetlights are still a problem. Driving into town, the only brightly lit building was the brand new central mosque, paid for personally by the Kremlin-backed local leader, Arsen Kanokov. It's a nouveau riche mosque with mirrored glass, faux-marble towers, and gold-plated crescents: new money and new religion in one prayer. Locals call it the KGB mosque, an attempt by the government to co-opt Islam. The young prefer renegade Salafi preachers. In 2005 Nalchik had been attacked by 217 Islamic militants, who had stormed the TV tower and government offices. It had taken the army days to defeat them, and there were one hundred deaths, including fourteen civilians.

"We were shocked when we found out the militants weren't Chechens but local lads from the university where I teach," a history professor, Anzor, told me when we had dinner that evening. He was doing a bit of moonlighting as my fixer. "I don't know what my students think about, it's like they speak another language to me. My generation were all Soviet. But my students, they don't feel Russian. There's nothing to bind them to Moscow."

The waitress brought more tough, smoked mutton. We were having dinner in the Sosruko restaurant, the town's most famous, named after a local mythical hero, a sort of Hercules. The restaurant, twenty meters high and concrete, is in the shape of the head of a medieval knight, with helmet and huge moustache, perched on a hill above the town and lit up in neon green, the only building well lit aside from the new mosque.

"When my pupils go to Moscow they have people on the street tell them to go home. But yet we're part of the Russian state. Not immigrants. So what does that mean: 'go home'? Meanwhile there's no work here for the young," continued Anzor, "and only the Wahhabis spend time with them."

The next morning I could finally see Nalchik clearly. The center was neat, with perfect beds of bright flowers in front of government buildings in Soviet elephantine neoclassicism. Mount Elbrus loomed over Nalchik like a bully threatening violence at any moment. The celebrity I had come to meet was one Jambik Hatohov, at the time the biggest boy in the world. Seven years old, he weighed over a hundred kilos. Tabloid hacks and television crews would fly in from across the world to take his picture.

I drove out of town to his mother's apartment in a suburb of Soviet matchbox blocks standing crooked on uneven dirt roads (the local FSB following, to make sure I wasn't meeting jihadists on the sly). The staircase was dark, the green paint peeling. The mother, Nelya, opened the door for me. Inside the apartment had been refurbished in the IKEA style, paid for by Jambik's media appearances. Jambik was in the bath when I arrived. I could hear him splashing and squealing and snorting. I went in to say hello. He was so overweight his penis was covered by flab, and his toes and eyes barely peaked out. He grunted rather than breathed. There was water all over the floor, and he was sliding up and down in a bath he could hardly fit in, splashing water everywhere. He charged me when I came in, and I was slammed against the door.

"He never had a father," said Nelya. "He needs a man in his life."

We went into town. It was the "day of the city," the state-sponsored party to instill local pride. There were fairground rides and sporting events. Jambik was known by everyone; he was a star. "It's our Sosruko, our little warrior!" locals would cry as we passed through the festival. Everyone gave him food: shashlik, smoked mutton, Snickers, pizza, Coke. They let us on rides for free. Jambik ate all the time, grunting. When Nelya tried to stop him he would scream like a burglar alarm and hit her with the full weight of his hundred-and-something kilos.

We stopped to watch a wrestling competition. There were fighters from several North Caucasus republics (Dagestan, Balkaria, Ingushetia), who represented themselves rather than "Russia." There were Olympic champions; the North Caucasus produces the greatest wrestlers in the world, and it's always a problem for the local wrestlers to feel they win their golds for "Russia." But for many young males the choice is between jihad and wrestling. Nelya hoped Jambik would grow up to become a wrestler, though the local trainers all told her he was too slow. Nelya thought he might make it in sumo.

After a while I noticed Jambik's speech was slow and slurred.

"How's he doing at school?" I asked Nelya.

"Oh, he's such a star they let him pass into the year above without taking any exams," said Nelya.

We flew Jambik to Moscow, where he appeared on Russia's number one talk show and pushed a Jeep for the cameras. He auditioned at Russia's top children's TV sketch show.

Meanwhile concerned doctors met with Nelya: Jambik was not a warrior, they explained, but a very sick child who needed help or he would die. She needed to put him on a diet, change their lifestyle. Nelya didn't want to know: he was her bloated, golden goose and their ticket to another life. I felt for her; I had seen what happened when she tried to deny Jambik food.

"God has willed him to be this way," she insisted.

When we parted Jambik hugged me so hard I could barely breathe. Later I heard that he had received an offer to study sumo in Japan. That had always been Nelya's dream for him. But the sumo never did work out for Jambik. Soon the family was back in Nalchik. A couple of years later an even bigger boy was born, in Mexico, and some of Jambik's star allure was lost. At the age of eleven he weighed 146 kilos.

• • •

"Switch on the news," said the text message form one of my producers on *Hello-Goodbye*. "The fuckers wrecked our set! Our set!"

A suicide bomber had blown himself up in the arrivals hall of Domodedovo international airport, where we had earlier shot *Hello-Goodbye*. On the news CCTV footage showed a blurred figure walking across the hall, then the shot was filled with a burst of blinding bright light, and when we saw the hall again it was full of blood. Thirty-seven people died. One-hundred-eighty were injured. A mass of worried messages jammed my phone: I was nowhere near the airport at the time, and the series had been scrapped long before the bomb went off.

Domodedovo is the newest of Moscow's three airports. It's all glass and light, swept marble floors, cappuccino bars, and bikini boutiques. When I made *Hello-Goodbye* I spent a lot of time in Domodedovo. I know every place the smoke alarms are dummies and you can have a crafty fag, when the best light floods through the glass walls to get the best shots, how to cut a deal with the customs guys so they go and buy you duty-free whisky. I know which flights bring in which type of passenger and what stories they bring with them. Our presenter, dressed in a bright orange shirt, would walk around the airport and talk to people parting or meeting: slow-kissing lovers parting as he leaves to work in San Francisco; funny lads off for a dirty weekend in Thailand; a secretary waiting for her boss, whom she is secretly in love with, to return from a business trip to London. A microcosm of the new, middle-class Russia, the first Russian generation that not only flies but even flies abroad as a matter of course, a generation's aspirations under one high-domed roof, in this bright new airport in a bright new nation.

So many of our stories were about women waiting for men. There was the fur-clad Anna, a former ballerina from Voronezh, who now danced at strip clubs in Zurich. Her Swiss banker boyfriend was coming to meet her family in Russia and her two children from previous men who had dumped her without leaving a penny behind. The banker wanted to marry her, but it was happening all too fast, and she wasn't so sure. Two weeks later we saw them again; they parted frostily, then he flew back to Zurich. She wouldn't tell us what went wrong, only: "Us girls called strip clubs Krankenhauser, loony bins, only mentally ill men go there."

And there was "the milkmaid," whose story became a YouTube hit. A woman of uncertain age, with golden teeth, a huge permed haircut, bright pink lips, and a fur coat over mud-splattered, knee-high white boots, she was a milkmaid on a cooperative farm. She was waiting for her boyfriend, a teenage Tajik who helped clean refuse at the farm. Their relationship was the scandal of the village: not only was she old enough to be his mother, but worse, she was a white woman going with a "churok," the insulting nickname Russians give to anyone from the Caucasus or Central Asia. The paranoia that men from the "south" will take away white women has grown into something of a Russian obsession: the "churok" women will blow us up; the "churok" men will take away our women; the "churki" will rebel and the Russian Empire will be no more.

But the "milkmaid" didn't give a damn about what the locals on the farm said about her lover. She reveled in all the details of their affair:

"At work I wear this little white robe, shows off my legs, he likes that!" she told us.

"I didn't give it up straight away, I told him he'd have to give me perfume first. That's what my mother taught me!"

And now she was pregnant. She told him when he came off the plane, on camera. We caught all his emotions: shock (he couldn't have been older than seventeen), anger, and then the joy as he hauled her up and twirled her: perm, fur coat, white boots, and all. Other people in the arrivals lounge began to applaud and cheer. That was right on the spot where the suicide bomber would blow himself up.

The arrivals hall was always the most difficult to film in. It has been under construction ever since I can remember. It has no natural light, is cramped and narrow. We had to drag and place contributors in front of a neon café sign to make the picture palatable. If they stood naturally the shot was awful, made positively ghoulish by the black-coated, grim-faced mob of illegal taxi drivers who leap on anyone coming out of customs and try to bully them into taking overpriced rides to town. Many of these taxi drivers are from the North Caucasus; the suicide bomber's victims were compatriots and coreligionists.

And as we shot *Hello-Goodbye*, there was always another reality just out of frame. For every London and Paris flight, there were far more from Makhachkala, Nalchik, Tashkent. Clans of gold-toothed migrants form the Caucasus and Central Asia squatted in the manicured halls, among hills of plastic sacks full of clothes and fruit they bring to trade in Moscow's markets.

"We don't want to see them," the producer at TNT would complain. "We've researched our audience. They don't want to hear about the people from the Caucasus or Central Asia. They don't relate to them. We need ethnic Russians."

Eventually, however, we had to deal with a serious story about Chechnya. One young couple we interviewed were parting for at least six months. The guy looked like a young Steve McQueen; the girl was spotty.

"Why so long?"

"There's war on where I work. I'm a soldier. I serve in Chechnya. She can't go there."

This is how they met. He was alone and bored at his post, a little brick hut high in the Caucasus. It was night, and he was drunk. He wanted to find a girl away from the front. He looked down at the serial number on his gun. Just for the hell of it he took out his phone and dialed the Moscow area code followed by the serial number. A sleepy girl answered.

"Who is this?"

He told her. She slammed down the phone.

"I just liked her voice," he said. "So I kept on phoning."

He called every day. Slowly she caved in. They sent each other photos of themselves on their cell phones. Two weeks before our shoot he had some leave and came to visit her. She was from a traditional family from the Caucasus, and he asked her father's permission to marry her. The father agreed. Now they both wore rings. The wedding was planned for when he would return from Chechnya in six months.

"This is my last tour of duty. I'm done with the army. In six months I come back and that's it, no more war."

"Do you still have the gun with her number?"

"The gun? I'll always keep that gun."

He blew kisses and she cried as he went through passport control. I have no idea what happened to them after that.

• • •

It was a while since I'd been back to the long, long bar by the train station.

"How's your show?" asked the girls.

"It got scrapped."

The ratings for *Hello-Goodbye* had sucked. Part of the problem was that the audience wouldn't believe the stories in the show were real. After so many years of fake reality, it was hard to convince them this was genuine.

Dinara skipped up to me with a squeal. She bought me a drink. Her hair was longer. She hadn't been able to get a proper job or resume her studies. Her face looked puffy.

"How's your sister?"

"Great," said Dinara. "Great."

"Is she still with the Wahhabis?"

"The nightmare's passed. I went back home and convinced her to join me here. Thank God, she loves Moscow, she doesn't want to do jihad any more. Now we work together, we're both pro-sti-tutes."

Dinara was delighted. Thank God. A story with a happy ending.

THE HEIGHTS OF CREATION

Though we are expecting Vladislav Surkov, the man known as the "Kremlin demiurge," who has "privatized the Russian political system," to enter from the front of the university auditorium, he surprises us all by striding in from the back. He's got his famous Cheshire Cat smile on. He's wearing a white shirt and a leather jacket that is part Joy Division and part 1930s commissar. He walks straight to the stage in front of an audience of PhD students, professors, journalists, and politicians.

"I am the author, or one of the authors, of the new Russian system," he tells us by way of introduction. "My portfolio at the Kremlin and in government has included ideology, media, political parties, religion, modernization, innovation, foreign relations, and . . ." here he pauses and smiles, "modern art." He offers to not make a speech, instead welcoming the audience to pose questions and have an open discussion. After the first question he talks for almost forty-five minutes, leaving hardly any time for questions after all. It's his political system in miniature: democratic rhetoric and undemocratic intent.

As former deputy head of the presidential administration, later deputy prime minister and then assistant to the President on foreign affairs, Surkov has directed Russian society like one great reality show. He claps once and a new political party appears. He claps again and creates Nashi, the Russian equivalent of the Hitler Youth, who are trained for street battles with potential prodemocracy supporters and burn books by unpatriotic writers on Red Square. As deputy head of the administration he would meet once a week with the heads of the television channels in his Kremlin office, instructing them on whom to attack and whom to defend, who is allowed on TV and who is banned, how the President is to be presented, and the very language and categories the country thinks and feels in. The Ostankino TV presenters, instructed by Surkov, pluck a theme (oligarchs, America, the Middle

East) and speak for twenty minutes, hinting, nudging, winking, insinuating though rarely ever saying anything directly, repeating words like "them" and "the enemy" endlessly until they are imprinted on the mind. They repeat the great mantras of the era: the President is the President of "stability," the antithesis to the era of "confusion and twilight" in the 1990s. "Stability"—the word is repeated again and again in a myriad seemingly irrelevant contexts until it echoes and tolls like a great bell and seems to mean everything good; anyone who opposes the President is an enemy of the great God of "stability." "Effective manager," a term quarried from Western corporate speak, is transmuted into a term to venerate the President as the most "effective manager" of all. "Effective" becomes the raison d'être for everything: Stalin was an "effective manager" who had to make sacrifices for the sake of being "effective." The words trickle into the streets: "Our relationship is not effective" lovers tell each other when they break up. "Effective," "stability": no one can quite define what they actually mean, and as the city transforms and surges, everyone senses things are the very opposite of stable, and certainly nothing is "effective," but the way Surkov and his puppets use them the words have taken on a life of their own and act like falling axes over anyone who is in any way disloyal.

One of Surkov's many nicknames is the "political technologist of all of Rus." Political technologists are the new Russian name for a very old profession: viziers, gray cardinals, wizards of Oz. They first emerged in the mid-1990s, knocking on the gates of power like pied pipers, bowing low and offering their services to explain the world and whispering that they could reinvent it. They inherited a very Soviet tradition of top-down governance and tsarist practices of co-opting antistate actors (anarchists in the nineteenth century, neo-Nazis and religious fanatics now), all fused with the latest thinking in television, advertising, and black PR. Their first clients were actually Russian modernizers: in 1996 the political technologists, coordinated by Boris Berezovsky, the oligarch nicknamed the "Godfather of the Kremlin" and the man who first understood the power of television in Russia, managed to win then President Boris Yeltsin a seemingly lost election by persuading the nation he was the only man who could save it from a return to revanchist Communism and new fascism. They produced TV scare-stories of looming pogroms and conjured fake Far Right parties, insinuating that the other candidate was a Stalinist (he was actually more a socialist democrat), to help create the mirage of a looming "red-brown" menace.

In the twenty-first century the techniques of the political technologists have become centralized and systematized, coordinated out of the office of the presidential administration, where Surkov would sit behind a desk on which were phones bearing the names of all the "independent" party leaders, calling and directing them at any moment, day or night. The brilliance of this new type of authoritarianism is that instead of simply oppressing opposition, as had been the case with twentieth-century strains, it climbs inside all ideologies and movements, exploiting and rendering them absurd. One moment Surkov would fund civic forums and human rights NGOs, the next he would quietly support nationalist movements that accuse the NGOs of being tools of the West. With a flourish he sponsored lavish arts festivals for the most provocative modern artists in Moscow, then supported Orthodox fundamentalists, dressed all in black and carrying crosses, who in turn attacked the modern art exhibitions. The Kremlin's idea is to own all forms of political discourse, to not let any independent movements develop outside of its walls. Its Moscow can feel like an oligarchy in the morning and a democracy in the afternoon, a monarchy for dinner and a totalitarian state by bedtime.

Living in the world of Surkov and the political technologists, I find myself increasingly confused. Recently my salary almost doubled. On top of directing shows for TNT, I have been doing some work for a new media house called SNOB, which encompasses TV channels and magazines and a gated online community for the country's most brilliant minds. It is meant to foster a new type of "global Russian," a new class who will fight for all things Western and liberal in the country. It is financed by one of Russia's richest men, the oligarch Mikhail Prokhorov, who also owns the Brooklyn Nets. I have been hired as a "consultant" for one of SNOB's TV channels. I write interminable notes and strategies and flowcharts, though nothing ever seems to happen. But I get paid. And the offices, where I drop in several times a week to talk about "unique selling points" and "high production values," are like some sort of hipster fantasy: set in a converted factory, the open brickwork left untouched, the huge arches of the giant windows preserved, with edit suites and open plan offices built in delicately. The employees are the children of Soviet intelligentsia, with perfect English and vocal in their criticism of the regime. The deputy editor is a well-known American Russian activist for lesbian, gay, bisexual, and transgender rights, and her articles in glossy Western magazines attack the President vociferously. But for all the opposition posturing of SNOB, it's also clear there is no way a project so high profile could have been created without the Kremlin's blessing. Is this not just the sort of "managed" opposition the Kremlin is very comfortable with? On the one hand allowing liberals to feel they have a free voice and a home (and a paycheck), on the other helping the Kremlin define the "opposition" as hipster Muscovites, out of touch with "ordinary" Russians, obsessed with "marginal" issues such as gay rights (in a homophobic country). The very name of the project, "SNOB," though meant ironically, already defines us as a potential object of hate. And for all the anti-Kremlin rants on SNOB, we never actually do any real investigative journalism, find out any hard facts about money stolen from the state budget: in twenty-first-century Russia you are allowed to say anything you want as long as you don't follow the corruption trail. After work I sit with my colleagues, drinking and talking: Are we the opposition? Are we helping Russia become a freer place? Or are we actually a Kremlin project strengthening the

President? Actually doing damage to the cause of liberty? Or are we both? A card to be played?

Sure enough, in the next presidential elections Prokhorov will become the Kremlin-endorsed liberal candidate: the SNOB project helps endear him to the intelligentsia, but as a flamboyant oligarch best known for partying in Courchevel with busloads of models, he is an easy target for the Kremlin. Again Moscow's chattering classes speculate: Is Prokhorov a genuine candidate? Is it better to vote for him, or does that mean you're playing the Kremlin game? Or should one vote for no one and ignore the system? In the end Prokhorov gains a fairly impressive 8 percent—before elegantly retreating from the political scene to wait for his next call-up. We are all just bit-part players in the political technologists' great reality show.

But Surkov is more than just a political operator. He is an aesthete who pens essays on modern art, an aficionado of gangsta rap who keeps a photo of Tupac on his desk next to that of the President. He likes to say the President has been sent to us from God, yet writes lyrics for rock groups such as these:

> *He is always ahead of us in scarlet silk on a pale horse.*
> *We follow him, up to our knees in mud and our necks in guilt.*
> *Along our road burn houses and bridges.*
> *I will be like you.*
> *You will be like him.*
> *We will be like everyone.*

And Surkov is also the alleged author of a novel, *Almost Zero*, published in 2008 and informed by his own experiences. "Alleged" because the novel was published under the pseudonym Natan Dubovitsky; Surkov's wife is called Natalya Dubovitskaya. Officially Surkov is the author of the preface, in which he denies being the author of the novel, then makes a point of contradicting himself: "The author of this novel is an unoriginal Hamlet-obsessed hack"; "this is the best book I have ever read." In interviews he can come close to admitting to being the author while always pulling back from a complete confession. Whether or not he actually wrote every word of it, he has gone out of his way to associate himself with it. And it is a best seller: the key confession of the era, the closest we might ever come to seeing inside the mind of the system.

The novel is a satire of contemporary Russia whose hero, Egor, is a corrupt PR man happy to serve anyone who'll pay the rent. A former publisher of avant-garde poetry, he now buys texts from impoverished underground writers, then sells the rights to rich bureaucrats and gangsters with artistic ambitions, who publish them under their own names. Everyone is for sale in this world; even the most "liberal" journalists have their price. The world of PR and publishing as portrayed in the novel is dangerous. Publishing houses have their own gangs, whose members shoot each other over the rights to Nabokov and Pushkin, and the secret services infiltrate them for their own murky ends. It's exactly the sort of book Surkov's youth groups burn on Red Square.

Born in provincial Russia to a single mother, Egor grows up as a bookish hipster disenchanted with the late Soviet Union's sham ideology. In the 1980s he moves to Moscow to hang out on the fringes of the bohemian set; in the 1990s he becomes a PR guru. It's a background that has a lot in common with what we know of Surkov's own—he only leaks details to the press when he sees fit. He was born in 1964, the son of a Russian mother and a Chechen father who left when Surkov was still a young child. Former schoolmates remember him as someone who made fun of the teacher's pets in the Komsomol, wore velvet trousers, had long hair like Pink Floyd, wrote poetry, and was a hit with the girls. He was a straight-A student whose essays on literature were read aloud by teachers in the staff room; it wasn't only in his own eyes that he was too smart to believe in the social and political set around him.

"The revolutionary poet Mayakovsky claimed that life (after the communist revolution) is good and it's good to be alive," wrote the teenage Surkov in lines that were strikingly subversive for a Soviet pupil. "However, this did not stop Mayakovsky from shooting himself several years later."

After he moved to Moscow, Surkov first pursued and abandoned a range of university careers from metallurgy to theater directing, then put in a spell in the army (where he might have served in military espionage), and engaged in regular violent altercations (he was expelled from drama school for fighting). His first wife was an artist famous for her collection of theater puppets (which Surkov would later build up into a museum). And as Surkov matured, Russia experimented with different models at a dizzying rate: Soviet stagnation led to perestroika, which led to the collapse of the Soviet Union, liberal euphoria, economic disaster, oligarchy, and the mafia state. How can you believe in anything when everything around you is changing so fast?

He was drawn to the bohemian set in Moscow, where performance artists were starting to capture the sense of dizzying mutability. No party would be complete without Oleg Kulik (who would impersonate a rabid dog to show the brokenness of post-Soviet man), German Vinogradov (who would walk naked into the street and pour ice water over himself), or later Andrej Bartenjev (who would dress as an alien to highlight how weird this new world was). And of course Vladik Mamyshev-Monroe. Hyper-camp and always playing with a repertoire of poses, Vladik was a post-Soviet Warhol mixed with Ru Paul. Russia's first drag artist, he started out impersonating Marilyn Monroe and Hitler ("the two greatest symbols of the twentieth century," he would say) and went on to portray Russian pop stars, Rasputin, and Gorbachev as an Indian woman; he turned up at parties as Yeltsin, Tutankhamen, or Karl Lagerfeld. "When I perform, for a few seconds I become my subject," Vladik liked to say. His impersonations were always obsessively accurate, pushing his subject to the point of extreme, where the person's image would begin to reveal and undermine itself.

At the same time Russia was discovering the magic of PR and advertising, and Surkov found his métier. He was given his chance by Russia's best-looking oligarch, Mikhail Khodorkovsky. In 1992 he launched Khodorkovsky's first ad campaign, in which the oligarch, in checked jacket, moustache, and a massive grin, was pictured holding out bundles of cash: "Join my bank if you want some easy money" was the message. "I've made it; so can you!" The poster was pinned up on every bus and billboard, and for a population raised on anticapitalist values, it was a shock. It was the first time a Russian company had used the face of its own owner as the brand. It was the first time wealth had been advertised as a virtue. Previously millionaires might have existed, but they always had to hide their success. But Surkov could sense the world was shifting.

Surkov next worked as head of PR at Ostankino's Channel 1, for the then grand vizier of the Kremlin court, Boris Berezovsky. In 1999 he joined the Kremlin, creating the President's image just as he had created Khodorkovsky's. When the President exiled Berezovsky and arrested and jailed Khodorkovsky, Surkov helped run the media campaign, which featured a new image of Khodorkovsky: instead of the grinning oligarch pictured handing out money, he was now always shown behind bars. The message was clear—you're only a photo away from going from the cover of *Forbes* to a prison cell.

And through all these changes Surkov switched positions, masters, and ideologies without seeming to skip a beat.

Perhaps the most interesting parts of *Almost Zero* occur when the author moves away from social satire to describe the inner world of his protagonist. Egor is described as a "vulgar Hamlet" who can see through the superficiality of his age but is unable to have genuine feelings for anyone or anything:

"His self was locked in a nutshell . . . outside were his shadows, dolls. He saw himself as almost autistic, imitating contact with the outside world, talking to others in false voices to fish out whatever he needed from the Moscow squall: books, sex, money, food, power and other useful things."

Egor is a manipulator but not a nihilist; he has a very clear conception of the divine:

"Egor could clearly see the heights of Creation, where in a blinding abyss frolic non-corporeal, un-piloted, pathless words, free beings, joining and dividing and merging to create beautiful patterns."

The heights of creation! Egor's god is beyond good and evil, and Egor is his privileged companion: too clever to care for anyone, too close to God to need morality. He sees the world as a space in which to project different realities. Surkov articulates the underlying philosophy of the new elite, a generation of post-Soviet supermen who are stronger, more clearheaded, faster, and more flexible than anyone that has come before.

I encounter forms of this attitude every day. The producers who work at the Ostankino channels might all be liberals in their private lives, holiday in Tuscany, and be completely European in their tastes. When I ask how they marry their professional and personal lives, they look at me as if I were a fool and answer: "Over the last twenty years we've lived through a communism we never believed in, democracy and defaults and mafia state and oligarchy, and we've realized they are illusions, that everything is PR." "Everything is PR" has become the favorite phrase of the new Russia; my Moscow peers are filled with a sense that they are both cynical and enlightened. When I ask them about Soviet-era dissidents, like my parents, who fought against communism, they dismiss them as naïve dreamers and my own Western attachment to such vague notions as "human rights" and "freedom" as a blunder. "Can't you see your own governments are just as bad as ours?" they ask me. I try to protest—but they just smile and pity me. To believe in something and stand by it in this world is derided, the ability to be a shape-shifter celebrated. Vladimir Nabokov once described a species of butterfly that at an early stage in its development had to learn how to change colors to hide from predators. The butterfly's predators had long died off, but still it changed its colors from the sheer pleasure of transformation. Something similar has happened to the Russian elites: during the Soviet period they learned to dissimulate in order to survive; now there is no need to constantly change their colors, but they continue to do so out of a sort of dark joy, conformism raised to the level of aesthetic act.

Surkov himself is the ultimate expression of this psychology. As I watch him give his speech to the students and journalists, he seems to change and transform like mercury, from cherubic smile to demonic stare, from a woolly liberal preaching "modernization" to a finger-wagging nationalist, spitting out willfully contradictory ideas: "managed democracy," "conservative modernization." Then he steps back, smiling, and says: "We need a new political party, and we should help it happen, no need to wait and make it form by itself." And when you look closely at the party men in the political reality show Surkov directs, the spitting nationalists and beetroot-faced communists, you notice how they all seem to perform their roles with a little ironic twinkle.

Elsewhere Surkov likes to invoke the new postmodern texts just translated into Russian, the breakdown of grand narratives, the impossibility of truth, how everything is only "simulacrum" and "simulacra" . . . and then in the next moment he says how he despises relativism and loves conservatism, before quoting Allen Ginsberg's "Sunflower Sutra," in English and by heart. If the West once undermined and helped to ultimately defeat the USSR by uniting free market economics, cool culture, and democratic politics into one package (parliaments, investment banks, and abstract expressionism fused to defeat the Politburo, planned economics, and social realism), Surkov's genius has been to tear those associations apart, to marry authoritarianism and modern art, to use the language of rights and representation to validate tyranny, to recut and paste democratic capitalism until it means the reverse of its original purpose.

At the height of his power Surkov's ambition grew beyond mere parties and policies or even novels. He began to dream of creating a new city, a utopia. Its name was to be Skolkovo, a Russian Silicon Valley, a gated community of post-Soviet perfection. Hundreds of millions were poured into the project. I found myself invited on a media tour to Surkov's city of the sun. We were taken on a coach and driven for hours outside of Moscow. At the visitor's center at Skolkovo a girl with clover-blue eyes showed us 3-D video projections of the future city: offices built into the landscape in the style of Frank Lloyd Wright, artificial lakes and schools, eternal sunshine and adventure sports, and entrepreneurs in sneakers. We got into the bus and drove across the real landscape: miles of snowy wastes and bare trees. Since Skolkovo's launch billions have been spent, but virtually nothing has been built (there are whispers and rumors the project was at least partly created to give Surkov's circle a mechanism through which to siphon off state money).

We were being taken to the hyper-cube, the only building of the future city already constructed. "We will soon arrive at the hyper-cube," our guide said. "The hyper-cube is just coming into view." It turned out to be a very modernist little structure, looking lost in an empty field. It had exposed concrete walls and large video screens. A PR man with a deep tan and the nasty smile common to upper-end foreign-service KGB men told us that all the corruption scandals related to Skolkovo had been solved. Behind him, on the video screens, the words "innovation" and "modernization" kept popping up. I asked whether the "modernization" project had failed: every week there were more arrests of businessmen and -women, and more than 50 percent of people were now employed by state companies. Polls showed that young people no longer wanted to be entrepreneurs but bureaucrats. The PR man shrugged and answered that the President was fully behind Skolkovo.

On the tour of Skolkovo we were accompanied by a young man named Sergey Kalenik, a member of the Kremlin youth group, Nashi, created by Surkov. Sergey wore a hoodie, goatee, and skinny jeans and looked like any hipster youth you find in Brooklyn or Hackney—then he opened his mouth and began to sing paeans to the President and how the West is out to get Russia. Sergey was from a humble background in Minsk, Belarus. He first made his name by drawing a really rather good manga cartoon that showed the President as superhero doing battle against zombie protesters and evil monster anticorruption bloggers: a nice example of the Surkovian tactic of co-opting hipster language to its own ends, trying to get the "cool" people on the Kremlin's side.

The cartoon was so successful Kalenik was introduced to senior government officials, and his career as a young spin doctor was launched. "Politics is the ability to use any situation to advance your own status," Sergey told me with a smile that seemed to mimic Surkov's (who in turn mimics the KGB men). "How do you define your political views?" I asked him. He looked at me like I was a fool to ask, then smiled: "I'm a liberal . . . it can mean anything!"

ACT II

CRACKS IN THE KREMLIN MATRIX

You think prison is something bad that happens to other people. And then you wake up and my God you're a convict.

On the evening before her arrest, Yana Yakovleva was sitting in the garden of her country dacha. It was Sunday. The last of the summer was slowly draining out of the light. The guests had left; there were empty wine glasses and wine bottles and plates with cheese and sushi from the picnic lying on the mown grass. Yana leant back in the chaise longue to catch the last of the sun. It was getting cold fast. Suddenly, very suddenly, she had the sense something bad was about to happen. It was so strong Yana suddenly realized she was crying.

Alexey, her lover, was moving about the garden collecting things. Yana wanted to call out to him, then changed her mind. She couldn't explain her sudden fear. They had been living together for two years, and she knew what he would say: he would tell her to snap out of it.

The next morning, a Monday, she drove the Lexus back into town still wearing the clothes from the weekend party: a short white frilly dress, pink heels, and a white handbag. They stopped for a cappuccino at the new coffeehouse on Frunzenskaya and skimmed through *Vedemosti*, the Russian version of the *Financial Times*. Then Alexey grabbed a cab to his job as a senior manager in one of the big new Russian energy companies, and Yana drove to the gym. All the while the sense that something bad was about to happen wouldn't go away, like a distant but ever-present ringing in her ears.

At the reception desk she noticed the girl behind the counter was staring at her in a strange way. Yana thought it rude; this was a private gym, and it wasn't the sort of stare members paid to receive. Near the door to the back office there was a small group of men in polyester suits. They didn't look like they belonged here. One was pacing back and forth, wringing his hands.

Her trainer had Yana box, run, and then finish off with abs. It hurt after the weekend's wine, and her trainer let her go easy on the abs. "See you Thursday," the trainer said. She usually trained three times a week. "If I make it," said Yana. It just came out; she wasn't sure why she had said it. "Oh, there's nowhere you could disappear to" laughed the trainer.

Yana showered and changed back into the white dress and pink heels. They would giggle behind her back at work, but it was her company, and there was no one to tell her what to wear. She had been running the company since she was twenty with one other partner. Now she was thirty-four, they had dozens of employees, and she could afford to turn up late wearing high heels. It was the sort of company the general public rarely notices but that makes good money: importing and reselling industrial cleaning fluids to factories and army bases. Yana came from a family of academic scientists; her father had taught chemistry, and now she made her money in the chemicals industry. Soviet knowledge transmuting smoothly to post-Soviet economics.

When she came out of the changing room the girl at the reception desk was staring at her even harder. It was embarrassing. Yana had decided enough was enough; she was going to tell her off. Then the men in polyester suits approached. The nervous one flashed his badge and said, "We're from the FDCS [Drug Enforcement Agency]; you need to come with us."

The first thought that went through Yana's mind was: "That explains why the reception girl had been looking at me funny. 'The FDCS have come for Yakovleva'—it makes me sound like I'm a drug dealer!"

Yana flashed the girl at reception a quick smile as if to say, "Hey, it's no big deal, I work in pharmaceuticals, we deal with the FDCS all the time," but the girl turned away.

Yana felt no panic. She had done nothing wrong, so why should she panic?

The FDCS had been visiting her office regularly over the last few months: the chemicals and pharmaceuticals industry, along with illegal drugs, were regulated by them. Men in masks carrying Kalashnikovs had raided the accounts department. No big deal: that happens regularly in Russia, to every business—when the organs want to find something, anything wrong in your taxes or your forms and registrations and extract some bribes.

Yana had never worried about it. Her company had done nothing wrong. And if they had done nothing wrong, what did she have to fear? It would be fine.

Yana followed the men from the FDCS to the front door. They looked awkward in their cheap suits in the up-market gym. The main one was sweating, but he had calmed down once he realized she wasn't putting up a fight. But why should she put up a fight?

Outside were two drivers. They had parked their old matchbox Soviet cars in front of her new Lexus so she wouldn't be able to make a getaway. It made her smile; it was like in some cops and robbers TV show.

One of the drivers walked up to her. He looked her up and down.

"It's nice to arrest decent looking people."

"I'm being arrested?"

"Well . . . held."

"I need to call my boyfriend."

"No phone calls," they told her.

They let her drive her own car to the FDCS headquarters. They sat in the back and let her drive. It was all very casual. She could sense she was entering a different world, one where the rules were different, where other people would tell her what to do. But she didn't feel panic. Just strange. She was trying to work out what the rules of this new world were. It felt curious. It tingled.

The office of the FDCS was in the north of town, a large gray Stalin building like an elaborately carved gravestone with the heraldic sign of the Kremlin's double-headed eagle at the entrance. The doors were heavy to push open. Inside were long office corridors and lots of men in polyester suits. They seemed to hush when they saw Yana, eyeing her as if she were someone terribly important.

They took her to an office room with a table and two chairs. They fussed over her: Did she want some tea? Something to eat? She asked for a chocolate bar, and they ran off to the local store to buy one. Her lawyer was there and told her to make calls. Yana phoned Alexey, but he wouldn't pick up. So she texted instead: "I've been arrested." And then a smiley face.

"You'd better ask him to bring you some clothes," said the lawyer.

This struck Yana.

"You think I will be here a while?"

"Not too long. We'll sort it out."

Then the detective came in. His name was Vaselkov, which sounds like the Russian word for "daisy." He had a face like a bulldog.

"We are charging you with a particularly serious crime," said Vaselkov.

"Which one?"

"Read this," he said and handed her a folder of ninety pages or so. "And then sign that you have understood everything."

Yana looked at Vaselkov. He stared into nowhere like an automaton. She opened the folder. Inside were photocopies of her company's accounts and transactions. Bills for buying and selling. Page after page of them. Just their accounts and bills. What they did normally every day. She couldn't understand. What was she being charged with?

"You have been trading in diethyl ether," said Vaselkov.

Diethyl ether was a chemical cleaning agent. Yakovleva's company had built its business around it, importing it from France and selling it on.

"Yes."

"It's an illegal narcotic substance. You are being charged with the distribution of illegal narcotics."

Some misunderstanding, thought Yana, just some misunderstanding.

"But we have a license for it," answered Yana, almost laughing. She was being charged with trading what she traded. Since when was a cleaning agent used in every factory a narcotic substance? It didn't make any sense. She had been trading in diethyl ether for over a decade. It was like telling a chocolate bar factory that chocolate was illegal. Or a jeans factory that jeans were illegal. She looked at Vaselkov, but he just stared back dumbly.

She continued reading through the charges. The paperwork was just her everyday accounts; that's what the men in masks must have been taking from the office. In the folder, page after page said the same thing: "bought 150 liters of diethyl ether, sold 100 liters of diethyl ether." It was what she did every day. What was she being charged with?

"If you have familiarized yourself with the charges, please sign," said Vaselkov.

She signed, but she didn't understand. Everything was starting to spin. Her synapses couldn't make sense of what was going on, a short circuit in logic. Chairs seemed lighter, walls flimsier. The world around us is made up of the association of words to things, and hers was buckling.

She kept on trying to square the logic in her head but kept slipping and falling whenever she tried.

She was still spinning as she walked into the corridor. Alexey was there. All she could see were his eyes. They steadied her. She moved toward him to embrace him, but someone pushed her on. "This isn't some dinner date," someone said. Alexey handed her a plastic bag with sneakers and jeans in it. Again someone pushed her to move on. She was losing control. She started crying. This time they put her in their own car, a broken-down old Lada.

They drove her to Petrovka 38, Moscow's main police station. Outside it is a lovely old nineteenth-century palace, with a grand triangular portico like on a Greek temple, standing on the corner of one of the tree-draped boulevards right opposite the Galeria restaurant where gold diggers meet oligarchs and the Bentleys are quadruple-parked onto the pavement.

Yana was pushed inside Petrovka 38 into a hive of cops. She had never seen so many cops in one place, men and women, young and old. But all somehow pasty and semolina-like, as if they were all distantly related or from one village, and all wearing blue uniforms against the seaweed-green walls. They were leading criminals back and forth and into cells. You could tell they were criminals: drunks and youths with smashed-up faces, gypsy girls and junkies. Everywhere the sound of locks turning, keys jangling, doors slamming. Yana kept thinking of the Count of Monte Cristo. She was taken into one room and then another. She felt like she was becoming a parcel, passed from one cop to the next. Turn around! Bend down! Put your hands to your head!

Shoes off—belt off—socks off—panties off.

Body search.

She was crying all the time by now. All the time. Couldn't they see she wasn't a criminal? Every cop she looked at, she tried to catch his eye. Couldn't they see she didn't belong here among all these criminals? Wasn't it obvious? Maybe if they could just see she wasn't meant to be here, it would change something? Everything?

But they just looked at her as if she were a parcel. In the morning she had been a businesswoman driving a Lexus in a frilly white dress. Now she was a parcel.

They put her in a dark cell. There were three bunks. She lay there for a while, stunned. When she turned to the wall, someone called through the door: "Turn around so we can see you." The next day they would take her to court to decide on bail.

"The court will sort it out," thought Yana. "The court will sort it out": she had grown up with that phrase. Courts were places where things were sorted out. She assumed she would get bail. She had no convictions. She had done nothing wrong. Why wouldn't she get bail?

They drove her to court in the back of a van. She hadn't slept or eaten. Her hair was a mess.

At court they put her in a cage in the accused stand. The judge looked matronly, with her hair in a bun and glasses. She looked like a sensible person. She would sort it out.

"Well?" said the judge.

"I don't understand the charges," Yana began. She tried to sound authoritative, but as she spoke she started to cry again. She didn't want to, it was just the absurdity of it all. The tears came from the effort to make sense of it. "I'm being charged with trading what I trade. It doesn't make sense. . . ." She was sobbing now.

"All right," said the judge. "Prosecution?"

The prosecutor was another man in a polyester suit.

"Yakovleva is a highly dangerous criminal. She has been hiding from us. We had to hunt her down. She needs to be put under arrest until the trial."

What had he just said? Hiding? Where? Where had she been hiding? At the gym? At work? What were they talking about? The prosecutor just smiled at her. The judge nodded and repeated what he had said word for word and said no bail was granted. She would await trial in prison. The next hearing would be in two months.

Everything was spinning again. The prosecutor walked up to Yana and whispered, "Bad girl, why did you hide from us?"

Black is white and white is black. There is no reality. Whatever they say is reality. Yana began to scream. The more Yana screamed, the more guilty she looked: she saw herself for a second, a redhead with red eyes screaming in a cage in a courtroom.

They took her back to Petrovka. They took her prints. Her hands were covered with ink. She cried out for some soap. Some soap! They laughed at her. Then someone threw some soap at her: a gnarly corner of industrial soap that was dirtier than her hands. Then they said, "When you're done with the soap we need it back."

They put her in another police van and drove toward the prison.

There was a small barred window at the back of the van, and through it Yana could see Moscow. She put her face to the barred window. It was the dead of night, and the streets were empty. She felt like she was being smuggled, not just out of the city but out of reality itself into a nightmare fantasy land. Or was she just leaving the fantasy? We live in a world designed by the political technologists. A fragile reality show set that can seem, if you squint, almost genuine. We move from gym to open plan office to coffee bar to French movie to wine bar to holidays in Turkey, and it could seem better than Paris: better because it's newer and more precious. And we can read *SNOB* or watch the reality shows on TNT, and it's a simulacrum of the whole democratic thing. It feels almost real. But at the same time the other, real Russia rumbles on like a distant ringing in the ears. And it can grab us and pull us in at any moment.

She noticed they were driving around and around the Garden Ring. She couldn't see the drivers, but by their voices she thought they were out of towners.

"Are you lost?" she called through the metal cage.

"Shut up." Then, after a pause: "We need to find the turning for Volgograd Avenue."

It had its humor, this new world. Hand in hand with everything else.

Yana directed them like they were learner drivers and she their instructor. Which lane to move into, where to U-turn, where to drive on. It felt good; for a moment she was in charge again.

They said "thank-you"; they were new in Moscow and couldn't get their bearings. These ring-roads were confusing, you could go round and round for hours not knowing where to get off.

And again Yana found herself wanting to prove to the drivers, to these provincial lads, that she wasn't a criminal. She tried to control the feeling: What did it matter what they thought? But it did matter. Because she needed some way to hold onto the life she lived a day ago. Just one day ago and that was disappearing.

She could hear the prison before she could see it. Triple iron gates opening. Huge locks and giant bolts turning. The great machine turning. Then the van was full of magnesium bright light that blinded her. There was the sound of dogs, many dogs, growling and howling and barking and scratching against the van. And there was the smell. The smell of prison. Mold and damp and cigarettes. She would never forget that smell.

• • •

All the while I'm shooting Yana's story I'm thinking: Will TNT let me show this? Lately they have been telling me they want more of the new Russian woman, self-made, independent. Enough already of the gold diggers. There is a new generation stirring. And Yana ticked all the boxes. She was tall and strong and flame-haired. TNT said they wanted more drama—and Yana's story certainly had plenty of that. And it was a love story, too. I really played up the love story angle when I pitched the film. But what about the rest? How much could I get away with? A wrongful arrest—maybe. Depending on how I could frame it . . . *Shawshank Redemption*?

This was the paradox: TNT wanted to find the new heroes. Capture (and advertise to) the new (lucrative) middle class. But TNT couldn't touch politics. And at one point the two meet. Crash. And so all the time I'm waiting for the call: "We can't show this. Sorry, Piiitrrr, we can't show this."

• • •

She woke to the sound of forty-six throats coughing. All she could see were women. There were so many and so close they seemed to split into body parts rather than form separate human beings: dozens of noses and scores of hands, feet sticking out from bunk beds, butts, thighs, and breasts. There were forty-six women in her cell, all packed together; it was like being in the subway at rush hour but with no way out. In the far corner was a kitchen and a television playing MTV as loud as any nightclub. Someone was dancing, twirling in between the bunks. There were voices shouting, swearing, singing, laughing. Above her someone was snoring and beside her someone was rustling paper bags. At the end of the room were the toilets, and the water was pouring out of five taps full strength all the time because something had burst, and everyone was coughing.

Then it was time for their walk. They went down the stairs and into the yard: a sequence of concrete corridors that led to a concrete sack of a space ten meters by ten with two saplings and bars over the top. She paced round and round, thinking of tigers in cages. She didn't talk to anyone, not at first.

At night she could hear the trains. The prison was right by the train lines. There were no windows facing the outside, but she could hear the signals and whistles of the train lines, and they would keep her up all night. Outside was suburban Moscow.

In the first days she just wrote. She curled up in her bunk and wrote letters to Alexey. Love letters. They kept her sane. They were sickly and sentimental, and she never intended to send them, but she needed to keep thinking about her life outside. She wrote about his eyes, how she dreamt of making love to him, how she wanted children with him, how they would be a family. Every time the door of the cell opened she would start up with the hope that the guards would say, "Yakovleva, you're free," but of course they never did.

She was allowed no visits from family, but her parents passed her a parcel with clothes. The clothes smelled so much of home; she burst out crying.

A woman, older, Eskimo-looking, came up to her.

"Don't cry," she said sternly. "It's the worst thing you can do." The older woman took out some photos from her pocket. "These are my children. I haven't seen them for three years. But I don't cry. We all want to cry."

It was the first time Yana had a conversation with another inmate. She wrote a letter to herself, a list of commandments:

1. Don't feel sorry for yourself.
2. Don't cry.
3. Don't think about your life on the outside.
4. Be patient.
5. He will wait for you. He won't leave you.
6. Smile.
7. He loves you.

In the following days she began to look around the cell more carefully. On every bunk there was a little micro-world. One woman was praying, another writing, another playing cards. Suddenly a group of half a dozen women got up at the same time and went to a corner of the cell, stood in a little circle, and began exercising. Squats, push-ups, abs. They looked like stumbling bears. They were doing every-thing wrong. Yana came up and asked whether she could join them. The next day she began to correct them, gently at first, just showing them how to do the exercises right. By the end of the week she was their trainer.

She began to get to know them. It turned out everyone here had the same recurring dream: they were trying to call someone and couldn't get through. She had that dream every night: trying to call Alexey on his cell phone but he was out of area. It was a relief to know everyone had the same dream.

Her cell was for first-time offenders. Half were twentysomething girls, virtually all in for drugs. They didn't know what to do with them-selves. They didn't know how to have a proper conversation; they just watched MTV and TNT and gossiped, but when Yana talked to them they all began to say how much they missed their parents. They had never had a relationship with them and now they missed them. There was an eighteen-year-old, Lara from Ukraine, who had been busted for a sack of weed her boyfriend had given her to take over the Ukraine-Russia border. She followed Yana everywhere. "What should I do with myself?" she would ask, over and over. At night she would come and stare at Yana lying in her bunk. Yana would wake and ask: "What are you doing?"

"I tried to read but I keep on getting these thoughts in my head."

The other half of the women were in their forties and accountants; they were in for white collar crimes like Yana. The elder women would fuss around the twenty-year-olds: "Make sure you wash the cups" and "don't swear." Most of the older women had worked in small businesses: estate agents, travel companies. It wasn't the thing to do to ask what exactly others were in for, and of course they all said they were "inno-cent," but after a while a couple of them told Yana what had happened. The companies had been fiddling taxes, but the male bosses fled the country in time to avoid getting caught, and it was the female accountants who went to prison. After all, their signatures were on everything. The women had been doing nothing more illegal than any other business in the country, the same double bookkeeping every small company needed to do if it wanted to survive. But either the tax police needed to fill some arrest quotas, or they wanted to scare someone else, someone bigger, and needed to make an example, so they had gone after these companies. Still other women were sure the hits on their companies had been ordered by rivals or bureaucrats who wanted to bankrupt them and then take over their companies. This was called "reiding" and was the most common form of corporate takeover in Russia, with more than a hundred recorded cases a year. Business rivals or bureaucrats—they have long become the same thing—pay the security services to have the head of a company arrested; while they are in prison their documents and registrations are seized, the company is re-registered under different owners, and by the time the original owners are released, the company has been bought and sold and split up by new owners. These raids happened at every level, from the very top—where the Kremlin would arrest the owner of an oil company like Mikhail Khodorkovsky, then hand the company over to friends of the President—right down to local police chiefs taking over furniture stores. It was the right to do this that glued together the great "power vertical" that stretched from the President down to the lowliest traffic cop.

Yana suspected this was what was happening to her. Of course she had heard of other companies being victims of "reiderstvo." But she had always assumed they must have been guilty of something to be attacked. They must have done something wrong. Something. She felt stupid now to have fooled herself that way.

The usual way out was a bribe. There was a whole network and industry of payoffs. Good "lawyers" were not those who could defend you in court—the verdicts were predetermined—but those who had the right connections to know whom to pay off in the judiciary and relevant ministry. It was a complex game; pay off the wrong person and you just wasted money. You had to find the real decision maker. And quickly a whole mass of middle men would begin to appear who want to persuade you that they, and only they, know how to pay off the right person. Yana knew her parents were looking for that person on the outside. They had found a "lawyer" who said he could help—he suggested she admit to the charges, and then he could get everything sorted. Meanwhile he told Yana's parents to sell their apartment to pay for the bribe, which would be near a million dollars. She smelled a rat. Something was wrong. Her company had done nothing wrong; shouldn't she stick to that? And what exactly was she meant to own up to? That she had traded what she traded? Own up to absurdity? If she even started to negotiate, it would be like giving away a part of her sanity, letting them own and dictate what the truth was. And then everything would start to slip.

She asked for another lawyer. He said the same thing. These were the rules. She understood the rules, didn't she?

It was Galya who first made Yana think there might be something bigger going on, more than just a case of common "reiderstvo." She had first met Galya at Petrovka 38, before her initial trial. She had been pushed into the cell, plump and trembling with tears. Over fifty. The sort of woman you see selling vegetables or hosiery at train stations. She was crying and spoke with a Ukrainian accent.

Galya, it turned out, was a cashier at a pharmacy. There are little pharmacies at train stations. One morning the FDCS had come and arrested her for selling food additives. Food additives! Yana's interest was piqued.

"What's your name?" asked Galya.

"Yana."

"Yana Yakovleva?"

How could she know her name? Yana had heard of stool pigeons. Was this one?

"When I was arrested," Galya explained, "the cops were talking to each other and said I was being taken down under the same law as Yana Yakovleva. They're all talking about you."

. . .

Though she was only just starting to work out the full picture, this was why Yana was in prison.

In 1950, in Leningrad, near the port, Viktor Cherkesov was born into a family of dock workers. A working-class kid, he joined the army straight out of school. It is there he is suspected to have joined the KGB; with no connections, it was a way up the ladder. The KGB sent him to study law at St. Petersburg University, in the same class as the young man who would become the President, who became his friend. Like the President he studied poorly. In 1975 Cherkesov joined the fifth department of the Leningrad KGB, which was in charge of arresting dissidents and nonconformist thinkers. For some KGB men, working in the fifth department was considered an embarrassment, compared to the heroics of real espionage. In the 1970s Cherkesov worked on cases rounding up, breaking, and jailing members of underground religious and feminist groups. He became head of the department. In 1982 he personally headed up the investigation of the Soviet Union's first independent trade union, SMOT. Vyacheslav Dolinin was one of those he interrogated:

Cherkesov was a gray, dim man. His only strength was he could lie without blushing. When a superior would come in, he would leap up instantly, he was very obsequious and dependent on them [remembers Dolinin]. He would threaten us: "we're not beating you, though we can use such measures." But he was not especially vicious and not a great detective. He didn't manage to find out the bulk of my dissident activities.

Igor Bunich was a witness in several of Cherkesov's cases between 1980 and 1982:

During interrogation Cherkesov followed the principle laid down by Alexander Shuvalov, the head of the secret police under the Empress Elizabeth in the eighteenth century: "Always keep the accused confused." At the start of an interrogation Cherkesov would lay out three pieces of paper on the table in front of a dissident. Each was a law the dissident could be charged with—all worded in a very similar way but carrying quite different punishments:

Law 190, "spreading anti-Soviet ideas," usually punishable with an enforced stay in a psychiatric ward;

Law 70, on "anti-Soviet propaganda," usually carrying five years' imprisonment; and

Law 64, on "treachery to the Soviet Union," which carried the death penalty (firing squad).

If the dissident cooperated and snitched, his case would be registered under Law 190, with a suspended sentence. If you didn't cooperate you would be charged under the other laws.

Other dissidents he interrogated described how Cherkesov's daughter would call during interrogations. He would pick up the phone, smile gently, and change his tone: "My pet, I'm interrogating now," he would say. He had that ability all KGB men have, to split his personality at will.

But Cherkesov was also a poor judge of history. In 1988, with perestroika in full swing, he launched an investigation into the new "Democratic Alliance," a group of activists who were calling for the end of the USSR. It was the final case ever tried in the USSR under the antidissident "Law 70." Cherkesov called a press conference saying he had discovered an important anti-Soviet conspiracy. The thing was a farce: the young activists were soon deputies in the Duma, and the law itself was rescinded. Within two years the USSR didn't exist.

After 1991 Cherkesov became head of the St. Petersburg KGB, supported by his friend, the future President, who was deputy head of the mayor's office. When the young President moved to Moscow to become head of the FSB (the successor to the KGB), Cherkesov moved with him and became his deputy. The rumor in Moscow was that when the President was inaugurated, Cherkesov expected to become head of the FSB. But he was overlooked for Nikolaj Patrushev, also a graduate of the 1970s St. Petersburg KGB, but from the much more glamorous counterespionage department. The president gave Cherkesov the FDCS, the least important of the security organs. Starting in 2006 the FDCS launched a series of moves to capture the chemicals and pharmaceuticals industries. Overnight a whole host of chemicals had their status changed from industrial or medical to narcotic. Pharmacies that traded in food additives were raided, veterinarians who gave ketamine to cats and horses were marched into police stations, and the heads of chemical companies like Yana were suddenly informed they were drug dealers. The plan was to "break" these industries. Yana was meant to swing from the gallows by the edge of the road, a warning to everyone of what would happen if they disagreed with the FDCS.

• • •

She had been there four months. Most of the time she would tell herself: "This is a game, a test"; that's how she coped. But once every two months they would wake her at 5:00 A.M. and take her down to the basement to await her trip to court to see whether she would be granted bail.

"*Yesterday was the worst day,*" she wrote in one of the letters to Alexey she never sent. "*The worst point is when in a dark, concrete, completely closed space 20 people start smoking at the same time. It's horrible. Waiting for the van and its cages, concrete, darkness, metal, handcuffs,* smoke, smoke. It's very hard to make yourself feel this is all a game and ev-eryone around you are just actors."

After two hours they put the women into a prison van and drove them, as if in a school bus, to various courtrooms around Moscow. When she saw Moscow everything suddenly became real.

"We drove along the Garden Ring. I could see people walking along the street, hurrying about their own business. And inside I screamed: 'I will re-turn. This world can't survive without me. I will return and forget all that has happened. I will cross it out.'"

And even more strongly she wanted to scream: "Pedestrians! Citi-zens! Stop! Help! Can't you see me? I'm here." Though of course she never did. And all passersby ever saw was a small prison van with dark, barred windows.

At the court they put her in a cage again. Her parents were always there, but the last time Alexey hadn't come. Her mother would always wear her best dress, which was a way of showing that their spirit hadn't been crushed. They looked good, and thus they were strong. Yana would repeat to the judge that she had no idea why she was in prison; none of the charges made sense. The judge would nod and give her another two months, and they would bundle her out again.

She had a new lawyer, Evgeny Chernousov. They had found him after he defended a few veterinarians in Yaroslavl against the FDCS. The vets had been charged with dealing ketamine, a drug they used as a painkiller for cats. Evgeny had managed to raise enough noise for the charges to be dropped. But there he had just gone up against provincial FDCS guys out to make a few quick bucks. Now he would be going against senior officials in a much bigger case. The plan was to make so much fuss it would become unprofitable for the FDCS to hold Yana: this was the opposite to what most prisoners did, which was to keep the case as quiet as possible and pay off the right person. Chernousov told Yana he would activate the human rights NGOs, business associ-ations. He was a former cop himself, and he took on cases no one else would. He used to catch criminals, and now he liked to catch cops. He had served in Afghanistan and Ossetia, and it had done something to his head. More than anything he loved a fight against the odds, and he seemed tipsy a lot of the time. He told Yana not to lose hope.

She was almost happy when they brought her back to prison after these excursions into reality. She knew that outside her parents and Chernousov were trying to change the world for her, but beyond giving direction to the overall plan there was nothing she could do from the inside. Her task was to stay sane. She had half a dozen fitness "students." They would exercise in the morning, and then again in the afternoon during their "walk." They would take old plastic bottles, fill them with grit, and use them as weights. They were getting better, slimming down. A couple had even stopped smoking. As the "trainer" she had a certain status, was allowed into the showers first. She even managed to convince the others to sometimes change the channel from TNT and MTV to the news. The trick was to keep herself busy all the time. Writing letters, reading newspapers, learning English, doing push-ups. Never a moment to spare. She had almost perfected this.

There were several big NOs for all prisoners: never cry; never talk about the future or release; never, ever, talk about sex. But sex was on everybody's mind. Tanya, an accountant on the bunk opposite her, would cut out pictures of men from magazines and put them beneath her pillow:

"Maybe I'll dream of one," she would say quietly.

Yana dreamt of Alexey every night. She would dream of his eyes when he had come to the FDCS headquarters to bring her bag. In her letters she worried he would forget about her: *"Does that make me an egoist?"* she wrote. *"But the only way I can keep myself together is to know there's someone waiting for me."*

When she went into the yard for exercise she became aware, in a way she never had been when she was free, of smells: *"In summer the two little trees in the yard smelled of heat and bread. Before I would go to a forest and not notice anything. Here there are just two thin trees yet how many impressions!"*

One time she was exercising in the yard with Sasha. Sasha owned a travel agency. She was a little younger than Yana, and they started talking about how they wanted children. They weren't supposed to talk about things like that, and Yana wasn't even sure how the conversation started. Sasha wanted two. Yana told her about Alexey and how she thought it was time to start a family, take a break from work. Sasha looked at her and said: "You're thirty-five; it's too late for children. There's no way they'll give you less than five years, that's the very minimum. Once you're in here that's it. It doesn't matter whether you're guilty. Forget about kids. . . . " Yana switched off and stopped listening to her and started doing star jumps so fast Sasha couldn't keep up.

Of those charged in Russia, 99 percent receive guilty verdicts. The women in Yana's cell would return after their trials broken, all found guilty. Their sentences were worse than anyone could have imagined: five years for possession of one gram of cocaine; four years for faking a prescription; eleven years for working as a cashier at one of the country's top construction companies whose owner had fallen out with someone in the Kremlin. They were often set up by their own lawyers: the lawyers would take the bribes, then use that as "evidence" that the prisoners were guilty (the bribes would then disappear). Yana's prosecutor, the one who had told the court she was dangerous and had been in hiding, had a reputation for being the fiercest.

"I'm stronger than him," she wrote to herself.

She would scour the news for reports about herself. Chernousov had told her they were writing letters to Duma deputies; there had been meetings and small pickets where human rights activists had defended her. But in Russia you can protest all you like; it won't change anything. You can scream and scream, but no one will hear you. There was one tiny paragraph about her in a liberal newspaper, and that was it.

Every day new white collar prisoners were brought to the cell. The last was a woman who had just won an award in Cannes for having Russia's best travel agency. "*Soon,*" wrote Yana, "*prison will become like a University get together. Now I'm afraid again. What should I be preparing myself for? For the worst? Should I be saying good-bye to everyone? Time is passing and nothing is changing. I'm the same as the others. It doesn't matter whether you are rich or poor. This system grabs people off the street, from work, from home, and eats them up. And no one knows when it will happen to them.*"

Then one day, as they were watching the news, she suddenly saw a report about herself. Not on one of the Ostankino channels, but on a slightly smaller one with an "opposition" reputation though actually owned by one of the President's oldest friends. There were five hundred people on Pushkin Square protesting against her imprisonment. There were posters with her face on them that said "freedom to Yana Yakovleva." A relatively famous musician played a resistance song on a stage. Chernousov was making a speech. The reporter said: "The FDCS appears to be arresting people who have nothing to do with drug dealing at all."

The next day her story was a double spread in one of the newspapers. When she came in after the shower everyone in the cell was gathered around reading it.

"Hey," they called out, "so you really are innocent."

• • •

Cherkesov had enemies.

He was trying to prove to the President that Patrushev, his rival and the head of the FSB, was a weak link. The President encouraged Cherkesov, handing the FDCS responsibility for investigating an illegal customs business on the China-Russia border allegedly managed by the FSB. This sort of investigation was way out of the FDCS's remit: Could the fact the President had entrusted it to Cherkesov mean he preferred him to Patrushev?

But Patrushev and the FSB were not going to go down easily.

Just as Cherkesov was investigating Patrushev, so Patrushev supported those who were fighting Cherkesov. So when the FSB heard about Yana's story, they made sure the police didn't close down the demonstrations, that the right TV channels and newspapers covered the protests. This was one of the reasons "liberal" papers and channels existed, to give one power broker a weapon to hit another power broker with. Every day Yana's story became better known. It was nicknamed the "case of the Chemists," to echo a Stalinist era purge known as the "case of the Doctors."

None of this ever would have happened if Yana, her parents, and Chernousov had not decided to fight back in the first place. Without the first dissident impulse, nothing would have appeared. But neither would that alone have been enough. To make something happen in Russia, you have to be both valiant protester and Machiavellian, playing one clan off against the other.

• • •

Shortly before she was released Yana had a dream. She and Alexey were lying on chaise longues in a strange country. Alexey was reading a newspaper. She got up and climbed a tall tree next to the chaise longue. The tree was very tall, and from the top she could see fields and forests. Suddenly she saw a grizzly bear was in the tree, too. He was coming toward her, growling. She froze in terror. He put his wet teeth right up to her face. And then he stopped. She thought he would eat her. Then suddenly he started to retreat. There was a great noise: below the tree a whole tribe of rabid bulls was running by, making the earth shake. Alexey kept on reading the newspaper as if nothing had happened.

She was awakened by the snores of the woman on the bunk above. She snored so hard her dentures popped out of her mouth and flew clattering onto the floor.

When Yana told the others about the dream, they all said, "It's a sign, the evil is retreating, but the danger is not over by a long shot."

The day of her release she was doing exercises with Luba, the Ukrainian girl who would stand next to her at night. Boxing, then some abs. "If you leave," Luba suddenly said, "I'm not sure how I'll cope without you."

"Where would I possibly go?" laughed Yana.

They went back in for lunch. They were all eating when the warden came in. "Yakovleva, get your clothes and your documents and follow me," she shouted. All the prisoners looked at each other.

"Probably another date with the inspector," joked Yana.

"They're probably going to let you go," said Tanya. "You'll be free."

"Shh," said Yana, "you know we never say that word."

They drove her back to the FDCS HQ in northern Moscow. Her lawyer was there, and her parents. Her lawyer said: "Look, we've done a deal. They will let you out on bail, but they are keeping your business partner in until the trial."

She didn't feel anything at first. She only turned and asked her mother: "Is Alexey here?"

"He knows you're being released but he's not here," her mother answered.

They went back to the prison to sign her out. She was still numb. Only when the TV cameras turned up at the prison did she begin crying. It was cold and the tears felt hot in her mouth; there were the people from human rights groups there and journalists; she was hugging all of them and she was crying out of gratitude to them. She had been inside for seven months, and now that she was outside it was suddenly like she had never been there. But it wasn't over yet: she had been granted bail, but the biggest battle was the trial that lay ahead.

Chernousov drove her back to the apartment she shared with Alexey. She knew their relationship was over. All those letters to him, the letters she never sent, they had been for her. She needed that illusion to keep her going. When they had spoken on the phone (four times over seven months), he was more distant each time. He wasn't even pretending he cared. She made excuses for him: he was afraid she would come out emotionally damaged. Their relationship had been between two independent grown-ups, and now he was worried he would have to look after someone frail.

"Ha," Chernousov grunted, "he's just a coward. Wouldn't even meet with me. He's afraid it might damage his career at the company."

Alexey was at the apartment when she arrived. They embraced formally. She gathered her things and put them into bags and waved good-bye as she left. She didn't show any emotion. She had dreamt of coming back to that apartment. That's what had kept her going. This was one final test, and maybe it was even the hardest. She passed it with a quick smile as she waved good-bye.

"Women always wait for men in jail," she told Chernousov, "but men never wait. There's been research on it."

The trial began a few weeks later. The fact that they were even allowed to call witnesses for the defense meant they had a chance. Essentially it was diethyl ether itself that was on trial. It was bizarre. The FDCS's scientists tried to prove it was a narcotic. Yana's scientists tried to show it wasn't. Of course it wasn't.

Meanwhile the battle that really mattered was starting to rage on the Olympus of the Kremlin. The conflict between Cherkesov and Patrushev became known as the "war of Chekists" (the KGB men). Cherkesov's men arrested the FSB generals involved in the Chinese border racket. In revenge Patrushev's men arrested the FDCS's top generals right in the middle of Domodedovo airport, surrounding them with masked gunmen and dragging them off to prison. (*Hello-Goodbye* was being filmed at Domodedovo at the same time, though they missed the standoff.) For a few rare months the thick stage curtain that separates the shareholders of the Russian state from the general public was pulled back. The country's elites were split down the middle between those who backed Patrushev and those who backed Cherkesov. With no instructions coming from the Kremlin, TV stations and newspapers had to choose sides. Cherkesov wrote an opinion piece in *Kommersant*, the country's main broadsheet, which became known as the declaration of the Chekist: "Only us Chekists have saved Russian from destruction," wrote Cherkesov. "We need to unify." Cherkesov had broken a cardinal rule—he had spoken publicly about an inner conflict. Why had he done it? Could the President have secretly encouraged him? Where was the President? Could he not keep his own clans under control? For the first time since he had become president, he looked weak. Was he losing his grip?

No. He was just waiting for his moment. Both men had compromised themselves: Cherkesov with the scandals around the FDCS and the letter in *Kommersant*, and Patrushev with the revelations about cross-border smuggling. Within one week both were fired. In one swing the President had got rid of two potential challengers, they had eaten each other up. Even the President's detractors could only step back and quietly applaud.

Yana won at her trial. The law was thrown out. Diethyl ether became legal again. She still officially runs her business, but she spends most of her time on an NGO she has set up called Business Solidarity: a sort of Good Samaritans for businesses that get into the same trouble she did. She connects them with the right lawyers, the media, me. She moved into a new apartment opposite my own. This meant whenever there was something left to film of her story, she could call me and I would grab the camera and run over to her apartment or wherever she was going.

Sometimes she takes me along to the trials. The courtrooms, to my surprise, are all brand new, with shiny bright tiles and high ceilings and lots of light. It's their modernity, their normality, that makes the actual trials so much more twisted. There are the little businessmen, all facing trumped-up charges, all with the same look of pure confusion, like they are being sucked into a whirlpool and into an underwater world where nothing at all makes sense. And Yana walks up to them and comforts them. They calm down when they see her; she brings if not the hope for justice then at least the promise of sanity. And as I scamper behind her she walks with ever-elongating strides through the corridors and courtrooms, seeming to get taller with every step, her huge, red hair filling up the room like something burning.

• • •

This is how I cut the story (with Yana's blessing). All the high-level political stuff goes. All the stuff about Cherkesov and the President and Patrushev. According to the film, she is released due to a bottom-up campaign against corrupt bureaucrats: proving that though of course there is corruption, one can fight it. It's an exception rather than the norm; in other words, there's hope in the country if you try hard. I focus on the love story, the strong woman facing huge challenges. The story is cut together with another story about a young mother who was told her infant would die of cancer if she couldn't raise $50,000 for his operation, which she moved heaven and earth to achieve. So it becomes a film about strong women, not just about political oppression. It's a compromise. It's a narrow corridor. But at least it's something. And the ratings are good. The country wants new heroes.

ANOTHER RUSSIA

The demolition ball keeps the time of the city, a metronome that swings on every corner. The city changes so fast you lose all sense of reality, you can't recognize streets. You look for a place where you went to eat a week ago, and before your eyes the whole block is being demolished.

Whole swathes of town are demolished in fits of self-destruction, wastelands abandoned for years and for no apparent reason, skyscrapers erupting before there are any roads leading to them and then left standing empty in the dirty snow. The search for a style is psychotic. The first builds of the boom imitated whatever the post-Soviets had seen abroad and most desired: Turkish hotels, German castles, Swiss chalets. When Ostozhenka, the area right opposite the Kremlin, was knocked down, it was renamed "Moscow Belgravia"; there are "Mos Angeles" and "Moscow Côte D'Azur." Dropped into the city as artificially and awkwardly as the political technologist's faux Western-style parties. Elsewhere you can spy a neon-medieval: behind high black gates peak out Disney-like towers tacked onto pink concrete castles, with rows of offices shaped like the knight's helmets, so they look like an army of warriors emerging from the ground. Often you find all the styles compiled into one building. A new office center on the other side of the river from the Kremlin starts with a Roman portico, then morphs into medieval ramparts with spikes and gold-glass reflective windows, all topped with turrets and Stalin spires. The effect is at first amusing, then disturbing. It's like talking to the victim of a multiple personality disorder: Who are you? What are you trying to say? Increasingly new skyscrapers recall the Gotham-gothic turrets of Stalin architecture. Triumph-Palace, briefly Europe's tallest apartment building, is a copy of the Stalinist "seven sisters." Long before the city's political scientists started shouting that the Kremlin was building a new dictatorship, the architects were already whispering: "Look at this new architecture, it dreams of Stalin. Be warned, the evil Empire is back."

But the original Stalin skyscrapers were made of granite, with grand mosaics and Valhalla halls leading to small, ascetic apartments. The new ones try to be domineering but come across as camp; developers steal so much money during construction that even the most VIP, luxury, elite of the skyscrapers crack and sink ever so quickly. That unique

Moscow mix of tackiness and menace. One time I see a poster advertising a new property development that captures the tone nicely. Got up in the style of a Nazi poster, it shows two Germanic-looking youths against a glorious alpine mountain over the slogan "Life Is Getting Better." It would be wrong to say the ad is humorous, but it's not quite serious, either. It's sort of both. It's saying this is the society we live in (a dictatorship), but we're just playing at it (we can make jokes about it), but playing in a serious way (we're making money playing it and won't let anyone subvert its rules).

I can hear the groan and feel the shudders of the excavator before I even turn onto Gnezdnikovsky Alley, the air already filling up with clouds of red-brick dust. A nineteenth-century, two-story palace folds so easily. The clumsy arm of the excavator pulls down a wall awkwardly, like a toddler playing, revealing for a moment the innards of an old apartment—the 1970s wallpaper, photographs, a radio—and then the demolition ball swings, and it's all gone for good. Gnezdnikovsky is just off Pushkin Square, what tourist guides describe as "Moscow's historic center." It should be untouchable. But the tremors of drill and demolition ball only become more frenzied with every meter closer you get to the Kremlin. Property prices are measured by distance from Red Square: the aim is to build your office or apartment as close to the center of power as possible, the market organized by a still feudal social structure defined by needing to be within touching distance of the tsar, the general secretary of the Communist Party, the President of the Russian Federation. The country's institutions—oil companies, banks, ministries, and courts—all want to crowd around the Kremlin like courtiers. This means the city is almost destined to destroy itself; it can't grow outward, so every generation stomps on the heads of previous ones. Over a thousand buildings have been knocked down in the center so far this century, with hundreds of officially "protected" historic monuments lost. But the new buildings meant to replace them often stand dark and empty; property is the most effective money laundering scheme, making money for members of the Moscow government who give contracts to their own development companies, for the agents who sell the buildings to the nameless and faceless Forbeses, who need some way to stabilize their assets.

A small crowd has gathered near the building site on Gnezdnikovsky. They put candles and flowers on the pavement in a little gesture of lament. These flash mobs mourning the death of old Moscow have become more frequent. In my spare time I've been filming the disappearing city, the last of Atlantis.

Alexander Mozhayev stands at the head of the little crowd, hair pointed in different directions, scarf down to his knees, a vodka bottle and a kefir bottle stuck out of each deep pocket of his sailor's coat. He is a member of what in another context might be a somewhat marginal profession, an architectural and urban historian, but here he has developed a slightly cult-like following as the guardian spirit of Old Moscow. Mozhayev and his friends have started salvaging buildings from the wrecking ball. They picket in front of wooden houses under threat, try to raise enough fuss that developers back off. But these victories are few and far between. Over several years they have saved three buildings out of three thousand. Mozhayev is young, a thirtysomething, but his voice is full of cracks and sandpaper tones, like the walls of Old Moscow itself. He takes out a bottle and says: "We're here to say a wake, to this building, to old Moscow, all these buildings are set to be destroyed."

Mozhayev and his followers put on the Pinocchio-like masks they wear for this lament and begin to howl into the air like professional mourners at a funeral. "Bastards, how long will you keep on destroying our city?" they cry. "Soon there will be nothing, nothing left!" (The little scene will then be posted online.)

He turns, and we follow him under an arch and into the last of the older, tender Moscow: the web of little lanes, courtyards, and alleyways that spread in a horizontal swirl between the great trunks of the gargantuan Stalin-era avenues. We pass through narrow arches and into suddenly spacious courtyards where teens play ice hockey on a skating rink poured between the houses. The light is different here, darker and softer, the fresh snow reflecting back the remains of the day to under-light the crumbling lions and angels stuccoed onto buildings. Everything here is scuffed, textured, tawny, ragged, and lived in. The lights are starting to come on in the houses, and parents call their children to come inside. Even the language here is different, full of singsong and caressing, affectionate diminutives: "Come here my dovelet," "my little bluebell." An almost rural mood of childhood, soft snow, and sleds. Here is the Moscow that existed before the Soviet experiment. Back in the eighteenth and nineteenth centuries St. Petersburg was the capital, the city of power, regime, order. Moscow was a backwater, the holiday city where you could sleep in late and spend the day in your pajamas.

Here we find places with names like Krivokolennaya, the street of the crooked knee, and Po-ta-poff-sky, a word that falls like snowflakes in the mouth. But my favorite of all is Pyatnitskaya: in English, the Street-of-All-Fridays. There is no pomposity on the Street-of-All-Fridays. It is full of little two-story, nineteenth-century minimansions, leaning higgledy-piggledy on each other like happy drunk friends singing on their way home to a warm bed. In every courtyard there is a bar, some little place with cheap vodka and smoky rooms. There are no office blocks, no narcissistic skyscrapers, no domineering malls. But there is an old metro station, a large, low, yellow, pancake-shaped building in which students share beers and boys chase girls. I love the street for its name. Friday is the best of days, Friday eve especially. When the working week melts into the days of rest. As the day darkens the mood lightens, the frowns turn to smiles, breathing comes better and deeper. Pyatnitskaya is a street dedicated to that moment, the materialization in space of a mood in time. Everything about the street says, "Let's drink, have a chat, swap stories: I haven't seen you for so long, I haven't been myself for so long." And then, later, I like to wander across town and over toward Pechatnikov, house 3, where you enter an arch near a pale, crooked baroque mansion with outsized angels and a window that leads nowhere, and inside is a long yard with tall houses around it that make you feel you've suddenly entered a deep valley; a long, low wooden house wrapped around the yard glowing with an orange light; and a bench collapsing in the middle.

"I call the courtyard of Pechyatnikov the time machine," says Mozhayev as we walk. "To anyone familiar with Prague or London or Rome or Edinburgh, these old Moscow courtyards are probably of little architectural significance. I'm not even sure they even qualify as beautiful. But in contrast to the new Moscow with its endless imitations, this world is real."

On the corner of Pakrovka three plump women who look like schoolteachers or doctors patrol an art nouveau apartment block, surrounded by their Labradors. They squint aggressively as we approach, then relax and greet Mozhayev when they see him. These little vigilante gangs have become common in Moscow, protecting not from burglars but from developers, who send arsonists to set buildings ablaze, then use the fire as an excuse to evict homeowners by claiming the houses are now fire hazards. The motivation is great: property prices rose by over 400 percent in the first decade after 2000. So these fires have become habitual in Moscow. Muscovites have taken to patrolling their own buildings at night: gangs of doctors, teachers, grannies, and housewives eyeing every passerby as if he were an arsonist. It's pointless for them to call the police; the largest groups of developers are friends and relatives of the mayor and the government. The mayor's wife is the biggest of the lot. The near mythical Russian middle class, suddenly finding they have no real rights at all over their property, can be thrown out and relocated like serfs under a feudal whim.

We follow Mozhayev as he climbs into the remains of a broken wooden mansion, recently gutted by one of these mysterious fires. In the palace the snow wafts through the burnt-out roofs into rooms with sky-blue wallpaper and the remains of an ancient fireplace now hung with icicles. Under open boards beneath our feet we can see bums sleeping in the basement. Mozhayev finds old notebooks from the people who once lived there. He begins to tell the story of the building, who lived here and who did what. His little audience listens closely. There is something almost hallucinogenic about his storytelling: the roof on the house seems to grow back, you can feel the fire burning in the hearth and hear the footsteps of lost aristocracy and the gossip of their servants, then see how the house was taken over by communists in 1917, hear the shots when the original owners were executed, and see the little palace be converted into a communal apartment—where everyone was arrested during Stalin's terror—then become a small hospital during the war.

"Old walls and doors know something we can't understand," Mozhayev wrote in one of his essays: "the true nature of time. The drama of human lives is written in the buildings. We will be gone; only places remain."

"Mozhayev is the city's memory," a girl with orange pigtails tells me when I ask her why she has come. "Before I had no idea about the city I grew up in."

But Russia has problems with its memories. There isn't a building that we walk past that wasn't the scene of execution squads, betrayals, mass murders. The most gentle courtyards reveal the most awful secrets. Around the corner from Potapoffsky is an apartment block where every one of the families had someone arrested during Stalin's terror. In the basement of what is now a brand new shopping mall was the courtroom where innocent after innocent was sentenced to labor camps, the courts working so fast they would get through two cases inside a minute. And those are just the Stalin years, not even encroaching on the dismal betrayals of later decades, listening at the door of your neighbors' rooms to report them tuning into the BBC or Radio Free Europe.

"Every new regime rebuilds the past so radically," Mozhayev says as we move back toward Barrikadnaya. "Lenin and Trotsky ripping up the memory of the tsars, Stalin ripping up the memory of Trotsky, Khrushchev of Stalin, Brezhnev of Khrushchev; perestroika gutting the whole Communist century . . . and every time the heroes turn to villains, saviors are rewritten as devils, the names of streets are changed, faces [are] scrubbed out from photographs, encyclopedias [are] re-edited. And so every regime destroys and rebuilds the previous city."

On the corner of Barrikadnaya a little baroque house is pushed out of the way by a constructivist apartment block of the 1920s, in turn dominated by a sneering, Stalin skyscraper, itself now outflanked by the dark glinting tiles of a huge, domed new mall, resembling the tents and spears of Mongol battle camps. And all these buildings seem to push and shove each other out of the way. If areas of London or Paris are built in a similar style—searching for some sort of harmony, memory, identity—here each building looks to stamp and disdain the last, just as every regime discredited the previous.

Whenever twenty-first-century Russian culture looks for a foundation it can build itself from, healthy and happy, it finds the floor gives way and buries it in soil and blood. When the Ostankino channels launch the Russian version of the British TV show *Greatest Britons*, renamed *Name of Russia*, it's meant to be a straightforward PR project to boost the country's patriotism. The audiences across the nation are to vote for Russia's greatest heroes. But as the country starts to look for its role models, its fathers, it turns out that every candidate is a tyrant: Ivan the Terrible, founder of Russia proper in the sixteenth century and the first tsar; Peter the Great; Lenin; Stalin. The country seems transfixed in adoration of abusive leaders. When the popular vote starts to come in for *Name of Russia*, the producers are embarrassed to find

Stalin winning. They have to rig the vote so that Alexander Nevsky, a near-mythical medieval warrior knight, born, we think, in 1220, can win. He lived so long ago, when Russia was still a colony of the Mongol Empire between the thirteenth and fifteenth centuries, that he seems a neutral choice. Russia has to reach outside the history of its own state to find a father figure. But though this was never mentioned in the program, what little evidence there is of his career shows that Nevsky made his name by collecting taxes, quelling and killing other rebellious Russian princelings for his Mongol suzerain.

How do you build a history based on ceaseless self-slaughter and betrayal? Do you deny it? Forget it? But then you are left orphaned. So history is rewritten to suit the present. As the President looks for a way to validate his own authoritarianism, Stalin is praised as a great leader who won the Soviet Union the war. On TV the first attempts to explore the past, the well-made dramas about Stalin's Terror of the 1930s, are taken off screen and replaced with celebrations of World War II. (But while Stalin's victory is celebrated publicly and loudly, invoking him also silently resurrects old fears: Stalin is back! Be very afraid!)

The architecture reflects these agonies. The city writhes as twenty-first-century Russia searches, runs away, returns, denies, and reinvents itself.

"Moscow is the only city where old buildings are knocked down," says Mozhayev, "and then rebuilt again as replicas of themselves with straight lines, Perspex, double glazing."

The Moskva Hotel opposite the Kremlin, a grim Stalin gravestone of a building, is first deconstructed, then after much debate about what should replace it, is eventually rebuilt as a slightly brighter-colored version of itself. And this will be the fate of Gnezdnikovsky, demolished and then rebuilt to house restaurants in the faux tsarist style, where waiters speak pre-revolutionary Russian, the menu features pelmeni with brains, and tourists are delighted at encountering the "real Russia." And so Mozhayev's walks become more than just about architecture, but about the way the whole society is governed. The glossy Moscow magazines that would never dare touch big politics instead talk about urban policy as a metaphor: "Give us back our city," they write, and through that express their much more general discontent.

Bells are ringing. Mozhayev stops and says a little prayer. He's Orthodox; always says a blessing before every swig. He brings us to a church. There is a crowd around the entrance, all holding candles reflected on the snow, which make this corner of the street look like it's been painted gold. Inside the prayers are coming thick with that almost Buddhist chanting of the Orthodox, there's a strong smell of incense, and people are crowding around the icons lighting candles. Your heart can't help but swell, and your skin prickles. There's something very true in the claim of the Orthodox that their version of the faith is closer to the original, less rational and more emotional and experiential. Everything presses in on you, the chanting and the people and the light, driving you toward the icons. And being, after all, someone who works in television, I notice how the experience follows the visual-emotional logic of my profession: you look deep at the icon of the suffering Christ, identifying your own experience with him just as the TV or movie viewer identifies with the close-up of the hero on the screen. And I remember something once told to me by the Russian émigré artist Vitaly Komar, that the genius in casting Christ as the main hero of the divine drama was that for the first time the viewer had a God he could truly identify with. "Christ is the precursor to Chaplin and all the other great loser-heroes of cinema and television," Komar said. "Before Christ all the Gods were either perfect, aspirational Apollos, or invisible: but this one is frail and broken. Just like you." (In his own paintings Komar had first satirized Soviet iconography with depictions of Stalin embraced by Grecian muses, and then, after emigrating, he searched for a new, divine symbolism.)

And as you stand in the church, finding in the image of the suffering Christ the comforting mirror for all your failures, you turn your head and see the image of a newborn baby and his mother, and your emotions move from comforted loser to the possibility of a new beginning.

Mozhayev's walk continues, across the boulevards all hugged with snow and past buildings covered in thick green gauze, a sign they are about to be destroyed. And all along the way Mozhayev is talking and swigging, bringing alive the alleyways and houses so they seem to teem with living ghosts. There's something mystic in his psycho-geography, his search for the Old, Holy Moscow, a city that doesn't quite exist, a search for something better and imagined.

It's well into the night as Mozhayev and I loop back toward Gnezdnikovsky. The excavators are silent. Mozhayev stoops down to wipe the top layer off the snow. Under the lamplight you can see how the next layer is a thick brick red from the dust of the day's great demolition:

"When we go to the barricades," jokes Mozhayev, "this will be the color of our blood."

The walk is over. We part and Mozhayev grabs a gypsy-cab home. I'd always assumed he lived somewhere in the alleyways of Old Moscow. Instead the car drives him deep into the suburbs. Shanson is playing on the taxi's radio. He drives far out from the magic of Mozhayevland, past hordes of rectangular apartment blocks, right to the MKAD, the final, outermost ring-road encircling Moscow.

Mozhayev's unkempt, twenty-story, 1980s block is right by the ring-road's edge. The elevator is out of order, and he climbs the stairs past lame graffiti and tin cans full of damp cigarette ends. The walk is sobering. He pants. His own home was knocked down a few years ago, replaced with high-rises. He is an émigré.

"You grow up sure that everything will always be the same: house, trees, parents," he will write later in another essay. "When my parents died I could remember them through the building that we lived in.

Buildings aren't so much about recollecting time as about the victory over time."

After the cold outside the building is overheated, and he is sweating heavily by the time he reaches his own floor. He tries to be quiet as he enters the apartment; his wife and children are asleep. The youngest (of three) is lying in his cot in the corridor. He makes his way to the tiny living room. Everywhere there are small artifacts of the wreckage of old Moscow, which Mozhayev has retrieved from demolition: shards of sixteenth-century designs of flowers from the basements of houses, wood carvings from the sashes of destroyed windows—firebirds, gentle giants, mouse-kings. They are laid out like exhibits from a long-lost civilization.

Outside the sound of rushing traffic on the MKAD rises. The high-rises merge with the darkness. Only the flocks of cranes still glimmer and swing around construction sites, working through the night, like catching a theater set between the acts. In the distance the thickest flock surrounds the ever-in-construction Federation Tower, the central skyscraper of "Moscow City," Russia's rebuttal to La Defense and Canary Wharf but built higher, faster, and with shoulder-barging, get-out-of-my-way insistence near the middle of the capital, so much taller and bigger than anything in the city that it redefines its dimensions, its very idea of height and size. "It is time for Russia to get up off its knees," the President's favorite sound bite goes, and the Federation Tower rises like the folklore warriors of Russian stories, growing "not by days but by the hour."

There's a cry as Mozhayev's newborn starts sobbing in his cot. Mozhayev lifts the baby up, rocks him up and down to stop the mewling. He's only a few months old and a half-caste. Mozhayev's wife is from Cuba; her parents were communists who moved to Soviet Moscow expecting a utopia. All three of Mozhayev's kids are black, the only black kids the other kids around here have ever met. They get smacked about, called nasty names. Mozhayev has been thinking about emigrating for them to have a normal life.

Montenegro, he thinks to himself; he's always liked the sound of the word "Montenegro." Or London. Or maybe farther.

INITIATIONS

Late morning smell of benzine coating the city, overburn of weekend nights coating the mouth, white Sunday snow turning to Monday sludge—I'm late. I grab the camera and run out of my top-floor apartment with its grand view of the bend in the frozen river, and beyond that, the great jagged tooth of one of the Stalin-Gothic skyscrapers. The dark green stairwell is full of cigarette ends and small brown puddles of melted snow knocked from boots. The apartment doors are padded for security, which makes them resemble asylum cells. Behind the padded doors are millionaire's apartments; everyone's done well in this city of baby-faced billionaires, but especially so on this block, the old Stalin gothic block reserved for party and KGB and diplomatic elite and great actors, the last to profit from the old order and the first to profit from the new one. Yet no one cares to band together and redecorate the stairwells. Care stops at the threshold of your apartment. You lavish and stroke your personal world, but when you reach the public space, you pull on your war face.

I ride the elevator, still lit with a dim yellow bulb, past the mad woman who sits on the stairwell shouting, "I am an egg, I am an egg," all day and night. "The KGB came and took me. They came and took me. I am an egg!" (What does she mean?, I always think to myself, Did they do something to her? Or is it just nonsense?) At the front door I pat my trouser pocket to check for the thin outline of my passport and realize it's not there. Always the passport, always the "dokumenti!" You can get stopped and checked for papers at any moment. It might only actually happen once or maybe even twice a year, but you still have to stand in queues and knock on doors to obtain the whole library of little stamps, regulations, permits—the legal stipulations and requirements that are themselves always changing. A little trick to keep you always on tenterhooks, always patting your pockets for your papers, always waking up worried that you might have lost them in a bar. Over time you begin to pat for the passport instinctively, your hand going down unthinkingly to check your pocket so many times a day you don't even notice any more. That's true power—when it starts to influence the unconscious movements of your arms.

I have to go back up to the apartment.

There are so many little initiations, so many ways the system wraps itself around you. My latest has been a driving test. I would never pass, my instructor had explained, if I didn't pay a bribe (this month $500, but about to jump to $1,000 if I didn't hurry). I protested that I wanted to learn and pass the test for real. He explained the traffic police would fail me until I paid up.

The instructor was a friend of a friend of my parents, and I was told to trust him by everyone I knew. He specialized in giving lessons to what he described as "nervous" types: actresses and ex-pats. I gave up the money, and he made the appropriate deal. I had assumed I would then receive the license in an envelope. To my surprise my instructor told me to go to the traffic center to take the test with everyone else.

The theory part of the test was held in a large, bright, new office room with very new computers. There were around twenty of us seated in front of computers completing simulations of various driving scenarios. I assumed, with a little relief, that my bribe had been lost in the works and set about using my common sense to answer the questions. To my self-satisfied surprise I received 18/20, enough to pass. Only later did it hit me that every computer in the room must have been a priori rigged to give 18/20: everyone in the room had paid for the right result.

Then came the test proper, a sequence of maneuvers around cones in a car park. I got into a car, an instructor's model with two sets of pedals, next to a traffic cop in uniform. He told me to start the car. I was so nervous and had completed so few lessons, I couldn't get the pedals right and kept on stalling. The traffic cop smiled, glanced over his shoulder, and managed the ignition himself. "Put your hands on the wheel and pretend to drive," he told me. I did as I was told, and while the traffic cop controlled the whole movement of the car from his set of pedals, I cruised around with an inane grin. After a while I had the sense I was almost driving the car myself.

Back in the apartment I find the passport in yesterday's trousers in the unmade bed. I keep it in a special inner pocket where it would be hard to steal. But that means the passport is permanently plastered to the sweat of my leg. The logo at the front is rubbing off. The edges are curled up. The plastic coating over my photo is peeling. I hurry back down to the street to hail a ride. The cars speed up as they turn the corner: Mitsubishis, Hummers, BMWs, Mercedeses, all with tinted windows. You're only someone as long as you at least pretend to have something to hide. One stops. The window starts to come down, and I crouch down to be at eye level; you only have a few seconds to evaluate the driver's face. A drunk? Nutter? Or worse, someone who will drive you to a lay-by and mug you? For all the little bits of paper and little forms you need to sign to survive here, everything comes down to these little moments of improvised trust and deals, "kak dogovoritsa," in which everyone understands the game though nothing is ever formalized.

300 to Three Station Square?

400?

350.

I sit in the front and try to size up my driver further. It's an odd relationship you have inside these cars: on the one hand you've paid and you should be in charge; on the other it's not a real taxi and the driver can get offended. This one has a beard and looks composed. He switches on the CD and it's playing psalms. I advise him to take care on the corner where the traffic police like to change the signs from "single lane" to "no way" overnight to catch out drivers and extract their rent—the city is an obstacle course of corruption, and your options are to get angry or play up and play the game and just enjoy it. The traffic has already curdled—my journey is short but this will be a long ride. A Muscovite measures out his life in jams, the day's success or failure judged by how many hours you spend in traffic. They have become the city's symbol. The only way to relieve the city would be to move financial and government centers out of the inner rings of town. But that would be out of keeping with the feudal instincts of the system. So the traffic becomes the expression of the stalemate at the center of everything: on the one hand the free market means everyone can own a car, but on the other all the cars are in jams because of the underlying social structure. The siren-wielding, black (always black), bullet-proof Mercedeses of the big, rich, and powerful are free to drive against the flow of traffic, speed through the acid sludge, driven by modern-day barons who live by different rules. The sirens are the city's status symbol, awarded like knighthoods to the most loyal bureaucrats, businessmen, and film directors (or for a certain price). As they pass us the driver and I both grunt, united, I sense, for a moment against a common enemy. I relax and tell him how much I like the psalms he's playing. But when we end our journey and I get out to go, he suddenly grabs my shoulder and pulls me around so we are face to face. His arm is strong and his grip hard.

"Don't worry, my brother," he tells me, "we'll clean the streets of all the filth, all the darkies, the Muslims and their dirty money. Holy Russia will rise again."

One bumps into these types occasionally, Eurasianists, Great Russians, holy neo-imperialists, and the like, few but quietly supported by the Kremlin to have a mouthpiece through which to keep the conversation away from corruption and focused on fury at foreigners (the Kremlin isn't keen to say these words itself).

I pass through the station and head for the St. Petersburg train and my latest story—about mandatory military service, the great initiation into Russian manhood. Every April and October the color khaki seems to suddenly sprout on the streets as bands of young soldiers appear in the cities; skinny, in uniforms either too large or small, with pinched red noses and red ears, scowling at the Maybachs and gold-leaf restaurants. They hang around at the entrances of metro stations where the warm air gusts up from the underground, shiver while sucking on tepid beer on street corners of major thoroughfares. They come shuffling up stairs and knocking on apartment doors and stalk through parks. It's the time of year of Russia's great annual hide and seek; the soldiers have been given orders to catch young men dodging the draft and force them to join the army. Military service might be mandatory for healthy males between eighteen and twenty-seven, but anyone who can avoids it.

The most common way out is a medical certificate. Some play mad, spending a month at a psychiatric clinic. Their mothers will bring them in: "My son is psychologically disturbed," they will say. "He has been threatening me with violence, he wakes up crying." The doctors of course know they are pretending, and the bribe to stay a month in a loony bin will set you back thousands of dollars. You will never be forced to join up again—the mad are not trusted with guns—but you will also have a certificate of mental illness hanging over you for the rest of your career. Other medical solutions are more short term: a week in the hospital with a supposedly injured hand or back. This will have to be repeated every year, and annually the hospitals fill up with pimply youths simulating illness. But the medical route takes months of preparation: finding the right doctor, the right ailment—because the ailments that can get you off change all the time. You turn up at the military center with the little stamped registration card that your mother has spent months organizing and saving for, then find that this year flat feet or shortsightedness are no longer a legal excuse.

If you're at a university you avoid military service (or rather you fulfill it with tame drills at the faculty) until you graduate. There is no greater stimulus for seeking a higher education, and Russian males take on endless master's degree programs until their late twenties. And if you're not good enough to make it into college? Then you must bribe your way into an institution; there are dozens of new universities that have opened in part to service the need to avoid the draft. And the possibility of the draft makes dropping out of college much more dangerous—the army will snap you up straightaway. When the bad marks come in, mothers start to fret and scream at their sons to work harder. And when they can see the boys might fail, it's time to pay another bribe, to make sure they pass the year. But there are a certain number of pupils the teacher has to fail to keep up appearances, and the fretting mothers start to put out feelers for the most desperate and most expensive remedy: the bribe to the military command. The mothers come to the generals, beat and weep on the doors of the commanders, cry about their sons' freedoms (money by itself is not always enough; you have to earn the emotional right to pay the bribe).

But all these options are only available for those with money and connections. For the others, for the poorer ones, it's hide and seek time. The soldiers will grab anyone who looks the right age and demand his documents and letters of exemption, and if he doesn't have them march him off to the local recruitment center. So the young spend their time avoiding underground stops or hiding behind columns and darting past when they see the soldiers are flirting with girls or scrounging cigarettes off passersby. You see teens sprinting through the long, dark marble corridors of the subway as cops give chase. When soldiers come by apartments, potential conscripts pretend they are not there, barricading themselves in, holding their breath until the soldiers go away. The soldiers eventually get tired and leave, but from now on every time you have your documents checked by police you will be trembling that they might ring through and see whether you dodged the draft. And every time you go into the subway, every time you cross a main road, every time you meet friends near a cinema, any time you leave your little yard, life becomes full of trepidation. And you will live semi-legally until you are twenty-seven, unable to register for an official passport and thus unable to travel outside of the country.

This is the genius of the system: even if you manage to avoid the draft, you, your mother, and your family become part of the network of bribes and fears and simulations; you learn to become an actor playing out his different roles in his relationship with the state, knowing already that the state is the great colonizer you fear and want to avoid or cheat or buy off. Already you are semilegal, a transgressor. And that's fine for the system: as long as you're a simulator you will never do anything real, you will always look for your compromise with the state, which in turn makes you feel just the right amount of discomfort. Whichever way, you're hooked. Indeed, it could be said that if a year in the army is the overt process that molds young Russians, a far more powerful bond with the system is created by the rituals of avoiding military service.

Those too poor, too lazy, or too unlucky to avoid the draft—or those for whom the army seems a better option than anything they have—are rounded up, stripped, shaved, and packed off to bases all across the country. At the end of the April and October call-ups the city streets are clogged with great trucks full of conscripts, decked with tarpaulins and open at the back. The new conscripts sit and stare at the city they are leaving, rubbing their heads as they get used to the lightness of their newly shaved skulls. Where he will be sent depends on the bribe a soldier pays. Some will go to Chechnya, to Ossetia, to the death zones everyone dreads. But if you pay in time, you'll avoid those. What no one will be safe from is hazing, known in Russia as the "law of the grandfather": dozens of conscripts are killed every year, hundreds commit suicide, and thousands are abused. (Those are just the official statistics.) This is why every mother wants to keep her son away from the army. New conscripts are known as "spirits." And as the tarpaulin-covered trucks pass through the gates of the army bases, the conscripts will hear the shouts of the older officers waiting for them: "Hang yourselves, spirits, hang yourselves!" they call. And the great breaking-in begins.

The Committee of Soldiers' Mothers, an NGO run by the mothers of conscripts past and present, is the refuge "spirits" flee to when they run away from camp. The headquarters are in St. Petersburg. I take the Sapsan, the new train as smart as a TGV with wider seats and so expensive no one but the new middle class can afford it, up to the northern capital. The Sapsan takes four hours to reach Petersburg, the normal train takes eight. Some laugh that the Sapsan was built especially by the President so his "team" could travel between the two cities in comfort. The country is ruled now by the "St. Petersburg set," the President's old chums who were raised and studied with him. As I leave the train station I drive into town through a city built like a theater set, the original Russian facade of European civilization as imagined by Peter the Great, with little of its content.

In the office of the Soldiers' Mothers the walls are lined with photographs of dead soldiers. I've come to interview four eighteen-year-olds who have recently fled from a nearby base called Kamenka. I'm late, but they're all waiting quietly and jump to attention when I walk in. They wear hoodies and the football scarves of Zenit, the St. Petersburg football team, and are desperate to prove they didn't just run away because of common hazing, that they're loyal, tough. They seem embarrassed by having to take shelter with fifty-year-old women. They never call the Committee of Soldiers' Mothers by its name, just "the Organization."

"You get beaten up, that's fine. I pissed blood but that didn't scare me," says one, the skinniest.

"Stools broken over your head. It's good for you," echoes another.

"They put a gas mask over your face, then force you to smoke cigarettes while you do push-ups. If you get through that you're a real man."

"I'm not red, . . ." they all repeat.

"Red" means "traitors." It's a prison word: in the 1940s Stalin started to fill up the ranks of the army with prisoners, infecting the system with prison code and hierarchies.

"You need discipline. But what happens at Kamenka has nothing to do with discipline."

"The 'grandfathers' beat you to extort money, not because they want to make a soldier out of you."

The conscripts spend most of their time repairing and repainting military vehicles, which are then sold on the sly by Kamenka's command. The "spirits" are essentially used as free labor.

The boys had run away after a night of nonstop beatings. The "grandfathers" had been drinking all day, and then at night they began to whack the boys with truncheons. The commanding officer came by but did nothing; commanding officers need the help of the "grandfathers" in their larger corruption schemes and let them have their fun. They go to great lengths to cover up for the "grandfathers." In one week, the Soldiers' Mothers told me, five "spirits" at Kamenka had their spleens beaten to a pulp. The commanders couldn't take the "spirits" to a normal hospital; too many questions would be asked. So they had to take them privately, paying 40,000 rubles (over $1,000) for each operation.

At 6:00 A.M. the "grandfathers" told the "spirits" they needed to each bring 2,000 rubles ($50) by lunchtime or they would kill them. One of the conscripts, Volodya, had decided to make a run for it. He slipped through the fence and made it to the road. His father had picked him up and brought him to the Organization.

Volodya mutters as he tells his tale. I have to keep on asking him to speak up.

"Of course it's because the commanding officer in the army is a darkie from the Caucasus. The darkies control the camp, it's all their fault," he tells me. The women from the Organization tut-tut and shake their heads. They hear this every day, especially in St. Petersburg, the skinhead capital, and especially among the supporters of Zenit, Volodya's team.

"Were the 'dembels' who beat you darkies?" ask the "mothers."

"No, they were white," admits Volodya.

The story might have died after he ran away; Volodya would have reported who had carried out the beatings. The army would have denied them. And that would have been the end of it.

But the commanding officer panicked. He drove into town, grabbed Volodya from the street in front of his apartment, bundled him into his car, and tried to bring him back to the base. Volodya's father had given chase in his car and collided with the commanding officer's car to stop him. There was a pileup. The cops turned up; TV cameras turned up. The Soldiers' Mothers managed to extract Volodya. Then the new minister of defense found out about the story. The Kremlin had just pledged to reform the military. The minister needed an example to show everyone he meant it. Kamenka was already under examination; three conscripts had died during military exercises in the previous month. Maybe that's why the commanding officer had panicked. Now the ministry had an excuse to ramp up the investigation, and the TV reporters were being encouraged to make films about it (a couple of years later the anticorruption minister of defense was himself tried for embezzlement, in the next round of Kremlin purges).

I have learned to play this game by now, feed off the scraps of freedom given by the system. I will intercut Volodya's story together with other tales of bullying: a reality show star who married an abusive husband, a kid picked on in his yard. And my producers are happy. They have worked out that these stories about the little man being beaten up by the state play well; this is the everyday reality of the TNT generation. They're commissioning more of them. Another director is shooting a film about a man in Ekaterinburg who was beaten nearly to death by traffic cops when he refused to pay a bribe; now he exacts his vengeance by catching traffic cops giving bribes on video and posting them online. Another film TNT is making is about a young woman killed when her car was crashed into by the head of an oil company; he got off due to his connections. Back in Moscow I have just filmed a story about teens beaten by the police. The whole thing was caught on cell phones, but the police have brought charges against the teens for beating THEM up. I hear the same chorus of confused despair from the teens that I heard from Yana Yakovleva: "It's like they can define reality, like the floor disappears from under you." The Kremlin has announced a new campaign to clean up the police, and the parents hope this will help save their children (and thus I'm allowed to shoot my story).

The victims I meet never talk of human rights or democracy; the Kremlin has long learned to use this language and has eaten up all the space within which any opposition could articulate itself. The rage is more inchoate: hatred of cops, the army. Or blame it all on foreigners. Some teens, the anarchists and artists, have started to gather and protest, rushing out of the metro and cutting off the roads and the main squares. They call their gatherings "Monstrations" and carry absurdist banners:

"The sun is your enemy."

"We will make English Japanese."

"Eifiyatoloknu for president."

The only response to the absurdity of the Kremlin is to be absurd back. An art group called Vojna ("War") are the great tricksters of the Monstration movement: running through the streets and kissing policewomen; setting cockroaches loose in a courtroom; graffiti-ing a penis on the underside of a bridge in St. Petersburg so when the bridge comes up the penis faces the local FSB; projecting a skull and crossbones onto the parliament building.

In any other culture this might seem flippant; in this society of spectacle and cruelty it feels like oxygen. Even the performance artist Vladik Mamyshev-Monroe has become politicized, posing in a magazine as a grotesque version of the President. He spent days immersing himself in the role: "When I became Putin, I felt myself become a totemic maggot, about to explode with shit. But I wasn't the baddie, I was the janitor, who needed to eat up everything, Russia, the USSR, so the new life could begin. . . . Putin will eat up our country. One day we will reach into the cupboard and reach for our clothes and they will turn to dust in our hands because they have been eaten by maggots."

But just as I feel I'm on a roll, my little corridor is cut off.

"We're sorry, Peter," my producers tell me at TNT, "we've been told to stop making . . . 'social' films. You understand. . . ."

They look a little uncomfortable when they say this (there's a new one among them, a redhead, who has replaced the raven-haired, who has married and left to live in London). I'm uncomfortable for their discomfort, and I find myself nodding. Of course I understand. I have learned to pick things up on the edge of a hint. I don't ask "why." I don't argue that ratings should be our priority. There are unspoken walls. The Kremlin wave of cleaning things up has finished. The 2008 financial crisis in the West has lowered the oil price, and there's less money for the Kremlin to indulge in toying with reforms. We need calm now. The economy is curdling.

As I am coming out of TNT toward evening, the neon lamps on the sushi bars are already lighting up dark mountains of dirty acid sludge: the chemicals the city puts in grit burn the paws of stray dogs. You can hear them whimper as they huddle by the warm pipes along the buildings. Two pork-faced cops, whom Muscovites have taken to calling "werewolves in uniform," patrol the corner. I try not to gawk and walk past in the Moscow style, face down and furious. The main thing is not to catch their eye—one of my many registrations has expired.

But they can still smell the fear on me—belching out the phrase that is their mark of power: "Documents: Now!" I know the script. They shepherd me toward the darkness of a courtyard. Then comes the ultimate Moscow transaction, the slipping of the bribe, a 500-ruble note already placed that morning among the pages of my passport (the rate has been going up as the economy worsens). But never offer money directly. Paying bribes requires a degree of delicacy. Russians have more words for "bribe" than Eskimos do for "snow." I use my favorite formulation: "May I use this opportunity to show a sign of my respect for you?" "Of course you may," the werewolves say, smiling suddenly, and slip the cash under their policeman's caps. All they ever wanted was some respect.

And though I still tremble quietly at the act, I have become good at this.

MIDSUMMER NIGHT'S DREAMS

An advertisement hangs on huge billboards over the city: a single, handsome, male eye staring out of a dark room through a crack in a door, both spying on the passersby and imploring them to release him. The advertisement is for one of Grigory's companies, office furniture (black sells best) to fill up the just-built offices of the new Moscow. At thirtysomething, Grigory is one of Moscow's young self-made multimillionaires, one of the boys who became rich in a blink during the 1990s, when being an entrepreneur, and not a bureaucrat, was the thing to do.

Moscow knows Grigory best through his great parties: oases where we escape the barons and werewolves for a night. Tonight's event is in honor of Grigory's marriage. He has taken over a mini-Versailles-like palace for the occasion. Near the entrance to the park teams of makeup artists from Moscow's film studios dress up the guests in motion picture costumes: tonight's theme is "Midsummer Night's Dream." The same crowd follows Grigory around from week to week, re-creating itself for his latest whim. Inside the park trapeze artists on invisible ropes swoop down and through the trees; synchronized swimmers dressed as mermaids with shining silver tails flip and dive in the dark lake. Geysers shoot up from the water: as the droplets fall they're lit up to create a rainbow in the night. Everyone wonders: Where are the bride and groom? A spotlight illuminates the lake. Grigory and his bride appear on opposite sides, on separate little boats made up like tortoise shells, both dressed in white. The tortoise shells move magically toward each other (pushed, I later learn, by frogmen). The boats meet in the middle; the lovers join hands and step barefoot on the water. They do not sink. Suspended on the lake, they turn and walk across the water toward us, their path illuminated by lasers. We gasp at the miracle and all applaud. The effect is achieved with a secret walkway installed specially under the lake, but it is still divine.

But when Monday comes Grigory will return to a world of corrupt officials demanding bribes. The world of businessmen is shrinking. Even the poster for Grigory's company seems to suggest a secret social edge: Is the eye peeking through the door a reference to "Big Brother is watching you"?

I first met Grigory through an old university friend, Karine. Back home I'd remembered Karine as wearing sandals and tie-dyed skirts, forever getting her curls in her eyes. Then she went to Moscow and was transformed: her hair up, back bare, designer heels replacing Birkenstocks. She'd changed after meeting some Russian guy. That was Grigory. When I first came to Moscow she introduced us. He was living in one of the new skyscrapers, his penthouse perched over the erupting city. The apartment had been specially designed for Grigory and was featured in glossy architecture magazines: open plan, all-white, a lot of plastic. A vision of the future—or maybe a lunatic asylum. Grigory would pace it with the walk common to many of Moscow's newly rich: a confident strut with the odd, sudden alarmed glances. He was small and lithe, with the eternally young face of a choir boy.

Looking around, I noticed the apartment seemed to have no signs of personal history: no old books, clothes, silverware, photographs. As if Grigory had emerged out of a void.

With time I found out more about him.

He grew up in Tatarstan. His dad was just another Soviet oil worker, a small cog in the great state energy machine. Growing up the young Grigory excelled at math and physics, the type of quiet boy who would spend hours on the toilet reading chess books, forgetting where he was, learning grand masters' games by heart. (I played him once; he beat me in ten moves.) His talents were quickly spotted, and in the 1980s he was dispatched to a special math and physics college in Moscow, to be taught by Nobel Prize winners, with others being crunched and molded into crack intellectual troops to glorify the Soviet Empire. It was perestroika, and the Soviet Union was creaking, swaying. Films and books and music from the West were starting to seep into the new black markets. Everyone pieced together his own version of the West, his own collage of freedom. Grigory got into Freddy Mercury, later films by Pasolini and Jarman, Dadaists, Greenaway—as far away from Soviet Tatarstan as you could possibly go. He was finishing his studies as the Soviet Union collapsed. For an older generation, for men like the President, the collapse of the empire was tragic. But for a twentysomething like Grigory, it meant that suddenly anything was possible.

Grigory began by making his own computers. They sold well. Soon he had a team of other students working with him. Got involved with banking. Then came the new world of threats, bodyguards. At the parties, people would whisper he was lucky to have made it through alive.

"The worst is when people owe you money," Grigory told me once as we drove through the woods outside of Moscow in a new, silver, sports car. "As long as you owe them, they'll never kill you. But if they owe *you* they'd rather kill than pay. I dream of being able to go outside without bodyguards. A normal life." (The bodyguard's Jeep was visible in the rearview mirror as we drove.)

"What is it you want from Moscow, Peter?" he asked me another time, as we were drinking bright blue cocktails.

"Well, you know, it's a booming city. It's up and up and up."

"Only a foreigner can think that. This city devours itself."

And then once, when he was thinking of resuming his studies, but this time in political economy: "There must be some way of working out how to make Russia work. Must be!"

Whenever I see Grigory he is accompanied by Sergey, who directs the human scenery around his boss: he brings artists, directors, actors, and foreigners so Grigory feels he's at the center of a bohemian feast. A personal tailor makes Sergey's clothes: capes, knee-high boots, tweed breeches, the cultivated getup of a twenty-first-century necromancer. He has a way of making his pupils shrink and dilate in hypnotic pulsations. He drives a green vintage Jag (whose very appearance is some sort of wizardry in this black-Jeep-and-Hummer-dominated town).

Sergey and Grigory studied together at the math and physics college, shared rooms. But after school, while Grigory had become a millionaire, Sergey had tried to be an artist. He discontinued that and joined a cult. He returned talking mystic riddles about the "materialization of dreams" and "re-dividing reality into segments you can travel through."

"I'm Grigory's healer, his wizard," Sergey likes to say. "The parties are mystery plays."

Sometimes Grigory smiles at Sergey's mystical obsessions, but with every week he seems to need him more, waiting for Sergey to take him by the hand and escape to a better world straight out of the movies they grew up on.

One evening Sergey delivers an invitation for another Grigory party. Guests are told to prepare for the art project of the year. The impossibly fashionable boys are all dressed in black this time. Grigory enters, and his court photographer (he has a stutter and is the only one here drinking as heavily as me) puts down his cocktail and scampers over. A burst of photographs: this is the Moscow way—all the rich have their own photographers. They take them on holidays, to parties, to family gatherings; you've only made it when your life becomes a magazine.

Grigory comes over and we toast the evening.

"Tonight is when we reveal the true face of Russia," says Grigory. "I present Sklyarov!"

A light comes on, illuminating a stage at the far end of the club. A man with a face like a gargoyle sits on a throne, dressed in tsarist robes. Rocking, he spits and mutters. A bulge on his forehead sticks out like a small, second head, pushing the eyes down into dark slits. The eyes dart around the room like a trapped animal's. This is Sklyarov. Sergey had picked him up outside a railroad bar in a polluted provincial town. Sklyarov was the local madman and a prodigious scribbler: conspiracy theories, nonsense political utopias, frenetic sketches of the ideal city. When Sergey showed Grigory the scribbles, he was inspired: this was the true voice of the new Russia. They flew Sklyarov to Moscow (he'd never flown before and soiled his seat), put him up in the best hotel on the highest floor, and told him people in the highest echelons of power were interested in his ideas. Tonight they are launching Sklyarov's book, his mendicant vision for the future of the country. Sergey introduces the mendicant as a great Russian prophet, a future leader of the nation.

Sklyarov begins to read extracts from his book. His hands tremble as he holds it; it's the hands that are the most appalling, caked with layers of factory soot, dirt, blood, the scum of railway toilets. The book opens with a description of life in his hometown, which in tsarist times had the most apt name of Yama, literally "the pit." Sklyarov, frightened at first, reads fast:

The psychological situation in Yama has become critical, acts of psychological violence are on the increase. The violence takes place on the pathological, material, political, moral, financial, and other levels. There is an increase in corruption among bureaucrats aimed at destabilizing the psychological arsenal of the people.

The thing works like a nonsense satire of Moscow. The impossibly fashionable boys and girls start to relax, applaud, congratulate Grigory on the art project of the year. Sklyarov reads on; the next chapter deals with his autobiography:

As regards the story of my own life, in all its facts, numbers, events, trials, tortures, pluses, minuses, flights, falls, ravelings, unravelings, realities, realisms, points of view, versions, dark, light and colored phases: I was born at four o'clock and twenty minutes, in the year 1972, in the town of Yama, in the then-Soviet Union. I was raised in the tradition, order and instructions of Communism, though my soul always rebelled against them. On October 28, 1979, I was made into a Young Pioneer. I took my Young Pioneer badge and flushed it down the toilet with the words: "Maybe you, toilet, can be a young pioneer."

Grigory stares up at the gargoyle. As the mendicant tells his story I start to notice how uncannily he and Grigory reflect each other: born in the same period, both children of one system they disbelieved, now in conflict with a new system ruled by corrupt bureaucrats. Grigory feels that he lives in an asylum, rebuilds his penthouse to look like one. Sklyarov spent all his formative years in real ones—his asylum diary takes up the bulk of his autobiography.

Sergey is as ever on Grigory's shoulder, smiling with his success. After the event the three link arms and pose for photographs; in this city they rhyme.

But every week Grigory seems to need rebirths ever more intensely. Every time I see him he is wearing a new costume, transforming himself for another of his fancy dress evenings—one night an elf, then

Hitler, Rasputin—escaping, changing, and mutating, clipping his hair short, growing it longer, brushing it to the side, then forward. (Only the bodyguards stay the same. Their boss is an eccentric, and I can never tell whether they hate or love him for it.) Sergey consults lunar calendars, arranges parties to match zodiacal principles. When Aquarius is in the sky he makes a deal with those who run the Moscow zoo and takes over the dolphinarium at night, the partygoers diving and swimming between slippery, pretty girls and dolphins. When the moon is new the theme of the party is "White." Grigory, carrying a white rabbit in a cage, announces "tonight is all about my rebirth, a new me." One week Grigory works as a waiter in a café ("I want to find out what it's like to be a normal person," he tells me), the next he's writing plays, flying so fast no role can stick to him, and all around him the city is churning, the demolition ball swinging, and Gotham-gothic towers erupting. And now the bully bureaucrats and Chekists are closing in, and on the news there is always the same message: "Our great President has brought stability." But all I see happening is that the brilliant boys like Grigory are being eaten.

Television is also increasingly affected. Originally TNT's formula for success was to remake hit Western reality shows like *The Apprentice* or *Dragon's Den*. They were successful across the world—why not here? But when TNT made Russian versions, they flopped. The premise for most Western shows is what we in the industry call "aspirational": someone works hard and is rewarded with a wonderful new life. The shows celebrate the outstanding individual, the bright extrovert. But in Russia that type ends up in jail or exile. Russia rewards the man who operates from the shadows, the gray apparatchik, the master of the *politique de couloir*. The shows that worked here were based on a different set of principles. By far the biggest success was *Posledny Geroi* ("The Last Hero"), a version of *Survivor*, a show based on humiliation and hardship.

Slowly Grigory, like thousands of other Russians, starts to discreetly shift to the safety and serenity of London. Every year he spends less and less time in Moscow. Away from Russia he settles down. Has kids. He posts photos of his new life on his Facebook page: at trance festivals in Arizona, among the snows of Iceland, in the Scottish highlands. Grigory now feels calm enough to ditch the bodyguards. And though he has all the money in the world he likes to travel across west London in big red public transport buses.

• • •

For all their restoration hedonism, there can be something so forced about the glittering whirligig of the grander, gaudier Moscow nights. One time there is even a "Putin Party" in Heaven, one of the clubs where Oliona does her hunting. Strippers writhe around poles chanting: "I want you, Prime Minister." (The President is briefly Prime Minister at the time, though still actually in charge, still the real President, just dressed up as the Prime Minister as at a masquerade.) The mood at the "Putin Party" is a mix of feudal poses and arch, postmodern irony: the sucking up to the master completely genuine, but as we're all liberated, twenty-first-century people who enjoy Coen brothers films, we'll do our sucking up with an ironic grin while acknowledging that if we were ever to cross him, we would quite quickly be dead.

So, midway during nights in the baroque clubs with their Forbeses and girls, at around 2:00 A.M., I tend to take my leave, pull on my coat and scarf, and slide and stumble across black ice to one of Mitya Borisov's bars. In earlier years I went to his little basement bar on Potapoffsky, then later to his one-room place on Herzen Street. There might be many of the same faces I'd seen earlier at the more glamorous events: Borisov's bars aren't "underground" places, and they're not particularly cheap. The food ranges from okay to abhorrent, the booze is warm and often the wrong bottle. Borisov himself may well be there, but he has been drunk for so many years that his puffy, drooping face stares past you when you walk in even if you once swore friendship.

He's too tight ever to have installed air-conditioning, and the bars are such a smog of sour Russian cigarettes it makes a chain-smoker choke. Even so, as soon as you are through the door you can breathe more easily than in all the other places.

Borisov's bars tap into the only unbroken tradition in Moscow, that of Soviet dissidents and nonconformists, a tradition that started off in Soviet kitchens and didn't have to reinvent itself after 1991 because it had never pretended to "speak Bolshevik" beforehand. It just continued out of the kitchens and into Borisov's bars. Borisov's father, a literature professor, served time (he'll tell you the story around 4:00 A.M.), and his first venue was an old apartment where you brought your own bottles and read your own poems. The clientele now range from an older generation in their sixties to their children and grandchildren. There's no face control, but Borisov might threaten to throw you out if you can't tell a decent rhyme from a bad one.

During the night I make my way from one of Borisov's bars to the next. He's put a bunch of places on one street so you never have to leave this world. There's Kvartira 44, decorated like a 1970s dissident apartment, with the same books you would have found in your parents' homes. (We're back drinking in kitchens—though now you have to pay for the experience.) There's Jean-Jacques, themed as a French bistro, John Donne as an English pub. But they don't feel like hollow pastiche so much as witty acts of imaginary emigration, like visiting a White Russian émigré locale in 1920s Paris or a nineteenth-century London pub full of exiled antitsarists. Between darkness and dawn we all want to escape from the President's Russia.

And if the mood is still with me the next day, I like to head down to the big yellow concert hall on Herzen Street and order a large Armenian brandy from the bar in the grand, scuffed marble foyer, with a little slice of lemon on the side (always insist on a fresh one). I avoid the stalls and stride right upstairs and take my seat among the gods with the pale, intense conservatoire students and the slight spinsters, usually music teachers, whose breath smells of brandy and who are quite convinced these concerts are just for them. And when I get to my seat and finally look around, I notice something unusual, namely the light. Most classical concert rooms only have artificial lighting. But here on Herzen Street there are great, arched windows that show the sky. Only the sky; you don't see any roofs. And if your timing is lucky it will just be approaching sunset and the sky will be turning brandy-tinted. As the music starts I always have the sense the concert hall is somehow lifting. And if the wind is blowing and the clouds are moving fast, you get the extraordinary feeling that you're flying on a zeppelin powered by brandy, lemon, wind, sky, and music.

ACT III

FORMS OF DELIRIUM

THE LOST GIRLS

When Ruslana Korshunova was first spotted as a potential supermodel at the age of sixteen, it was her eyes that caught everyone's attention. Large and a wolf blue, the light of her Siberian ancestry: somewhere far off, a white midwinter sun on snowy wastes. Their power was heightened by a slight physical defect: in the bottom inside indent of each of Ruslana's eyes there was a slight cup, which led to them always being filled with liquid and thus always shining, giving the impression she might be about to cry or maybe had just been crying—though whether in joy or sadness you could never tell. The rest of her face, in stark contrast to those deep, light, blue, complex eyes, was all innocence. The eyes of a thirty-year-old woman, more actress than model, in the face of a child.

At the age of eighteen she became the star of a campaign for a "magical, enchanting perfume" from Nina Ricci. You might even remember the ad. It's in the style of a fairy tale. Ruslana, in a pink ball gown with bouncing curls, enters a white palace room. The room is empty apart from a tree, withered and bare but for a bottle of perfume shaped like a pink apple, which dangles from one of the branches, and a high mountain of dark, red apples in front of the tree. Ruslana sees the pink apple, and the camera zooms in as she gasps with teen excitement. She climbs the apple mountain, higher and higher, up to the very top, stretches, and reaches for the object of desire.

Two days before her twenty-first birthday she was dead. It was all over the tabloids, cable channels, and glossies: "Russian supermodel dies after plunging from near her ninth-floor apartment in downtown Manhattan. Her death is a presumed suicide. There was no note."

The moment her body hit the ground the story exploded into a clusterfuck of rumors. Was it drugs? Love? Mafia? Prostitution? She had burst into a thousand Ruslanas—the addict, the whore, the spurned lover. And through all these rumors the magical face of the girl stared out at me.

I had "access," that magical word all documentary makers and TV producers crave. A friend of mine knew Ruslana's friends and family. In the months since her death they had refused documentary makers, but they would make an exception for me. I phoned TNT, excited. It was the story that had everything. There would be supermodels, suicide, and parties. There was Moscow, New York, London, and Paris. Glamour and tragedy. It was the easiest commission I ever had. I was even given a larger advance than usual to produce the film.

"But don't make it too dark," TNT said, "Remember we need positive stories."

• • •

She died on Water Street, at the corner of Wall Street, Manhattan, where the financial district meets the East River. The evening I arrive is cold and wet. During the day it's crowded here with office workers, but after 6:00 P.M. it goes quiet quickly. Just the last clerks in pall-bearer black suits hurrying home, the coffee bars already closing. Ruslana's apartment is the only residential building on the street. It's a twelve-floor concrete jagged thing, the floors at different angles that fold awkwardly to fit onto the corner. Few families live here, just the tired travelers of trade and commerce, the foot soldiers of globalization: a Pakistani wool trader, a Malaysian PhD student. Jobbing models handed Ruslana's apartment down to each other.

The police report of her death shows photographs of her rented rooms: there are no books, no photos on the wall, no paintings. The door was locked from inside. The door to the balcony was open. There were cigarette butts on the floor—she would always smoke there. The balcony was covered with thick black netting from the building site next door. On the floor of the balcony there was a kitchen knife. There was a long cut through the netting: she must have taken the knife and sliced it open. The balcony is set at an angle away from the street. She couldn't have jumped from there; any fall would have been broken by the floors beneath. There was a small gap through the scaffolding to the building site. It was so small only a lithe girl could make it. When the police arrived none of them could slither through.

Next door the frame of the new fifteen-floor office building was already built. A concrete shell, complete with stairs and dividing walls, but with no front. The police report doesn't specify how long she spent wandering the empty building site. Several levels up one of the floors juts out into the street like a diving board. Could it have been from there? The police report doesn't specify where she jumped from.

The street was nearly empty the Saturday she died. It was the hottest day of the year, a headache-making hot New York high summer. On weekends the bankers are away, and in high summer anyone who can flees the financial district. At 12:45 a city laborer working on the street heard a loud thud: "I thought a car had hit a person. I turned around and there was a girl lying in the middle of the road," he told police. She was lying right out by the dividing lines, 8.5 meters away from the building—8.5 meters. The supermodel didn't take a step off and fall. She took a run and soared.

The night before her death Ruslana was with Vlada Ruslakova, the Chanel girl. I'm lucky to catch her in New York—she's about to fly off again, to somewhere in Asia. They're nothing like their images on paper, these girls. Brittle, with lost looks not quite sure on what to focus. I suppose it's only when they strike a pose for work that they become resolved; until then they are oddly in-between. But Vlada's face is perfectly proportioned: she holds the center of the shot very well during the interview.

"We had dinner in Manhattan, at our favorite bistro. We were planning for her to maybe come to Paris in a few days' time. Later that evening I took a plane to Paris myself for a shoot. She texted me when I landed—to see if I had arrived okay. That must have been morning in New York. And then a few hours later . . . a few hours later I saw on the news she was dead."

"Did you notice anything out of the ordinary?"

"No. But she had spent much of the last year in Moscow. So we hadn't seen each other much recently."

"Was she upset about anything?"

"No."

"Was she high?"

"No!"

"Why do you think she killed herself?"

"I refuse . . . I can't . . . I don't believe she did."

Vlada describes Ruslana as "sweet," "honest," and "intelligent." "Like a child." She repeats this: "like a child." Behind me Ruslana's mother is there during the whole of the interview. Vlada only agreed to talk because the mother asked her to, and I can't quite tell whether she's revealing all she knows. I can hear the mother gasping for breath like one holding back tears throughout our conversation. When it's her turn to give an interview, she runs out of the room weeping after just a couple of questions.

"I should never have let her go. Never. She was a child. She wasn't right for this world."

The mother has the same eyes, the exact same eyes, as Ruslana, and as I talk to her it can seem as if Ruslana is somehow present. She speaks in a small, sharp voice that cuts the ears ever so slightly.

Valentina hates the media, TV, journalists—anyone who had taken possession of and tried to tell her daughter's story.

"Why do they all say she was a drug addict, a prostitute? How dare they? How can you just take someone and talk about them when you never knew them? What right do they have?"

I tell her I will be different. Samples of Ruslana's organs and blood are kept in a vault under the New York coroner's office. Valentina allows me to send blood samples for a full test to see whether there are traces of heavy drug use. She also insists we test for Ruffinol and chloroform or any other drug that could have been administered to knock her out.

"She would have never killed herself," both Valentina and Vlada insist. "She wasn't like *that*."

• • •

Ruslana grew up in Almaty, Kazakhstan. The family was Russian: Ruslana's father was a Red Army officer, and Kazakhstan happened to be the last place he was stationed before the breakup of the USSR. He then went into private business.

"We were wealthy. One of the first to be really wealthy," the mother tells me as we walk through New York. "But he was killed."

Ruslana was only five at the time. She had a younger brother, Ruslan. Ruslan and Ruslana.

"You gave them the same names?"

"Yes—it's beautiful. Don't you find?"

Valentina looked around for work. She found door-to-door sales; American cosmetics companies were just expanding in Kazakhstan. Their business was dipping in the west but rising in the east. Valentina enrolled. She attended training to make her into a model salesperson: you can sell anything to anyone, they preached, as long as you believe. They taught her the "secrets" of sales success: make the customer say "yes" three times when you first chat with her, she can just be agreeing about the weather, that way she will be tuned into saying "yes" when you offer lipstick or anti-ageing cream. In the post-Soviet space such companies were hugely successful: the promise of money, secret knowledge, and Western beauty all in one package. (The catch was that the sales reps were actually being conned; they had to buy the cosmetics in bulk and see if they could sell them. They felt like salespeople, but actually they were the customers.)

"I was one of the best," Valentina tells me, and I can almost hear the corporate training pride. "I made it to the level of middle manager."

Valentina sent Ruslana to the local German-language school, considered the best in Almaty. It was prestigious to attend one. Ruslana had braces, got good marks, and was preparing for university in Germany. She had hair that reached down to her knees.

"Such beautiful hair," remembers Valentina. "I would help her wash it. Until the age of fifteen she never washed her hair alone."

When the call came from the modeling scout, Valentina laughed it off. Modeling wasn't their sort of thing; it smelled of prostitution. Ruslana was going to university after all. But the scout kept on calling. She explained that modeling was the best way to pay for a university education, even in England or America. Ruslana would go straight to the West; she wouldn't be held up in Moscow. They would try her at London fashion week.

"London, I'll finally see London!" Ruslana told her mother as she begged to go.

• • •

The scout's name is Tatyana Cherednikova. I find her in Moscow. She is on her way to the airport, and we talk in the back of the car. I expected someone in a designer dress and heels. Tatyana is quite the opposite. She wears a fleece with a reindeer pattern on it and snow boots. We listen to a CD of Christmas carols on the player. It's approaching the Western date for Christmas (the Russian date is in January). Tatyana converted to Protestantism during her travels in Europe and America.

"It's all about hard work and honesty," she tells me about her new faith.

I ask about Ruslana.

"Of course I feel guilty. There she was, happy with her mum, preparing for university—and up I pop and say *Hey, come to modeling land, it's wonderful out here.* . . . And then it all ends up the way it did. . . . But I really thought it would be a good way for her to make money for university. It is for lots of girls. It's a chance."

She says this simply—there's nothing duplicitous about her. I ask her how she found Ruslana.

Tatyana spends 50 percent of her life on the road. Her life is an endless progression of cheekbones, legs, buttocks, lips. She sees thousands of girls a year. Maybe three will make it to the top. The former Soviet Union is her territory. In the Cold War it was spies who knew this country, studied it, poured over every detail: every block of high-rises, every muddy road, every factory. Now it is modeling scouts. Voronezh, Karaganda, Alma Ata, Rostov, Minsk—these are the great wells of beauty, raw girl crude to be pumped and refined. Many have never heard of these places. Tatyana knows them inside out. The Soviet Union occupied 20 percent of the world's land mass; its former states produce 15 percent of the world's oil. But over 50 percent of the models on the catwalks of Paris and Milan are from the former USSR.

In 2004 Tatyana had gone to Kazakhstan. She was on the jury of Miss Alma Ata. Local businessmen invited her down; they wanted her to choose one of the girls, many their mistresses, and whisk her off to Paris. But the girls were all breasts and bums: oligarch lolls. Nothing that would suit the needs of Paris and Milan. She had gone around all the agencies while she was there, too; no one had stood out. A disappointing trip.

Tatyana was on the flight back. She had finished the paperback she was reading quicker than she thought. She flicked through the in-flight magazine.

And then she stopped. In between the whisky ad and the piece on Kazakh flora was a photo of a girl. Amazing. The photo was in dubious taste: a semiclad waif in tribal garb, posing like some cross between Lolita and Mowgli in a jungle of plastic trees. But the girl herself—she was amazing. Her blue gaze went on forever, so powerful and deep that everything—Tatyana, the plane, the clouds—seemed to be caught inside it: small toys suspended inside this young girl's gaze.

As soon as Tatyana landed, she phoned her colleagues at a Moscow casting agency. "Find that girl," she said. "Find that girl."

But Ruslana wasn't a model. No agency had heard of her. In the end they found the photographer. Ruslana had been friends with the daughter of the editor of the magazine. They had taken the photographs for fun, for a piece about Amazons. Tatyana spotting the photos was magical chance. Fairy-tale stuff.

"She was hired by a London agency straightaway. She was doing the shows in London, Paris, Milan. Just in the holidays, in between school. Later, when she went full time, she would ring to say thank-you. It's rare to hear 'thank-you' from a model. Ruslana was different."

"Why do you think she killed herself?"

"She was the most emotionally stable model I knew. The most balanced. The best educated. It just doesn't make any sense."

The traffic is becoming congested, and we barely make Tatyana's flight. She rushes to the departure area.

Before she goes she turns and says: "If you see Ruslana's mother give her my love. Tell her I think of Ruslana every day. And if you need to find me I'm at church most Sundays."

• • •

I find video of Ruslana's first trip to London, her first trip outside the former Soviet Union. A teenager—no, child—in a hoodie on a blustery London day, snapping photos of Tower Bridge, grinning goofily, laughing widely, and trying to hide her braces as she does so. Then she takes the hoodie off, and down it tumbles: that heavy, golden, knee-length hair. They nicknamed her "the Russian Rapunzel" in modeling land.

Masha was her best friend during those first European days. We meet up during Moscow Fashion Week. Passing backstage during the shows, I'm struck by how young the girls look. Not even nymphet-like, just skinny like prepubescent boys.

Masha is twentysomething, but she still looks fifteen. She has Bambi brown eyes. She met Ruslana in London on her seventeenth birthday. It was Ruslana's first season modeling.

"Who would wash her hair?" I ask to break the ice.

"We all took turns in the apartment. When we first met I had the sense Ruslana was my child, she was so innocent," says Masha.

They shared digs in six-to-a-room flats in London, Paris, and Milan. Those were the days of casting upon casting. Life squeezed into measurements (32–23–33), tense girls eyeing each other's legs-hips-breasts, desperate to be the one who is picked: every rejection a slap saying your body's wrong, you're wrong. We think of models as ideal; they think only of how they don't quite fit.

"Ruslana would cry; she took rejection personally. But then she'd pull herself together. Wrote poems to console herself."

Some poems still survive online:

Instead of moaning at the thorns,
I'm happy that a rose among them grows

Often they went hungry: agencies only provide a small allowance for food. That gets spent quickly.

"In Paris and Milan there'd be these dinners, rich men would pay to come, we could join in for free. Ruslana and I would go: it was our only chance to eat."

"And?"

"The men could tell we weren't like THAT. For lots of girls modeling is just a chance to meet a rich guy. It's not as if the men have to work hard to sleep with someone. All that stuff was happening around us."

Some girls, the Russian girls from god-knows-where who grew up with no running water, go nuts, sucked into the whirlpool of champagne, cocaine, debauchery. But not Ruslana.

"We were the dunces," says Masha, "the ones who went to bed early."

Success came quickly for Ruslana. Within a year she had her first hit for *Officiel*. The long hair spun into seaweed chains, entwining her body. Her face made over to cross the line from childhood to sex. But not Lolita-like; rather the stuff of folktales. And again that gaze: the taiga, Baikal, snowy wastes.

Then came the ad that took Ruslana and transformed her life. Nina Ricci. The magical tree. The pink apple . . . and stardom. The ad catapulted Ruslana into the jet set. Jerry Epstein, the head of Bear Sterns, famous for his love of teenage girls (he was later jailed for statutory rape), flew her down to his private Caribbean island. The new Russian mega-rich were especially keen to be seen with the new Russian supermodel. She spent more and more time in Moscow, found herself in the VIP lounge of all the clubs. The dream life of all the gold diggers and wannabes: she was living it. It was Moscow she fell in love with, felt most at home in. Her rise chimed together with the city's.

She met Alexander at a club (though no one can remember whether in New York or in Moscow). He was one of the handsomest Russian tycoons on the scene, and she fell blissfully in love.

Luba, a former Miss Chelyabinsk, knew her during the affair. Luba's Moscow apartment is drowning in her collection of cuddly bears. A little pug yaps throughout our conversation. "I never had toys when I was small," says Luba. "Now I'm making up for it. I have over two thousand bears. Every city I visit I buy new ones."

She tells me about Alexander.

"He's not that young, but he is gorgeous. Girls drop at his feet. He's been with so many of my friends. All of them perfect."

Friends, experienced models like Luba, warned Ruslana not to fall in love. But she was certain this was the real thing. She wanted marriage, children, a steady home.

"That was the thing about Ruslana," says Luba. "There was something childish about her. She believed. And she liked that he was older, she missed her father."

Ruslana told friends Alexander wanted to marry her. Introduced him to her mother. They lived together.

When Alexander dumped Ruslana she kept on texting him, hoping for an answer. She couldn't eat, couldn't sleep. Lost weight. She would ask friends to persuade him to change his mind. Her Facebook page was full of poems of unrequited love:

I gave love and forgave hurt,
Hid pain in my heart in anticipation of the miracle.
You left again, leaving in return
A castle of pink dreams and ruined walls.

And:

Don't be silent my love, don't be silent.
My soul yearns for you.
Turn back. Glance back.
My bright little sun.
I can't breathe without you.

In the end Alexander's assistant contacted her and told her not to bother him again.

And just as suddenly as Alexander dumped her, Ruslana's career stalled. The calls dried up.

"She couldn't understand," says Luba. "Suddenly she was one of a thousand girls. A no one."

She went back to New York to look for more work in the last months before her death. There was a new boyfriend, Mark, a Russian luxury car dealer in New York, but better known as a guy who parties with all the models.

"I'm probably the only girl Mark hasn't had an affair with," says Luba. Ruslana had fallen for another playboy, though this time a much poorer one. "That was Ruslana's problem," repeats Luba. "She believed."

• • •

Elena Obukhova used to be a model. Now she's a psychologist. "Look at these girls, they're all lost. Moscow is full of them. I'd have lots of clients: it's a very specific journey. I would understand them better than a regular analyst."

Elena too was discovered by chance, on the street in Tashkent, Uzbekistan, where, like Ruslana in Kazakhstan, she was one of the blonde ethnic Russian girls left after the empire fell. We walk through a spring Moscow, all the men looking around at the giant blonde beside me.

When we come to shoot the interview she's different than the younger girls I've interviewed: she has a language to talk about herself in, stares down the camera instead of searching in the air for words.

"I was fifteen and I remember listening in at the kitchen door. The scout was trying to convince my parents to let me go to Milan. I couldn't understand why he had chosen me, just like that on the street. I thought I was too tall, ugly, everyone at school would tease me. And now I was listening in at the door, just praying my parents would say yes. Italy! I hadn't been to Moscow, let alone Italy. And my poor father, he couldn't understand what was going on, he thought a model and fashion designer was the same thing."

Her parents let her go eventually, though only after she had finished school. She was sixteen going on seventeen when she reached Milan.

"Oh, I was so confused. People were nice and nasty at the same time. I mean, they talked nicely but said nasty things. I had thought everyone would be fascinated by me, I would be like a movie star. But it's the opposite. No one cares about your personality. You become a picture. That was hard, because growing up I had been used to talking about myself, gesticulating, shouting, laughing. The first thing you learn in modeling is to put on a mask, strike an array of poses, pouts, smiles. And before you know it you've lost the ability to talk normally, laugh naturally. But you're sixteen, seventeen, eighteen, everything inside is boiling over, but your profession is all about suppressing that."

"And the men?"

"Oh the men. They flock around. You're a prize—but they're sleeping with the girl on the photo, not you, and you begin to become your image and just become even more lost. And then there is a very common type you come across whose life is dedicated to making models fall in love with them. They're these pseudo-romantics, who imitate a tortured inner world and con models into romances, one after another, which no doubt makes them feel a little more self-worth. It seems all perfect with cars and private planes and flowers and you begin to think it's real, and when you hit reality you are just dashed to bits. And you get to this point where you're so confused as to who you are, what's real and what's fake, that, and I realize this sounds odd, but you begin to feel the only way you can become real again is to kill yourself. My method was hanging. I stood on the windowsill and jumped off. The rope must have given way, and I came to hours later bruised but alive. I just felt shame, so much shame."

But when I put forward that love and career were the catalyst for Ruslana's suicide, her friends and mother all turn to me and say in a chorus:

"Not Ruslana!"

"She wasn't like that!"

"She wouldn't kill herself over some guy!"

"She was looking forward to university, didn't care if modeling was behind her. None of that mattered to her!"

Back in the United States the drug tests we sent out have returned: Ruslana had no signs of illegal drug abuse over the last months. But neither had she been drugged with anything that could have knocked her out.

But the more Ruslana's family and friends interrogate the police account of her death, the more skeptical they become. Why didn't the police look in the actual building that she jumped from? Why didn't they specify the actual place she leapt from? How could she have jumped 8.5 meters? How? She wrote incessantly—why no note? She'd hinted to friends she was owed money from old contracts; could one of those have led to some sort of conflict?

I help the mother find a postmortem expert to go over the evidence again. He asks for samples of Ruslana's organs: histology tests will show whether her organs had stopped functioning before she hit the ground. He will reinspect the autopsy to see if it yields fresh clues.

• • •

A few months pass. I get a call. Another model has killed herself, this time in Kiev, Ukraine. She was Ruslana's friend; her name was Anastasia Drozdova. She too threw herself from a high-rise block of flats.

Luba knew both girls well. She chain-smokes backstage at a fashion show, chews her lips: "First Ruslana, now Anastasia. I'm wondering which of my friends will be next?"

I phone TNT: "There's been another suicide. I'm on my way to meet the parents now."

The producers at TNT are cautious. "Two suicides is a little depressing for us. We need positive stories. Please keep that in mind."

I sit with Olga, the mother of the second girl, in a Kiev café. She's slight, a former ballerina. A waitress takes our orders, the process torturous: how to decide whether you want extra cream when you've just lost your daughter?

"I got home late. She wasn't there. I found a note: 'Forgive me for everything. Cremate me.' I ran to the police station. A cop said casually: 'You the mother of that girl who threw herself from the block of flats?' I didn't know what to say. They showed me a bag with trainers. They were hers. Then there could be no doubt."

Back at the mother's apartment she shows me home video of Anastasia as a child. The apartment is in a regular 1960s panel block, but inside it's done up nicely with new floors and a European, open kitchen. Anastasia paid for it as a present to her mother. When she was growing up they had shared bunks in the dormitories where dancers were housed by provincial ballets. The father had left when Anastasia was young. The mother had sent Anastasia to ballet school.

"At least she would have one profession to fall back on," says Olga. "During the USSR being a ballerina was a steady job. That's less the case now."

The home video shows Anastasia practicing ballet when she was fourteen. She's taller than the others, awkward, trips during her pirouettes. Olga winces at her mistakes; she herself is petite, every movement light and exact.

"She was a little uncoordinated, too tall and gangly to be a dancer. She was picked on by teachers; it was all one long humiliation. But everyone would tell her she should try modeling, her lankiness would be perfect there. She would nag: 'Let me try, let me try.' I made her wait until she graduated and then I couldn't hold her back."

In Moscow Anastasia placed in the top five of the Elite Model Look competition. Her ballet training meant she had ideal posture and movement. She was flown to the all-European tournament in Tunis, and ranked in the top fifteen.

When Olga saw her get off the plane from Tunis, she knew that was it, her daughter was a different person now: "She had seen a new world, yachts and cars and wealth I could never give her. What can you say to a child who's set to be earning more than you? What could I teach her?"

In the first years Anastasia would return home bubbling over with stories about Europe, all the people she had seen and all the parties that she'd been to. She decided to make Moscow her base. And slowly she changed.

"She began to be more, how shall I say, materialistic," says Olga.

The mother's friends are less gentle on the daughter:

"*I need a man with money, with a top car, who can give me a house and holidays,*' that's how she began to talk," says Rudolf, a former Ukrainian high-jump champion and Olympic bronze medalist, who dated Olga. "She could be very specific in her desires. But in a way I could understand her. A model is like a sportsman. You have to grab everything when you are young."

Anastasia was trying to play the Moscow game. She had affairs with wealthy married men who promised to house her in smart places on Rublevka. Anastasia would tell friends she was "made." Her favorite phrase was "I'm going to cling on in Moscow, cling on!"

But she wasn't any good at playing that game at all. She kept falling in love, wanted to be the only focus of a man's attention. But she was in relationships a priori based on other rules. And so she was always in a muddle and getting hurt. Her relationships with married men kept breaking down; she would be housed in some penthouse and then would find herself out again, crashing with friends or sharing small flats with other girls. Her modeling career went sidewise. It wasn't a disaster, but neither did she become a cover girl. By the time she was twenty-four, the age of her death, she knew her career in modeling was ending.

In the last year of her life her behavior started to change radically. She became aggressive. On her last trips to Milan, in the spring before her death, she would miss castings, get into fights with other girls. Her agents would get calls from their Italian partners complaining about her behavior. They couldn't understand it; she had always been professional.

When Anastasia came home that final summer she was unrecognizable. Terribly thin—her hips just eighty-two centimeters. Silent, with her head down. She looked like she knew some awful secret but couldn't tell anyone about it. She had always been the buoyant life of any party; in restaurants she would laugh so loud people at other tables would turn around and stare. Now she wouldn't leave her room. In 40-degree heat she sat scrunched up under a duvet. She complained of stomach cramps and switched off her phone. She didn't wash her hair for a whole week. When she had an interview for a new job she broke down when she couldn't decide what she should wear. She walked around the flat, rocking, repeating, "there's no way out."

"It wasn't her, it was some different person," says Olga. "She'd always told me what was going on in her life. Now she was silent."

After Anastasia's death her mother searched her room. It was strange walking inside without her there. She didn't really know what she was looking for. A diary, clues, anything. She came across a folder she'd never seen before. There were two "diplomas" that looked like university diplomas, but the name of the institution caught Olga's eye: the "Rose of the World." The Rose of the World? What sort of name was that?

One diploma was for passing the foundation course, the other for the advanced course. There were papers with Anastasia's writing on them—saying how she must transform, change herself, become a different person. There were pages and pages on which she listed the worst traits in her personality: laziness, lack of aims, drugs, the wrong men. And there was a postcard, with a note addressed to Anastasia:

"*When you understand who and what you really are, then everyone around you recognizes you without a word of opposition. Anastasia: you're on your way. Your lullaby is 'winter's end.'*"

What did it mean, "You are on your way?"

Now Olga remembered the Rose of the World. A year and a half before Anastasia had mentioned that she had started to attend what she referred to as "psychological trainings" in Moscow.

When Olga asked her what went on there, Anastasia was vague—something about remembering childhood experiences. Telling all your secrets. She explained that she had signed a contract promising not to tell anyone what went on at "the Rose." But she explained that these courses would transform her, perfect her; if she could pass them she could do anything, anything at all.

Olga told Anastasia she was a healthy girl and didn't need any self-perfecting. She should stop.

Olga thought little of Rose of the World back then, but now she wanted to know more. After the funeral she took Anastasia's friends aside to ask whether they knew anything.

Did Olga know Anastasia had spent another year at the Rose of the World? they asked. She'd been going until a few months before her death.

No, Olga answered, she hadn't known. Anastasia had told her she'd stopped going over a year ago.

Did Olga know how much money she'd spent there?

No.

Thousands of dollars, thousands and thousands. And did Olga know Ruslana went there, too? They went there together. Ruslana stayed three months, Anastasia over a year.

"We think it might be a sect," said the model friends. "Though we can't quite be sure."

Olga started to look online.

"Trainings for personality development" is how the Rose of the World describes itself. "Our seminars will teach you how to find your true self, realize your goals and achieve material wealth," its Web site states—lit up by photographs of happy, shiny people standing on the top of a hill, shot from the bottom up, their arms out embracing a strong wind so it looks like they're almost flying.

The Rose also specializes in corporate training.

Olga went through Anastasia's papers from the Rose. She found the names of two men mentioned there and matched their numbers to Anastasia's phone (a gold-plated Vertu, given to her by some lover). One number didn't answer; another did. When he picked up the phone and Olga told him who she was and what had happened to Anastasia, he was shocked. But, no, he didn't think the Rose was that important. He couldn't say exactly what happened there, he also had signed some papers, but he mentioned there was lots of crying. He had only finished the first basic course before he quit. Anastasia had stayed much longer.

On Internet forums and in chat rooms there is some discussion, though not much, about the Rose. A couple of people write that it changed their lives forever and they are transformed. Others write that it's a con. Still others write that they think it might be dangerous. The posts in the chat rooms are all anonymous.

• • •

When I tell my editors at TNT about the Rose they aren't particularly excited.

"Find out anything you need, Piiitrrr. But why should our audience care about life-trainings for Muscovites?" says one producer.

"How much did you say they cost? 1,000 a go?" adds another.

"How does that relate to a provincial single mother? Our audience? It's not part of her world, nor is it anything she aspires to or understands. Keep it brief," says the third.

"But what if it *is* a sect?" I answer back.

"Russian sects are crazed freaks on communes in Siberia. What do this lot do: corporate trainings? That's not like any Russian sect we know. And Piiitrrr, we still need more positive stories."

• • •

Everyone who has been at the Rose has pledged themselves to secrecy. I need someone to go in and blend with the girls there, make friends with the employees and those who have been there a while. There must be some gossip since two students have now died. I want someone Russian, preferably the same age as the girls.

I approach an undercover reporter, Alex (not his real name), who is excited to help out. Alex is meant to be the best in the business, has penetrated gangs and corrupt state institutions. We pay just under $1,000 for the foundation course. It will last three days. After each day of the trainings Alex will meet with me and Vita Holmogorova, a professional psychologist and member of the Russian Association of Psychotherapists, to go through all the events and thoughts. Based on Alex's testimony, recordings, and interviews I do with present and former adepts and the psychotherapist's analysis, I slowly start to piece together what happened to Ruslana and Anastasia at the Rose.

• • •

The Rose of the World runs its trainings in a Soviet-gothic palace at the All-Russian Exhibition Center (VDNH) in northern Moscow. VDNH was commissioned by Stalin to celebrate Soviet success, with great gothic pavilions and statues dedicated to every republic from Armenia to Ukraine and every accomplishment from agriculture to space. Now it is rented out to petty traders selling anything from kitsch art to kitchens, furs, and rare flowers. Stray dogs hunt in packs between gargantuan statues of collective farm girls and decommissioned rockets. The Rose's trainings are in the old Palace of Culture.

When you walk in at 10:00 A.M. there's a table with name tags on it, just like at a professional conference. You're directed up the grand staircase toward the main hall. It's closed. All the participants of the training stand around in the foyer looking a little awkward. There's some tea. There are roughly forty people: a few stolid fortysomething businessmen and a lot of younger women in their twenties who are clearly well looked after. Suddenly you're startled by *Star Wars* music blasting from inside the hall itself. The doors burst open. The music is really loud, so loud it almost hurts. A woman is standing at the entrance:

"The doors to our auditorium are open! Come inside! Come inside!"

She shouts this over and over as you enter. Inside it's almost pitch black, and all around the sides are people shouting: "Quick, quick, take your seats, put your bags away." This is the "group of support," volunteers who have been at the Rose several years. They're shouting at you all the time, and they seem to be everywhere in the darkness. From the moment you walk in you're lost, disorientated, somewhat stunned.

You take a seat on chairs that spread in a fan several rows deep around the stage. The volunteers are seated in the row behind you—so you can't see them but their voices are shouting at the back of your head: "Sit down! Hurry! Hurry!"

Then everything is silent.

A bright light comes on up on the stage, and the "life coach" enters. He has a face like a teddy bear and wears an earpiece microphone and a slightly baggy suit with a bright tie that looks too loud. One of those silly ties you get as a joke for Christmas. He talks fast, very fast, and in provincial Russian with some grammatical mistakes. His accent is so hokey and he looks so comedic with his baggy suit, soft face, and silly tie that at first you find him funny. He talks about nothing in particular. How his mother was a seamstress. How he's from the sticks. He tells a few stories, like a bad comedian. Everyone is looking at each other—what have they signed up for? This is a "life coach?"

He keeps on talking very fast, the microphone pitched at a level that slightly hurts the ears. Your head begins to ache mildly. He brings out a huge white board and draws flowcharts, complicated shapes and arrows showing how you will transform and what your personality consists of. You try to keep up with all the formulas and arrows and flowcharts, but at some point you start to get confused, lose your orientation. The more clever and alert you are, the more you focus on what he's saying and drawing, but it never quite makes sense, and you get confused all over again. This is the point of the introduction. The shouting, the darkness, his jokes, and the frenetic drawing: your brain starts to get scrambled.

After a period (you're not sure quite how long) of this a woman gets up to leave the room.

"Where are you going?" the life coach says, suddenly angry.

"The toilet."

"You can't go," says the life coach.

Everyone thinks he's joking.

"But I need to," smiles the woman.

The life coach shouts back at her: "You want to change your life? And you can't stop yourself from going to the toilet? You're weak."

Everyone is shocked. The woman explains that she really does need to go.

"Off you go then," he says, light again, and waves her away.

What was that?

He talks on, jovial. A few minutes later another woman wants to go to the bathroom. When she's at the door the life coach, stern again, says:

"Forget about coming back if you leave."

She turns back.

"Why?"

This time he screams louder, longer, waving his arms in front of her face: "Why? We've come here to transform. Change. I could just wander off and grab a snack. But we're here to perfect ourselves. You're weak. You're just weak!"

"That's ridiculous," says the young woman who wants to go to the bathroom. At first everyone in the audience backs her up; the life coach is being a tyrant. In her time Ruslana was one of the loudest and brightest in the audience, the first to pick a fight with the life teacher.

The life coach starts to negotiate with the audience. Their transformation starts now, today, he argues, this minute. Don't they want to change? Defeat all their fears and inner demons? Be free? Together they can do it. And the only person holding them back is the woman who wants to go to the bathroom. She's betraying them. They've spent how long now discussing this? Ten minutes? Fifteen? So she didn't really need to go, did she? It's all in her head.

"Yes, she didn't really need to go," repeat the volunteers from the back of the room.

The woman looks uncomfortable. What if they are right?

And without you noticing, the life coach has brought the audience around to his side, and the whole audience is calling on the person who needs the bathroom to be strong, she can make it, if she can make it they all can. She sits back down. Everyone applauds. They have crossed a little Rubicon together. The life coach has their attention.

"In the next days," says the life coach, "you will feel discomfort, fear, but that is good, that's because you are changing, transforming toward a brighter, more effective life. You're like a plane, experiencing turbulence as you rise higher and higher. We all know you can't grow without discomfort. Don't we?"

The life coach calls up anyone who is ready to join him on the stage. Ruslana had been one of the first to try this. He asked her why she came, what were her aims, what was holding her back in life. She said her problem was men: she couldn't get any relationship right. And then the life coach ploughed into her: it was her own fault she let men leave her, she had an "inner monologue" that made her a victim. Ruslana tried to fight back—she was the innocent party, she explained. But the trainer spun her words back at her: she wanted everyone to think she was a "good girl" and that made her weak. The more you push back against the life coach, the more he argues: "Ha, the fact you're fighting me shows how scared you are to admit you're wrong! Scared to change!"

You find yourself first outraged and then slowly nodding.

Then everyone stands and has to recite together, like in an army, the "Commandments of Training":

I will not tell anyone what goes on here.
I will not make any recordings.
I will not be late.
I will not drink alcohol for the duration of the training.

Smokers are told to stand. There are seven or so out of the forty. Anastasia and Ruslana were both smokers. Alex is, too. The trainer tells the smokers they have a chance to change their lives and quit. Those who promise to quit can sit. A couple (the stubborn ones) keep on standing. And the trainer begins to lay into them again; he keeps talking for ten, twenty minutes, until their legs are hurting, and they face a challenge between the physical pain they are experiencing and not giving in to the life trainer. Meanwhile the volunteers and some in the audience begin to shout at them: "Come on, sit down, you're taking up our time."

Eventually everyone sits down.

There's a lunch break. It's packed lunches or takeout; you're not allowed to leave the building. Many are outraged and upset at the trainer—but no one leaves. People have come here for different reasons: some are midlevel professionals who want the training to give them a boost. This is what the trainer promises: to make you more "effective," borrowing the language of the Kremlin and the political technologists. Others have been brought here by friends or lovers who have been through the courses themselves and insisted they come too.

"My girlfriend said she would leave me if I didn't do it," says one young man.

After lunch you go back into the hall and there's some ambient music playing. "Who's strong enough to tell their darkest secret?" asks the life trainer. He seems suddenly gentle now, caring. Everyone is sworn to secrecy, he repeats; this is one community. Someone stands up and tells how she was sacked at work. Someone else how a girl-friend left him. Then a woman stands up and talks about how she was raped when she was still a child, raped repeatedly. She breaks down afterward and cries; the volunteers cradle her. It's the first time she has told anyone. There's a hush around the room. There's a lot of crying. When it was her turn Ruslana talked about her father: how she had felt when he departed. Anastasia remembered her parents' divorce when she was young. For the first time the models had a place where someone would listen to them. They felt for the first time that they could be themselves. No one even knew they were models here.

And now the trainer moves in for another kill: all these events were your fault. If you were sacked—your fault. Raped—your fault. You're all full of self-pity; you're all victims. Now break into pairs, he orders, and tell each other your worst memories, but retell them as if you're taking responsibility, as if you're the creator, not the victim, of your life. This will go on for hours. And as you retell the worst mo-ments of your life as if you were the creator, the one who made every-thing happen, you start to feel differently, you feel lighter, more powerful. Now you look at the life trainer a little differently. He's bullied you and then he's lifted you up and then confused you and made you cry, and now something else entirely. Without noticing you have been in the room twelve hours, but the time has just flown past, you've lost all sense of it.

You feel soft by now, somehow rubbery. You feel very close, closer than anyone you have ever known, to the other people in your group, as if you've always been meant to meet them.

"Transformation," "effective," "bright": as you walk home these words ring through your head like gongs. You think about seeing the trainer tomorrow. You want to please him, to let him know you didn't smoke, as you had promised. You feel a wave of warmth when you think about him. He's tough, but he means well.

You get home toward midnight. Your relatives or roommates notice that you seem strange, but you shrug it off. It's just that they've never seen you outside your comfort zone. You do the homework: detailed notes on everything you don't like about yourself. Everything you want to change. You get to sleep at 1:00, maybe 2:00 A.M.

At night you dream about the trainer.

In the morning you're there early. So is everybody else. When the doors open everyone rushes in, keen to show that they made it here on time. The doors are shut at 10:00 and any spare chairs removed. One guy comes in late, but there's nowhere for him to sit. The trainer screams at him:

"You promised to be on time. You made a pledge. Why are you late?"

"I was hesitating whether I should come at all," says the young man.

"Yesterday I saw you didn't confess to any painful memories. You just looked at the others as if they were a show. That's how you see everyone, entertainment, and now you want to run off. Is that the case?"

And if you were sympathetic to the young man when he was late, you now find yourself shouting: "A show! You think we're just a show for your entertainment!"

The young man squats in the corner of the hall, ashamed. "Yes," he admits later, "I was just afraid to leave my comfort zone."

The trainer begins to draw more diagrams—arrows that show how you are going in one direction, and the people you know at home and work are going in another. That's why they might not understand you after you do the trainings. You're changing; they loved you for the person you were before, but you're growing. This is a test for them: only the ones who really love you will be able to cope, to love the new you. And for those who don't accept you, you should ask yourself: Are those relationships holding you back? Should you lose them?

The girl who yesterday talked about unspeakable things that happened in her childhood takes the microphone and says she regrets confessing now: some people in the hall seem wary of her, she says. But instead of feeling sympathy, everyone in the hall turns on her: "You're just a victim," they shout. "You're enjoying showing off your feelings." The life trainer doesn't even have to tell them anymore what they should think.

Now the trainer's talking about death. Death is no big deal. The other day some Russian tourists died in a bus explosion in Egypt. Is it a good or a bad thing? Well? It's neither. A friend of his died recently. It's neutral. Just a fact of life. Everyone here will die. You all, you all will die.

"Who remembers that girl Ruslana?" says the life trainer. "The model who killed herself? Jumped from a skyscraper. I knew her well. Her 'inner monologue' was 'suicide.' You know she had five attempts at suicide before she came to us?"

(This is new: none of her friends, colleagues, or family remember suicide attempts. Quite the opposite: they all say how well-balanced she appeared.)

"And did you know," he continues, "her mother was taking money from her? She once borrowed 200 bucks from me to pay for her apartment in New York. And she was a supermodel!"

(New again: everyone else has told me how close she was to her mother.)

"Ruslana," says the life trainer, "was a typical victim."

After he says this one girl puts up her hand.

"But don't you feel bad that one of your students killed herself?"

"Sometimes it's better to commit suicide than not to change. And the fact you're feeling so sorry for this girl means you're a victim too. It was her choice to do it."

And everyone in the room agrees: it was Ruslana's own choice to do it. And who could possibly disagree with that?

Toward the middle of the day your head will start to feel light, like bubbles are rising through it. There are role-playing games and team-building games. Everyone has to walk around the room shouting at each other, "I need you, I like you," if they think the person is transforming, or "I don't need you, I don't like you," if they think the person is not. The girl who felt bad after she told everyone what happened during her childhood now takes the microphone and admits she's a victim and she's ready to transform. Everyone's applauding her, the life trainer is saying how proud he is of her, and you're sitting there just waiting for him to praise you and frightened that he won't.

During the lunch break you're told to sit quietly for half an hour. Not a sound. Just think about all your mistakes in life. All the relationships you messed up, all your failures in your career. When you come back inside the hall there's dancing, lots of fast dancing with loud, banging music, and you're happy now and hugging people. Then the music changes to ambient. You're told to stand in two lines opposite each other. You look into the eyes of the person opposite. You look for one, two, three, four minutes. Longer. It's uncomfortable to look into the eyes of someone you barely know. You feel it's the first time you have really looked into someone's eyes. "Now take a step to the right, look into the next person's eyes, imagine they're your mother," says the life trainer, "how she raised you when you were small. Her lullabies. How she felt when she sensed you growing inside her womb, how she looked at you when you were in the cradle." Everyone softens. "Now imagine the eyes of someone you have lost. A loved one." Ruslana thought of her father, Anastasia of her best friend, a fellow model who had died in a car accident the previous summer on the road between Kiev and Moscow. Everyone's eyes are wet. "Now take a step to the right, look into the eyes of the next person, and imagine it's the person you've lost, and think of all the things you didn't have a chance to tell them." Everyone is crying by now. The volunteers are walking around with tissues. You use dozens and put them in your pockets, and your legs grow wet from the number of wet tissues you are using. "Now take a step back to the left, look into the eyes of the person opposite, and imagine, for a moment, the person you lost is back with you, they've returned. Now you may hug them." At this point everyone breaks down.

You're lying on the floor. The trainer tells you to close your eyes. Breathe deeply. His voice takes you through a deep wood; the wood is your life, then you find a hut, in the hut there's a room, and in the room are all the times people have let you down, betrayed you; beyond that is another room, where are all the times you let others down; and now you're running, running free through the woods, ready to change, to lead a bright, effective life.

As you walk home you feel warm inside. Everything around you, the whole evening, seems to be dissolved in a slightly fuzzy light. People look beautiful. The trainer has given you homework: you've been told to walk through town and hug at least ten strangers. And you do it. You can do anything. You feel free. They look at you funny, but no one reacts badly. You've made them smile. You can break free of all barriers and limits, you can change. A bright, effective life. You won't be a victim. You'll take responsibility.

At night you lie awake buzzing so powerfully you can't sleep. After a couple of days of the training many women find their periods have suddenly started earlier than usual. The life trainer has warned that you will suffer from stomach cramps, and you get these, bad. The people you live with say they can't recognize you. You smile. They say you've changed. Of course you have. Looking back forty-eight hours, you can't even remember the person you were before the training started.

You're back at the training next morning a good half hour before it starts. You want to be the first to tell the life trainer you've managed to hug ten people as he told you to. The others are there, too. No one has slept. Everyone is so glad to see each other. When you go inside the hall everyone swaps stories about how they hugged people on the street. Others rang their neighbors' doorbells and said they wanted to be friends with them, phoned long-lost friends or parents they barely speak to. The ones who failed in the homework confess to failure. You attack them for being weak, victims, not transforming. The life teacher barely says anything; he just stands at the side: you're doing it all yourselves now. And then you're playing another game. You're in little groups of seven all screaming at each other, "I am your aim" or "I am your obstacle," and you have to scream past your obstacles to reach your aims. Everyone is screaming, but instead of being painful it's like rocket fuel, and now you've been told to stand opposite each other and the other person is shouting at you, "What do you want? What do you want?" And it's like that for forty minutes. Your desires start to come out of you like intestines, first cars and houses and all the easy stuff and then the silly stuff like painting the floorboards yellow or dressing up like a fairy queen, and then the really heavy stuff about wanting to hit your mother or stab the ex who dumped you. By the end you just feel free, and for the first time you can see what you really, really, really want. Then the life trainer comes out and says if you want your dreams, now that you've finally realized what they are, you can achieve them if you pay another $1,000 and come to the advanced course.

There's a one-on-one consultation afterward with a volunteer. You sit at a table with that person, who says that if you sign up for the advanced course this week, then you can get a hundred dollar discount. You say, "there's something funny with my head right now, I can't think critically," and the volunteer says, "but that's good you're not thinking critically, the trainings are all about learning not to think, your thinking holds you back, you're learning to use your emotions, don't you agree?"

"Yes . . . but I'm not thinking. . . ."

" . . . and because you're not thinking you should sign up now. Don't you want to live a bright life? Transform? Become effective? Take responsibility?"

And every time you hear those words your whole body starts to rush.

You delay a bit, though there are plenty who are signing on already. The next day comes the phone calls. Alex is sitting with me and the psychotherapist Vita in her office when the calls from the Rose start to come in. Alex switches on the speaker. There's a woman from the Rose on the other end.

"Alex, don't you want to live a bright life? Full of real emotion?"

"Of course. But I don't have money at the moment. I'm sorry, I can't go."

"But that's your challenge. Find the money. That shows you can be strong."

Alex is half laughing: in a way the manipulation is so crass. But he doesn't hang up.

"Come on, Alex," says the volunteer from the Rose. "Don't you want to change? Transform? Take responsibility?"

The words set off a Pavlovian reaction inside Alex. He starts to relive the last few days, the most intense days of his life, all his most intense experiences, most secret memories. He hangs up the phone, and though on the one hand he can tell quite clearly that the people at the Rose are toying with him, all of him is still desperate to go back there.

"Those bastards. They reach into your most sacred places and then wrap it around them."

He starts to laugh, then cry. Then laughs again, but in a way that sounds very forced. His pupils are dilating. He seems to be splitting in two.

Ruslana and Anastasia would be called by the Rose of the World daily. When they were with friends they would get a call and then leave to talk and not come back for hours. At first their friends thought the girls were talking to boyfriends or parents; when they found out it was the Rose they were confused. Why talk to them when you're with your friends already? One time, sitting in a London restaurant with Masha, Ruslana was talking to the Rose, then put the phone down and ran into the street and started stopping people to retie their laces. She came back grinning and slightly sweating. It wasn't that the task they'd given her was so weird, it was just the way she dropped everything, the dinner, their conversation, to run and do their bidding.

Alex's friends keep a close watch over him the next few days; they're worried a call from the Rose will entice him to go back. Over the next weeks his sleep is ruined; he starts to wake up in the middle of the night and yearns to go back inside the training. Alex is the only one from the group not to have signed up for the advanced course. Every time anyone mentions words he heard inside the training he starts to feel nauseated. He dreams of the life trainer, can hear his voice.

The real problems start in about two or three months. Alex loses his appetite. He starts to skip deadlines and fuck up at work, shouts at his editor. Everything hurts. He starts to cry in the middle of the day, for no reason.

"I just can't find my way back to myself," Alex tells me when we meet. He's shaved his hair off and lost weight.

At work they tell Alex he needs medical help. When Alex goes to see the doctor, he takes one look at Alex and prescribes a course of antidepressants, massages, acupuncture.

Alex had only spent one course at the Rose. Anastasia and Ruslana went back for more. Each course costs a little more than the previous one, and each one is far more intense. The volunteers and life trainers at the Rose told people they were getting better, stronger.

Anastasia at first seemed happier than ever. "I can do anything now, anything," she told her friends. When they went out clubbing she would say, "You've just got to grab the guy you want, just grab him and take him."

As the models moved further into the Rose, they were instructed to bring more pupils. This is how the Rose gets new clients: adepts are expected to bring in more people. Ruslana tried to persuade Masha. She insisted so much that Masha ended up agreeing. Then she couldn't go after all due to a family thing. Ruslana got angry. Masha had never seen her angry. Ruslana swore. Ruslana cursed. She had never used swear words before. She'd stopped being the gentle girl Masha had known. Masha missed the old Ruslana.

Soon after Ruslana had to go back to New York for work. Anastasia kept on attending courses at the Rose. She signed on for the master course. One of her first challenges was to bring in at least twenty people, or she would be thrown out. This was her "exam"—and she failed it. Try as she might, she couldn't get people to come. She was told she was letting everyone else down. She drifted away from the organization. That was in February. By May she was displaying all the signs of the depression that killed her. "I've failed," she would say. She was a victim. She hadn't been able to transform.

The cruelest part was that in the last half year she had met the man she always dreamed of.

Kostya picks me up in his new Maserati. He's a former Olympic judo champ who now "works in oil."

"Those fucking trainings fucked her up," he says. "Every time she visited them she would come back cranky, nuts. She'd promised she'd stopped going. . . ."

He wanted her to move in with him, was ready to settle down. But now she'd found her perfect man Anastasia couldn't be happy with him. Her mind was starting to slip and tangle. When she and Kostya went out on the town, she would have awful attacks of jealousy, would cry if she saw him so much as talking with other women. A month before she died he left her at his home and went off on a business trip. When he came back she was gone. She was having so many panic attacks she couldn't stand to be alone. She told friends she would hear the voice of her friend who had died the year before. She went back to her mother, to Kiev. She kept on complaining of stomach cramps. Kostya phoned her constantly the last few days before her death. Her phone was off.

"Those fucking trainings fucked her up," he repeats as he lets me out of the Maserati. "I'm going to get my boys to see to them." It's all words. He never does.

• • •

"We really gave the opportunity for Anastasia to change. But some people you can't change. She wouldn't let herself transform. And let's be honest—I hear she was into drugs. Blame modeling. Her lifestyle. Not us."

It's taken me a while to find Volodya, the only senior person from the Rose of the World who agrees to speak to me. He was Anastasia and Ruslana's "chairman" from the volunteer group when they attended. Now he's branching off to start his own training. He's only in his twenties, boyish. Wears a white track suit top and jeans. He has the slightly glazed look of the true believer. He also had a brief affair with Ruslana when she was at the Rose. I ask whether that's normal.

"Oh, that's normal. Happens all the time. The trainings are intense. People open up."

"Do people ever go through depression after the Rose?"

"That's normal. We call it a rollback. Ruslana had one. She would cry at night. Would wander about town, not knowing where she was going. You have to go through that to grow. Like turbulence on a plane as it takes off. But by the time Ruslana went back to New York in March she was okay."

Volodya's claims contradict what his own boss, the life trainer, said about "Ruslana": he had argued at the training that she was a "typical victim." When I raise this with Volodya he simply says the life trainer is confused. Ruslana wasn't the suicidal type, he says.

"So does anyone ever have any serious medical trouble after the Rose?" I ask Volodya.

"Of course they do. That's normal. Sometimes it can be pretty rough. Not everyone can transform. But Ruslana was now a different person. She told me she wanted to fight for money she felt was owed to her from various contracts. She was new. Look—when I first started going to the trainings I quit my job, left my girlfriend. I fought with everyone I knew; my parents still think I'm in a sect. But I'm happy. I'm real. But people around you, they can get offended when you become strong. I'm sure Ruslana was murdered. Sure of it."

The latest tests from Ruslana's autopsy have arrived. They say there is no new evidence pointing to her being dead before she hit the ground; the neck muscles had no injuries, the thyroid and hyoid bone of the neck had no injuries. The scleras of the eyes were white without any petechia, ruling out strangulation. Meanwhile I have been doing some background checks about the Rose. On a small corner of its Web site, behind several tabs you would never think to open, is a small reference saying the trainings are based on a discipline called Lifespring, once popular in the United States. What the site doesn't mention are the lawsuits brought against Lifespring by former adherents for mental damage, cases that caused the US part of the organization to go bankrupt in 1980, though spin-offs would quickly reopen under different names. In Russia Lifespring is in vogue; few have heard about its past. When I contact Rick Ross in New Jersey, head of the Cult Education Forum and the world authority on Lifespring, and tell him about what happened to Alex, Anastasia, and Ruslana, he replies that he has seen the pattern dozens of times: "These organizations never blame themselves. They always say, 'It's the victim's fault.' They work like drugs: giving you peak experiences, their adherents always coming back for more. The serious problems start when people leave. The trainings have become their lives—they come back to emptiness. And just like with drugs, some will just move on. But the sensitive ones, or the ones who have any form of latent mental illness, break."

To what extent were Lifespring courses responsible for the models' suicides? When Anastasia's mother meets with lawyers to ask about the possibility of opening proceedings against the Rose, she is told that proving in court that someone was forced into suicide in this case, after she is already dead and has left no accusatory letter, is nearly impossible. But what is clear is that the Rose's advertising doesn't provide information about the risks associated with Lifespring, and the organization preys on those members of society—young, lost women—who are vulnerable. Girls from the former Soviet bloc are particularly fragile. Six of the seven countries with the highest suicide rates among young females are former Soviet republics; Russia is sixth in the list, Kazakhstan second. Emile Durkheim once argued that suicide viruses occur at civilizational breaks, when the parents have no traditions, no value systems to pass on to their children. Thus there is no deep-seated ideology to support them when they are under emotional stress. The flip side of triumphant cynicism, of the ideology of endless shape-shifting, is despair.

"When was the last time you spoke to Ruslana?" I ask Volodya.

He pauses as he tries to recall.

"Come to think of it—it was the day she died. It was late in Moscow, I was in a bar. It was kinda loud. I asked if there was any reason for her call—could she call back later? She said there was no real reason. She just wanted to chat. She would call back. I can't remember the exact time, but it must have been inside the last hour before her death.

I think I must have been the last one to speak to her. I didn't notice anything abnormal."

• • •

In March Ruslana went back to New York to look for work. Her social media posts from the time mix the light and breezy with messages full of confusion and self-hatred:

"My own fault—that I allowed in. My own fault—that I fell in love. My own fault—that I allowed my heart to be broken. My own fault."

And then:

"Life is very fragile and its flow can easily be ruined. I'm so lost: will I ever find myself?"

One day before her death, Ruslana starred in a photo shoot on a roof in midtown New York. A weird day: first rain, then sun so hot the camera burns. The photographer's name is Erik Heck. On a final trip to New York I visit his Harlem apartment, and he shows me grainy 8mm video of Ruslana's last day. The Ruslana I see in this shoot is completely different from her previous work. She's a grown woman, not a fairy-tale princess. For the first time I catch a glimpse of the real person. "She'd always been told to play different roles. What I saw in her was more than that, a timeless beauty," Heck says. "I shot her when she wasn't watching, she had no time to pose. That's when you get the best work. She was free."

A day later she was dead, three days before her twenty-first birthday. Her mother is still convinced it's murder. Each new pathology test proves nothing new, but leaves just enough room for speculation.

More than two years after her death, the Nina Ricci ad with Ruslana in it was still used in Russia, her face hanging over Moscow with "a promise of enchantment." The perfume is a hit with teens. It smells of seductive, adult musk, mixed with childhood scents of toffee, apples, and vanilla.

A BRIEF HISTORY OF SECTS
IN POST-SOVIET RUSSIA

The Rose of the World wasn't the first sect I had encountered in Russia. As the Soviet Union had sunk, so sects had bubbled to the surface. Indeed, it was the Kremlin that had given them an impetus, via the power of Ostankino. In 1989 a new show appeared on Soviet TV. Instead of the usual ballet and costume dramas, the audience suddenly saw a close-up of a man with 1970s porn star looks, black hair, and even blacker eyes. He had a very deep voice. Slowly and steadily and repeatedly he instructed the viewer to breathe deeply, relax, breathe deeply. "Close your eyes. You can cure cancer or alcoholism or any ailment with the power of thought," he said.

This was Anatoly Kashpirovsky. He was a professional hypnotherapist who had prepared Soviet weight-lifting teams for the Olympics. He had been brought to late Soviet TV to help keep the country calm and pacified. To keep people watching TV while everything went to shit.

His most famous lecture involved asking the audience at home to put a glass of water in front of their TV sets. Millions did. At the end of the program Kashpirovsky told the audience the water was "charged with healing energy" from his through-the-screen influence. Millions fell for this.

But Kashpirovsky was only the beginning. There was Grabovoy, who had a show on television and claimed he could raise the victims of Chechen terror attacks from the dead; there was Bronnikov, who claimed he had found a way of making the blind see with an inner vision. The sect the TNT personnel were referring to when they mentioned "communes in Siberia" was that of Vissarion, a former postal worker from Krasnodar who became convinced he was the returned Christ. In the 1990s he had founded a colony in the mountains near the border with Mongolia: "The Abode of Dawn City." It's still there. While still a film student I had helped out on a British documentary about it.

We flew into Abakan and drove into mountains that look like giant, frozen waves. Vissarion and his forty-five hundred followers had built their settlement up in the peaks. You have to climb for two hours to get there. There are no roads. The members of the sect live in wooden houses they built themselves, cutting down and sawing the trees. They plant their own food; they don't drink alcohol or eat meat; and they all have clear, crystal blue eyes and powerful shoulders and look ten years younger than their actual age. As first they filled me with wonder. Then they told me they were there to wait for the apocalypse. Only their mountain would be safe when the seas flooded the earth.

"You're lucky to have come for Christmas," they told me.

Both the Western and Orthodox Christmas had passed.

"Christmas?" I asked.

"Yes, Christmas is now on Vissarion's birthday."

Many of Vissarion's followers were former minor bohemians, actors, rock musicians, painters. They were educated, but now they mostly read Vissarion's works. Vissarion had written a New New Testament, in which he had united all the different religions (Buddhist, Christian, Hindu, Judaism) into one meta-story. Just as Surkov had gathered together all political models to create a grand pastiche, or Moscow's architecture tried to fit all styles of building onto one, Vissarion had created a collage of all religions. His followers would study transcendental meditation in the morning and whirl like dervishes in the afternoon. Vissarion also provided them with textbook drawings to explain everything from reincarnation to evil (see diagram, page 180).

On Christmas day Vissarion came down from his house, perched highest on the mountain, to meet his followers. He was dressed in flowing velvet robes, like he was playing "Jesus Christ Superstar" in an amateur production. He sat down at the front of a great wooden hall and answered questions. Someone was having problems with his wife; Vissarion told him to listen to her more. Had they tried talking about their childhoods to each other?

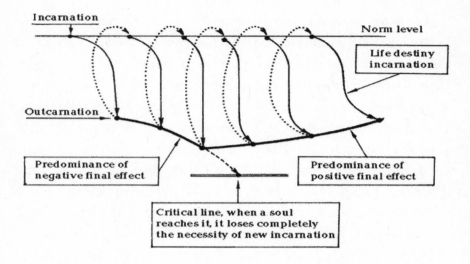

"Can't you see his wisdom? Isn't he the heir to the new consciousness?" his followers asked me.

We weren't the first, or the last, to film Vissarion. Camera crews from around the world went up and down the mountain near Abakan regularly. Every few years Vissarion would announce the coming of the apocalypse. When it didn't come he would tell his followers it was thanks to their prayers and efforts. No one from the Abode of Dawn protested at this. They enjoyed it. And the TV crews coming to the mountain only confirmed their sense of self-importance.

Closer to Moscow, Sergey, Grigory's "wizard," took me to meet Boris Zolotov, his guru and the author of *The Golden Way*. We drove for miles out of Moscow into the murmuring Russian forest. It was night when we arrived. "The Golden Way" was painted (in English) on the road, illuminated briefly by our fog-lights. An arrow pointed the way to a disused holiday resort for Soviet factory workers: a few low, prefab buildings fenced in by concrete walls and spiky wire. We headed for the largest building. In the green corridor was a huge pile of shoes: dirty sneakers, high heels, winter boots, sandals. We left ours, too. Through the double doors I could hear laughter and little shrieks.

Inside was a disused gymnasium. It was bright. Most people in the room were lying down, and everywhere was the smell of unwashed feet; people had been here for days. They lay in a half-moon shape around a stage, upon which, on a swiveling armchair, sat a round, grey-haired man. He wore a yellow shell suit. This was the teacher—Boris Zolotov. He spoke, and the people in the hall repeated the words back to him:

The energy of time and matter were put into the earth's core, forming an energy track in the base matrix of the planet, creating the path of circumstances into a state of light.

Where Vissarion spoke in plain, almost childlike Russian (to followers he considered children), Zolotov's idea was to remake language to re-create consciousness. He had been a theoretical physicist in the USSR, and he spoke in a montage of science and mysticism about the "materialization of dreams" and "redividing reality into segments you can travel through."

Zolotov's "method" was to stage experiments in which his followers would penetrate to the new level of consciousness: sweating orgies where the old, ugly, young, and beautiful rub and kiss and caress each other in a communal bliss. They spent whole days talking to each other in grunts, howls, meows, and belches. And always Zolotov sat in the middle, conducting the sweaty chaos. Many of his pupils had been with him since the early 1990s; when the Soviet floor gave way millions of Russians just kept falling and falling, deconstructing reality to the point where they thought they could see the very core of the universe.

"The new consciousness could only appear here," Zolotov would say, "in this country which is the graveyard of all ideologies." This idea united all the post-Soviet sects: all the suffering, all the shocks Russia had gone through made it the place where the new man, the future, could be born. And the sects also tapped into an even deeper myth: the idea that Russia will be the birthplace for a new, messianic consciousness. In the fifteenth century, when Moscow became the capital of what would become the Russian state, it pronounced itself the last bastion of Orthodox Christianity, the true faith of Christ: Europe was mired in the heresy of Catholicism, Byzantium had fallen to the Turks, but Ivan III's Muscovy was to be "The Third and Final Rome," the inheritor of holiness from St. Peter's Rome and Byzantium. Russian literature and thinking brims with the messianic. Dostoevsky's heroes profess that Russians are the only "God-bearing people" and that the second coming of Christ will take place in Russia. Berdyayev said that Russia was the bearer of a "vigorous messianic consciousness" rivaled only by the Jews. International communism was the most geopolitically ambitious expression of this idea: Moscow as the shining city on the hill of socialism, the churning forge of the new era to end all eras. Stalin built his seven great Gotham skyscrapers, which dominate and define the circumference of the city, to echo the Seven Hills of Rome. Any idea, not necessarily religious, finds itself magnified here to an iconic extreme: The Russian white supremacist will see Russia as the last bastion of white-ness in the world; the Russian nihilist will become *the* nihilist; Surkov's triumphant cynic-mystic becomes post-Soviet superman, the political technologist who can see through all ideas to the "heights of creation."

But if Moscow is the place where the Messiah will return, then of course it has to be the place where the devil will come to challenge him. Bulgakov envisioned the devil coming to Stalin's Moscow, strolling down its boulevards as if they were his own. It's as if the only way the city can make sense of itself is in the messianic; it has to envision itself as the place of the great battle of good and evil.

It was an idea that I again saw expressed while watching a theater production of Surkov's *Almost Zero* at the Stanislavsky Moscow Arts Theatre. It had been nearly impossible to find a ticket; black market ones were going for thousands of US dollars. In the end, I managed to obtain entrance for two bottles of champagne and a promise to one of the theater's leading ladies to let her use my parents' London home rent-free. It turned out that the fee wasn't even worth a proper seat. The ushers let me in after the lights were dimmed. They gave me a cushion and told me to sit on the floor by the front row. My head spent the night knocking against the perfumed thigh of some model, her bald partner seeming none too pleased. The audience was full of these types—the hard, clever men who rule the country and their stunning female satellites. You don't usually find them at the theater, but they were there because it was the thing to do. If they ever bumped into Surkov, they could tell him how much they liked his fascinating piece. But it was soon apparent that the staging of *Almost Zero* had transformed the novel. In passages that were added in, the actors talked straight at the audience, accusing it of being at ease in a world of killing and corruption. (The hard men and their satellites stared ahead, unblinking, as if these provocations had nothing to do with them. Many left at the interval.) And the Egor in the play was noth-ing like the Superman of the book, but rather a man wracked by self-loathing, miserable in his shiny life with its casual humiliations. A man in hell.

"Isn't it obvious Moscow is the Third Rome? The holy city?" asks Rustam Rakhmatullin.

I sit opposite Rustam in a café: a little wooden building with neon soft drink signs that reflect in our Lipton tea and Rustam's glasses. I order chicken soup, but it's just cold bouillon and I leave it standing to the side. Through the windows I can see a roundabout of two motor-ways, so heavily congested that black smoke hangs above the cars. Above the little wooden café are 1970s apartment buildings, the blocks of concrete naked, as if someone started building them and got bored halfway through and left. Rustam looks like an insect with thick glasses. He talks like a computer.

"Moscow is a perfect web, if you take the map of Moscow," he says. "Spin it around and you can see how it matches up perfectly with Jerusalem. Take a map of Rome, and Moscow matches onto that. This city is an expression of God's thought."

Rustam is no city madman. He is a scholar, a columnist in an establishment newspaper. We are talking about his new book, *The Metaphysics of Moscow*, which will go on to be a best seller and win highbrow literary prizes. He will later host a show on TV. He teaches the "metaphysics of the city" at a local university. The book is a kabbalah of Moscow's streets, where nothing is accidental: the yard where in the eighteenth century a feudal lady killed fifty of her serfs, two hundred years later becomes the home of a saintly prison doctor who sacrifices everything to improve the lot of prisoners, thus "cleansing" the original sin. And so on for five hundred pages.

Rustam is one of the good guys. He works with Mozhayev to save old houses, campaigns against corruption in city government. But he catches the broader zeitgeist, the growth of the associative, irrational, and magical. For if the likes of Zolotov and Vissarion were provincial oddities, now as Moscow becomes ever more full of its own uniqueness, as it watches itself transform with new money as fast and as strangely as looking down at your own body and seeing it change from flesh to gold in one sweep under your very eyes, so the center of the capital begins to swirl with mystic, messianic clouds.

In the compound of the Night Wolves, the Russian equivalent of the Hells Angels, ships' connecting rods have been refashioned as crosses ten feet high. Broken plane parts have been bolted to truck engines to make a giant stage; crushed Harley-Davidsons have been beaten into a bar; boats' hulls have been molded into chairs; and train parts have been made into Valhalla-sized tables. The crosses are everywhere: the Night Wolves are bikers who have found a Russian God.

"We only have a few years to rescue the soul of holy Russia," Alexei Weitz says. "Just a few years." Weitz is a leading member of the Night

Wolves. There are five thousand of them in the country, five thousand Beowulf-like bearded men in leathers riding Harleys. It's Weitz who has done most to turn them from outlaws into religious patriots, riding through Moscow on Harleys with icons of Mary the Mother, of God and Stalin.

"Why Stalin?" I ask. "Didn't he murder hundreds of thousands of priests?"

"We don't know why he was sent by God. Maybe he had to slaughter them so the faith could be tested. It's not for us to judge. When you cut out a disease you have to cut out healthy flesh too." As we speak Weitz is changing from his office clothes into leathers. The biking movement in the USSR sprang up in the late 1980s, utterly anti-Soviet, pro-freedom, pro-Steppenwolf, and by association pro-American. In the 1990s it remained a fringe subculture, though connected to biker gangs in Europe and beyond. The patriotic shift came late. The legend goes that Aleksandr Zaldostanov, the Surgeon, the Night Wolves' leader, met a priest on the road who told him he needed to change his life, help save Holy Rus. Weitz, whose day job is as a leader of a Kremlin-funded political party, a "Just Cause," helped give that impulse form. The Night Wolves are a top-down organization: if the Surgeon and Weitz say they are now Orthodox, everyone follows suit.

Weitz drops six lumps of sugar into his goblet and tells me his story. "I trained as an actor. I received the classic Stanislavsky method acting training. My teacher used to say I can be both tragic and comic at the same time. It's a rare gift." He breaks off to quote a line from a Russian movie version of *The Cherry Orchard*, replicating the original perfectly. He pauses, waiting for me to clap. "My breakdown came in 1994. I was starring in *The Cherry Orchard*, we were on tour in London—we were staying in a hotel at Seven Sisters. You know it? Nice area—and I just couldn't take it anymore, there were just too many roles. Too many 'me's."

"You mean too many theater roles?"

"Oh no, that was fine. I'm a professional. Something else. For a while I'd been seeing visions, religious visions. I could see devils and angels on people's shoulders. I could see serpents wrapping themselves around people as they spoke, their true souls. I could see the things others can't. People's auras, the colors around them. . . . You're looking at me like I'm crazy. I just have gifts. I was finding my way to the true faith. I couldn't be both an actor and a man of God."

When he came back from London, Weitz gave up acting. He became more devout. But he still needed a job, so a friend found him a position at a new political consultancy. Using the Stanislavsky method he started training politicians "to manipulate public consciousness" with "verbal and non-verbal forms of influence." "I applied the principles of method acting. First they had to decide where they were headed. What they wanted. . . . Where are you headed, Peter?" he suddenly asks.

I don't know.

"You're headed to death. We're all headed to death. That's the first thing I would make them realize. . . . That's the thing about us bikers. We live with death every day. We're a death cult. We know where we're going. Russia is the last bastion of true religion," continues Weitz. "Stanislavsky used to say: 'Either you are for art, or art is for you.' That is the difference between the West and Russia. You are imperialists, you think all art is for you and we think we are all for art. We give, you take. That is why we can have Stalin and God together. We can fit everything inside us, Ukrainians and Georgians and Germans, Estonians and Lithuanians. The West wipes out small peoples; inside Russia they flourish. You want everything to be like you. The West has been sending us its influencers of corruption. A Russian who is trained in a Western company starts to think differently: self-love is at the root of Western rationality. That is not our way. You have been sending us your consumer culture. I don't think of Washington or London as being in charge. Satan commands them. You have to learn to see the holy war underneath the everyday. Democracy is a fallen state. To split 'left' and 'right' is to divide. In the kingdom of God there is only above and below. All is one. Which is why the Russian soul is holy. It can unite everything. Like in an icon. Stalin and God. Like everything you see here in the Night Wolves, we take bits of broken machinery and mold them together."

He stops for a moment. I must have been looking at him strangely, my goblet of tea held in midair. The switch from Stanislavsky to the kingdom of God had happened so smoothly that I didn't have time to readjust my face. "Or at least I'm trying to piece everything together," Weitz says, more quietly. "It's a work in progress. Maybe we won't be able to manage it."

But there is also a very practical side to the Night Wolves' mix of politics and religion. In the 2000s international biker gangs began to consider spreading their influence in Russia. Most prominent among them were the Bandidos, originally American but now global, who offered to make the Night Wolves their local chapter. The Night Wolves want to rule by themselves, and to keep their own bikers in line they needed their own creed. So they started to build up a nationalist siege mentality. They changed their insignia to Russian and began to spread stories that the Bandidos wanted to flood Russia with drugs. It's hard to fathom how real the foreign threat to the Night Wolves is. There are thousands of Night Wolves and no more than a few dozen Bandidos in Russia. But to hear Weitz speak of it, they are surrounded.

When Surkov finds out about the Night Wolves he is delighted. The country needs new patriotic stars, the great Kremlin reality show is open for auditions, and the Night Wolves are just the type that's needed, helping the Kremlin rewrite the narrative of protesters from political injustice and corruption to one of Holy Russia versus Foreign Devils, deflecting the conversation from the economic slide and how the rate of bribes that bureaucrats demand has shot up from 15 percent to 50 percent of any deal. They will receive Kremlin support for their annual bike show and rock concert in Crimea, the one-time jewel in the Tsarist Empire that ended up as part of Ukraine during Soviet times, and where the Night Wolves use their massive shows to call for retaking the peninsula from Ukraine and restoring the lands of Greater Russia; posing with the President in photo ops in which he wears Ray-Bans and leathers and rides a three-wheel Harley (he can't quite handle a two-wheeler); playing mega-concerts to 250,000 cheering fans celebrating the victory at Stalingrad in World War II and the eternal Holy War Russia is destined to fight against the West, with Cirque du Soleil–like trapeze acts, Spielberg-scale battle reenactments, religious icons, and holy ecstasies—in the middle of which come speeches from Stalin, read aloud to the 250,000 and announcing the holiness of the Soviet warrior—after which come more dancing girls and then the Night Wolves' anthem, "Slavic Skies":

We are being attacked by the yoke of the infidels:
But the sky of the Slavs boils in our veins . . .
Russian speech rings like chain-mail in the ears of the foreigners,
And the white host rises from the coppice to the stars.

And as I work on my film about the models and the Rose of the World, I start to notice how the new mysticism is seeping into everything on TV.

On the Ostankino channels the President's personal confessor, the Archimandrite Tikhon, dressed in a long black cassock and walking through Istanbul, is telling a prime-time tale about the fall of Byzantium, of how the great Orthodox Empire (to which Russia is the successor) was brought low by a mix of oligarchs and the West. Professional historians howl in protest at this pseudo-history, but the Kremlin is starting to use religion and the supernatural for its own ends. Byzantium and Muscovy could only flourish under one great autocrat, the Archimandrite states. This is why we need the President to be like a tsar.

Even supposedly science-based programs are not immune. There is a spate of prime-time documentaries about "psychological weapons." One is *The Call of the Void*. It features secret service men who inform the audience about the psychic weapons they have developed. The Russian military has "sleepers," psychics who can go into a trance and enter the world's collective unconscious, its deeper soul, and from thence penetrate the minds of foreign statesmen to uncover their nefarious designs. One has entered the mind of the US president and then reconfigured the intentions of one of his advisers so that whatever hideous plan the US had hatched has failed to come off. The message is clear: if the secret services can see into the US president's mind, they could definitely see into yours; the state is everywhere, watching your every thought. The most expensive documentary ever shown on Russian television is called *Plesen* ("Mold"). It argues that mold is taking over the earth, that it has been doing so since the days of Moses. It is the devil's weapon, mentioned in ancient mystic texts, an invisible but omnipresent enemy whose evil spores have been invading our lives, causing death and disease. When the film ends large numbers of fearful people go out and buy the "mold-cleaning machines" that were advertised in the film; its manufacturers were among the producers. Under siege from psychic spies and airborne fungi, audiences are kept in a constant state of panic and medieval ecstasies. The more rational critical language is pushed off TV, the fewer critical films are made about the past and present, the more the mystic narratives take hold.

"The financial crisis has the Kremlin worried," Anna, a friend who used to work with TNT and now makes entertainment shows at Ostankino, tells me when we meet for a drink in a bar called Courvoisier. "Spiritual stuff is always good to keep people distracted. And the ratings will be good—our people love some mysticism when things are bad. Remember the 1990s."

Eventually even Kashpirovsky makes a return to mainstream television, hosting an eleven-part documentary series about immortality, ghosts, and "bending time." And while I am still editing my material about the Rose, I find out that the Lifespring movement in Russia is gathering strength. The largest of the Ostankino channels has created a pilot with another life trainer (much more successful and slick than the Rose of the World's) in which the humiliations and transformations from the trainings are turned into a show. The head of Ostankino loves the format. All the tears and conflicts make for great TV.

THE CALL OF THE VOID

"You look tired, Piiitrrr."

"You should take a holiday."

"You're too, how shall we say. . . ."

"You're too *emotional* about this story."

I'm at TNT to talk about the edit of the models' story, and it's not going well. The curly haired, redhead, and straight haired producers are too nice to say it, but I think they think I've become obsessed. They're not altogether wrong. I've spent so much time deciphering what happens at the Rose, it's all I think and talk about. Whenever I pass a high-rise I think of those girls and how they felt before they ran and leapt.

The project is so late that no one even mentions the deadline any more.

"We did say we don't want too many negative stories."

"You know we need a happy ending."

"Where are the positive stories?"

"How soon can you find them?"

I say I will do my best.

• • •

"How long are you going to keep making films with TNT?" asks Anna, the friend who has moved from making shows at TNT to the big leagues at Ostankino. "It's child's play. If you want to make real films you have to come and work with Ostankino. When can you come for a meeting?" TNT's success has meant many who work there are being wooed by Channel 1: the spiky comedians, the presenters, the "creative producers" are all getting contracts.

I had barely been inside Ostankino since my first visit almost a decade earlier to meet the political technologists who defined reality on the upper floors. But the great spire of the television tower had always acted as a compass for me, guiding me whenever I would be lost in town, always due north and steady among the sudden candle-flame domes of just-built cathedrals, glowing red stars of Stalin gothic towers, the erupting skyscrapers, turning cranes, and swinging wrecking balls that give a sense of perpetual movement to the horizon.

My meeting was scheduled for late, after 10:00 P.M., but the flat, wide train station of a building was still blazing with light when I arrived. In a country of nine time zones, stretching from the Baltic to the Pacific, comprising one-sixth of the world's land mass, where television is the only force that can unify and rule and bind—the great battering ram of propaganda couldn't possibly ever rest.

The lobby had been given a gleaming tile and glass makeover. The old grubby cafeteria was gone, and there was a coffee bar with the full range of beverages. Green tea with jasmine, cappuccinos, and cognac served with a slice of lemon. There was a banging coming from something being built to the left of the main doors: a new Orthodox chapel, I was told.

I was met by an assistant, and as we rode up in the elevator the doors would open, and every floor was a different civilization. The doors open once, and you find yourself on a floor with a black chrome news studio as new as a private jet. The doors open again, and you're back in 1970-something, with beige corridors and mature women with bleached hair up in a high bun. Another floor is under reconstruction, another bright blue. Ostankino is renovated piecemeal, the whole great thing split up into a thousand little fiefdoms, each carrying on at its own rate of history.

Then it's our floor, and the corridors begin. Left, right, left, down some stairs. As I walk I realize I'll never find the way out again. All those doors. All the same.

My meeting is at Red Square Productions. It wins the commissions for the big factual entertainment shows for Channel 1 and is owned by the wife of the head of Channel 1. There's a small anteroom before you enter the personal office of Red Square's creative director. I'm asked to wait. I have CDs of my latest programs in my hand, and I shuffle them. I wait over an hour. I'm pissed off and want to go out for a cigarette, but I'm worried I won't find the way back. It's nearing midnight when I finally go in.

The door is heavy, and inside the office are wooden shelves with lots of books and a long table and beyond that, wide windows looking over the Moscow night. On the other side of the table sits a thin, pale, young man in a light suit with floppy black hair. He never stops smiling. This is Doctor Kurpatov, Russia's first self-help TV psychologist. He has made a fortune with his show, on which people come to cry and be told how to change their lives. He can teach you anything, from how to conquer your fears to how to have good sex to how to love your child or make a fortune. He is a master of neuro-linguistic-programming and hypnosis, bereavement counseling, and philosophy. All along the walls of the office are his self-help books. And now he's not just a star with his own show, but the creative director of the production company closest to the head of the most important channel. Now he has to choose the programs that will keep the whole nation calm, happy, overcoming its fears.

He asks me to sit down and tells me how much he likes my work. I know he's lying, but he's just so nice, nodding and agreeing at all the points he should be and engaging just enough to make me feel he's genuinely interested. He says it must be odd for someone from

London working inside Russia. I say "oh yes!" and tell him so many of my adventures and misadventures I don't even notice half an hour has passed and all my discomfort at being at Ostankino has quite gone.

The next day his assistant phones to say Dr. Kurpatov really liked me and Ostankino wants to make me an offer. Whatever personality test that meeting was all about, I have passed. Would I like to helm a historical drama-documentary? With a real, big, mini-movie budget for actors and reconstructions and set designers? The sort of thing you make when you're right at the top of the TV tree in the West and that TNT could and would never even dream of making. The genre is new in Russia, and it's only now with Ostankino so flush that it can afford to do this. I've been wanting to emigrate away from straight observational documentary for a while, to think more about costumes and camera angles and a little less about funerals and sects and suicides.

The story is to be about a World War II admiral who defied Stalin's orders and started the attack on the Germans, while the Kremlin was still in denial about Hitler's intentions and hoped for peace. The admiral was later purged and largely forgotten. It's a good story. It's a really good story. It's the dream project.

I tell her I need time to decide.

She says no rush.

• • •

The models project is so late, I'm so over budget, and the advance is so long spent that I've been asking for money from family to keep production going. With the end of the oil boom, places like *SNOB* have long stopped paying. I have had to move out of my old place with its grand view of the Moscow River into a smaller, grubbier, lower apartment. It's right by one of the markets where traders from the North Caucasus sell replica designer suits and stolen phones. At night they get into fights with racist football fans underneath my windows. People in this part of town wear plastic Chinese slippers and carry their things in plastic bags. The warm little stores sell herring from open containers with a film of filth. The smell of the herring swells down the street, infused into the heat.

One morning I wake with the taste of burning in my mouth. There is smoke everywhere. I run to the kitchen to see whether the stove is on fire, but it's fine, and now I look up and notice the smoke is outside on the street, too. Thick and prickly, green and yellowish, rubbing up against the closed window, pouring slowly through the open one I never shut in summer. It seems like the whole street is on fire. I push out onto the little balcony and see that it's not just the street but the whole city. Buildings and sickly trees and the fly-over of the third ring-road are all half lost in haze. The smoke stings my eyes. It smells of fire and pine and forests, but mixed with gasoline, with traffic jams and perfume and something industrial. And it smells of peat. The peat fires are back.

This happens some summers. The peat fields around Moscow catch fire, and the smoke blows into town. Smoke so thick you can wrap it around you like a coat. Asthmatics, old people, and children are rushed away to relatives in the country. But then the smoke will go there, too. And they have to travel farther and farther, toward Petersburg or Bryansk or Monaco.

Out on the street the city seems abandoned. You almost push your way through the smoke. The first sign of another life-form is the sound of something going clack-clack-clack. At first the sound is startling. Then I realize: high heels. A girl goes by, dressed in heels, a bikini, and a dust mask. It's that hot. And then more and more people emerge and disappear back into the smoke: a wedding party with the confetti being thrown up into the haze, where it seems to be lost forever. A cop looking quite lost. Couples kissing.

I buy beers and return to the apartment. The camera, the old beaten metal-cased Z-1, the picture resolution of which is past its sell-by date since the arrival of hi-def, is on my bed. There are tapes all around it with castings and tasters from my search for TNT's positive stories. Many of the tapes are about Alexander: a blind football player, the star of Russia's first blind football team. I had hoped his story would be inspirational. He's someone who has overcome things: blind since childhood and now a potential para-Olympian.

On the tapes he looks like a Viking god with his long, red hair. He talks loudly and goes everywhere with his girlfriend, a quiet girl who teaches music to small children. When they walk she guides him gently beneath the elbow, around pillars and through doors. She's part blind herself, with glasses as thick as the bottoms of bottles, but she can see more than Alexander.

Blind boys usually go out with girls who are partially sighted. The boys, especially the football players, act tough, but it's the girls who are in charge. They can see. The blind boys are always worried their girls are looking at someone else. Or even kissing and touching someone else in the same room.

Alexander supports Dynamo Moscow. Every weekend he takes his place in the stands among the hard-core supporters behind the goal. He doesn't listen to radio commentary, as most blind supporters do: he tells me he can feel what's going on during the game with an inner football vision.

Dynamo Moscow is known for having racist supporters, and I soon find out Alexander is no exception.

"I can hear those darkies in the street. I can hear their language in the metro. My yard used to be full of the sound of Russian . . . when I hear those darkies I just come up and take a swing. Just like that."

When he fights he swings wide and wildly. But when he connects it's powerful.

"We believe Russia is a great empire that other powers want to tear away parts from. We need to restore our power, occupy our lost lands, grab Crimea from the Ukrainians," the football supporters say, then in the same breath: "We want a Russia for Russians, all these darkies from the Caucasus and Central Asia need to go home."

This has always been the paradox of the new Russian nationalism: on the one hand wanting to conquer all regions around, on the other wanting an ethnically pure great power. And all that comes out of this confusion is an ever-growing anger. There are more of them, hooligans and skinheads, lighting up the square opposite the Kremlin with their flares in marches of hundreds of thousands, chanting "jump if you're not a darkie." And when they jump together, the pavement trembles.

All the positive stories I touch on seem to tumble into negativity. On my bed there are more tapes, about a girl called Katja who has told me she managed to quit injecting amphetamines after a near-death experience. But when I begin to film her it turns out she's been lying to me and is smoking morphine boiled down from prescription painkillers (illegally bought from pharmacies paying a cut to corrupt FDCS agents). Katja is always asking me for money, claiming she's just been mugged or has someone after her she needs to pay off.

A bunch of girls from Kiev who call themselves Femen and who protest sex tourism by stripping down and running about naked at state events to highlight the sexism of the system sounded perfect for TNT. But suddenly they start protesting against the President. "The patriarchal is political," they tell me when I call them. TNT would never touch them now.

I am running out of money. And I am considering joining Ostankino.

For every *Call of the Void* or blatant propaganda show Ostankino makes, there's some edgy realist drama, some acerbic comedy. You can laugh and ignore the propaganda and watch the good stuff, and that's what people I know do. There's nothing bad about the film Channel 1 wants me to make; it's a good story. And yet I realize that though my film might be clean, it could easily be put next to some World War II hymn praising Stalin and the President as his newest incarnation.

Would my film be the "good" program that validates everything I don't want to be a part of? The one that wins trust, for that trust to be manipulated in the next moment?

But then again—so what if the other shows on Channel 1 are propaganda? Lots of good people make big shows and films for Ostankino, and no one holds it against them. We all have to carve out our little space. You make your own project, keep "your hands clean," as everyone here likes to say, and the rest just isn't your concern. It's just a job. That's not you.

• • •

Growing up I had never really thought too much about my parents' life in the Soviet Union, why they had emigrated. The USSR was just someplace people left. My father was being arrested for spreading copies of Nabokov and Solzhenitsyn. Who wouldn't want to leave that sort of suffocation?

But what exactly was it that they were rejecting? I had always just assumed "dictatorship" but had never thought much about how the system really worked. Now I remembered a story my mother had once told me.

She was fifteen. It was 1971. Their teacher at her very ordinary suburban Kiev school announced that today they would receive a very special visitor. He was from Radio Komintern, one of the propaganda elite who broadcast Soviet ideas to the West.

The man was in his thirties and he wore jeans and a leather jacket. Only the coolest, most rebellious, yet best-connected (only the best-connected could afford to be rebellious) were able to get hold of jeans and leather jackets—they only came from the West, and it was a privilege to go there or even know someone who went there. This man was nothing like their square teachers. He sat on the edge of the teacher's desk and smirked that knowing smirk that my mother would later recognize as the mark of the KGB boys, and that I now see on the

President and the men around him. The smile of the men who know they can see through everything.

The special visitor told the kids how Russia was surrounded by enemies, how they needed to be careful of Western agents and Western influences.

Then he went to smoke in the corridor. The kids followed him. He gave them cigarettes, which they lit with trepidation, but their teachers were so in awe of the special visitor they didn't dare stop them from smoking with him. He talked about how he had Beatles records at home (my mother had always been scared to even say the word "Beatles" in public). He told them he had even been abroad (no one in my mother's school had ever been abroad). In 1968 he had been in Prague, part of the Soviet forces that had "liberated" Czechoslovakia from counterrevolution. He told the kids about how they would go drinking in the cafés of the old town (my mother tried to imagine "cafés in the old town" but struggled to form a picture in her mind).

And he told them how one time, when he was sitting in a café, some Czechs ran in and started shouting, "Russians go home! Russians go home!"

This struck my mother. She had always believed the stuff about the Soviet Union "liberating" Czechoslovakia. She believed the Soviet Union stood for global social justice.

"You mean they weren't happy to see you?" she asked.

He looked at her like she was an idiot.

Everyone who grew up in the Soviet Union had a moment when they woke up. That was my mother's. And as she began to look at the world around her, she slowly saw how everyone was pretending, was faking belief, being one thing in the morning and another in the afternoon. But scared, too. Fear and irony together. And so many voices at the same time. One you in the morning at the Komsomol. Another you in the afternoon reading Solzhenitsyn. One you at work being a good socialist and another listening to the BBC in secret in your kitchen, yet everyone knowing you listened because they were all listening themselves.

Whenever I ask my Russian bosses, the older TV producers and media types who run the system, what it was like growing up in the late Soviet Union, whether they believed in the Communist ideology that surrounded them, they always laugh at me.

"Don't be silly," most answer.

"But you sang the songs? Were good members of the Komsomol?"

"Of course we did, and we felt good when we sang them. And then straight after we would listen to 'Deep Purple' and the BBC."

"So you were dissidents? You believed in finishing the USSR?"

"No. It's not like that. You just speak several languages at the same time, all the time. There's like several 'you's.'"

Seen from this perspective, the great drama of Russia is not the "transition" between communism and capitalism, between one fervently held set of beliefs and another, but that during the final decades of the USSR no one believed in communism and yet carried on living as if they did, and now they can only create a society of simulations. For this remains the common, everyday psychology: the Ostankino producers who make news worshiping the President in the day and then switch on an opposition radio as soon as they get off work; the political technologists who morph from role to role with liquid ease—a nationalist autocrat one moment and a liberal aesthete the next; the "orthodox" oligarchs who sing hymns to Russian religious conservatism—and keep their money and families in London. All cultures have differences between "public" and "private" selves, but in Russia the contradiction can be quite extreme.

And as I walk around this fog-asphyxiated Moscow, I see how the city's topography articulates these splits: the bullying avenues with their baron-bureaucrats, bribes, and werewolves in uniform, where the only way to survive is to be as corrupt as they are, and just a few meters away the gentle courtyards with an almost bucolic mood and small-town ideas of decency. Before I used to think the two worlds were in conflict, but the truth is a symbiosis. It's almost as if you are encouraged to have one identity one moment and the opposite one the next. So you're always split into little bits and can never quite commit to changing things. And a result is the somewhat aggressive apathy you can encounter here so often. That's the underlying mind-set that supported the USSR and supports the new Russia now even though the USSR might officially be long gone. But there is a great comfort in these splits, too: you can leave all your guilt with your "public" self. That wasn't you stealing that budget/making that propaganda show/bending your knee to the President, just a role you were playing; you're a good person really. It's not so much about denial. It's not even about suppressing dark secrets. You can see everything you do, all your sins. You just reorganize your emotional life so as not to care.

And always the buildings express this mind-set. In the fog above my head, balconies stick out seemingly suspended in the sky. Russians put all their shit on balconies, detritus on show. Satellite dishes, jars of gherkins, broken toys, punctured tires—all on the balcony. The English stack their sentimental junk and dirty secrets far away in the garden shed; the Germans have "Keller," basements, deep underground to hide all their dark memories. But in Russia you just throw it on the balcony; just as long as it isn't in the flat itself, who cares if the neighbors see? We'll deal with all that rubbish some other time. It's not even part of us.

But it's not everyone who can, or who wants to, pull off this psychologically acrobatic self-division. At some point in the 1970s, during her late teens, my mother had laid down on a bed and thought she was losing her mind. All those people she was meant to be, without any center. She could feel herself splitting up into little bits. Then began her journey to find the small bands of Soviet dissidents. They had their own vocabulary. They talked about "poryadochnost," "decency," which in practice could mean not being an informant. About "dostojnstvo," "dignity," which in practice could mean not making films or writing books or saying things the Kremlin wanted but you hated. And for many in the 1970s the only way out was prison or emigration. And sometimes it still is.

• • •

I've been keeping the windows shut against the peat smog, but it still penetrates through everything. My clothes, hair, glasses, and camera are all full of the smell. I wash the clothes over and over, but still can't get the smell out. I shave off my hair. But it's in my scalp, my fingers. A national emergency has been announced. The Kremlin youth groups, the Nashi, are shown in the papers putting out the fires with a great hose; then it turns out those shots were faked, too. On the Ostankino news they say the President has the crisis under control, but the emergency services fail repeatedly: the fire engines haven't been repaired for years and break down. People have started putting out the fires themselves, vigilante groups with buckets fighting great screaming fires in the crackling forests of middle Russia.

I have told TNT I can't find their positive stories. I have run out of money. Maybe I could beg them for more, but the truth is I don't want to. Another director will come in and finish up the work, splice in the positive stories. They are better at it than I am, and they will do it much faster than I ever could. I've fucked up. I've failed. The three producers, the curly haired and the redhead and the straight haired, are angry at first, and then they pity me.

The little TNT island of happy neon is shrinking. There's less and less factual, even "factual entertainment," on the network. Sitcoms are the thing now. They're brilliant; but they have nothing to do with any Russia I have encountered. A hospital comedy is set in a hospital so spotless and shiny it could almost be teasing the viewer. And always that canned laughter. The more asphyxiating the country gets, the more canned laughter TNT erupts in.

I have told the people at Ostankino I won't take up their offer. "Ostankino will only give you this chance once," they tell me. They say that to everyone.

I just need to leave. I need to go back to London, which is measured. Where you don't have to split yourself up into little bits. Where words mean things. Looking around I notice how many of my friends have left. Grigory. My first producer from TNT. Even Vladik, the performance artist, lives in Bali now. Before he left he wrote a public letter asking the President to resign: "It is time to save millions of people from this simulacra of power." What role could there be for a performance artist, where to watch a piece of grotesque performance art you just have to switch on the TV? Vladik had been outdone.

OFFSHORE

London. Chancery Lane. The Court of the Rolls: a squat new glass-and-steel building just behind the gray spires of the Old Bailey. Court number 26. Next door runs the humdrum affair of *Plenty of Fish Media vs. Plenty More LLP*. Across the hall a case dealing with a toilet paper patent. Nearly empty courtrooms with fluorescent lighting and IKEA desks. But court 26 is crammed to overflowing with oligarchs, political technologists, Chechen ministers in waiting, wannabe revolutionaries, and God knows how many security guys. Unidentified stunning females enter, glancing this way and that: gold diggers dropping in on the trial to meet a potential Forbes. It seems like the whole of the Russia I have spent a decade among is crammed into this little English courtroom. I spot Grigory, the young Moscow millionaire who threw the Midsummer's Night parties. He's wearing orange trousers and a peacock blue cardigan. "I thought I'd drop in to have a look at them all," he says. "You could never get so close to so many of the powerful in Moscow. Only in London."

This is the largest private litigation in history: $5.8 billion. Boris Berezovsky, the "Godfather of the Kremlin," the original oligarch, the man who created the Russian system and molded the President before being exiled by his own creation and fleeing to London—versus his protégé, Roman Abramovich, the "Stealth Oligarch," who outgrew the old master to become one of the President's new favorites. And who has also moved to London, though not to seek asylum, but to become one of the UK's richest men, a timid, unshaven, baggy-suited herald of the twenty-first-century Russia that buys up sports clubs, castles, German ex-chancellors, and newspapers. Abramovich owns Chelsea Football Club. He owns the largest private yacht in the world. He's worth $9 billion.

Berezovsky served the writ on Sloane Street, Knightsbridge. He was shopping at Dolce and Gabbana and saw Abramovich at Hermes next door. He ran to his Maybach, grabbed the writ, bustled past Abramovich's bodyguards, and threw the paper in Abramovich's direction: "This is to you, from me," the shop assistant heard him say. Now when Berezovsky arrives at Chancery Lane he skips and struts into court, a whirr of jokes and gesticulations, always in the center of an entourage of pretty women, chin-stroking advisers, giant Israeli bodyguards. In the morning before testifying, when he sees a traffic policeman outside the court ticket his Maybach, he calls out with a laugh: "Stop—we can do business together!"

"This is a very Russian story," says Berezovsky when he takes the witness stand, "with lots of killers, where the President himself is almost a killer." The ostensible cause of the complaint is Sibneft, an oil company. It was privatized for $100 million in 1996, and by 2005 was worth $13.5 billion. Berezovsky claims Abramovich and he were co-owners until Abramovich "acted like a gangster" and took Berezovsky's share away, when he was on the political ropes, threatening to jail one of Berezovsky's friends unless he gave up his part of the company. Of course there's nothing on paper to prove the company was Berezovsky's, but didn't everyone know they had a verbal deal? Hadn't the press always described Berezovsky as co-owner? (They had, and I have spent so long in Russia I think it perfectly normal for the actual beneficiary to never appear on paper.)

"I know it's hard for you to imagine a world where two men shake on it and that's it," explains Berezovsky, patiently, to the judge, Elizabeth Gloster, "but this is Russia."

Berezovsky delights in explaining how he acquired the oil company in question, using his Kremlin influence at a privatization auction, negotiating furiously in the corridors, getting one rival to bid lower in return for favors, another to withdraw if he paid off his debts.

Abramovich's lawyer, Jonathan Sumption, who in his spare time writes history books about medieval wars and is described in the papers as "the cleverest man in England" (he is being paid a reported record $12 million for this case), rocks backward and forward and moves in for the kill:

"You made a collusive agreement with one of the bidders and bought off the other: would it be fair to say that the auction was stitched up in advance?"

"It's not fixed," insists Berezovsky. "I just find the way through! In my terminology, it's not fixing."

Abramovich, bottle of cold water pressed to his temple against a headache, explains that it was not he but Berezovsky who was the gangster, the political godfather he would have to pay extortion money to when Berezovsky was vizier in the 1990s Kremlin. But as soon as Berezovsky lost his influence, he lost his access to money. Thus the President and his network find it so hard to leave the Kremlin now; the minute he retires, they might lose everything. There are no Western-style property rights in this system, only gradations of proximity to the Kremlin, rituals of bribes and toadying, casual violence. And as the trial wears on, as court assistants wheel in six-foot-high stacks of binders with testimony and witness statements until they fill up all the aisles between the desks, as historians are called by both sides to explain the meanings of "krysha" ("protection") and "kydalo" (a "backstabber in business"), it becomes apparent just how unsuited the language and rational categories of English law are to evaluate the liquid mass of networks, corruption, and evasion— elusive yet instantly recognizable to members—that orders Russia. And as I observe the trial from my cramped corner among the public seats, it takes on a dimly epic feel: not just a squabble between two men, but a judgment on the era.

"I was the first victim of President Putin's regime," pleads Berezovsky. "And then step by step he increased the number of victims." And with a rising passion he reels off the names of all the jailed businessmen and women, murdered journalists, and dead lawyers.

And then Abramovich, speaking quietly, explains how back in the 1990s he would sell oil at base prices to his own companies in Cyprus and then to others at a market rate.

"If Russia in the 1990s was corrupt on a scale of four out of ten," argues Berezovsky, "now it is corrupt ten out of ten. It is corrupt totally!"

Some $50 billion (sometimes more) is now moved illicitly out of Russia every year. Over the decades the tricks have multiplied: the state pipeline company, run by a friend of the President, buys pipes at inflated prices from a company that then turns out to be a shell owned by the state pipeline company's management; state banks invest pension funds in companies that then mysteriously go bust. (The money just disappears! The banks deny all prior knowledge that the deals would sour.) The latest economic model is to create "hyper-projects," which can act as vehicles for siphoning off the budget. The cost for the Russian Winter Olympics in Sochi was $50 billion, making it $30 billion more expensive than the previous summer games in London, and five times more expensive than any Winter Olympics ever. Some $30 billion is thought to have been "diverted." There is also a "hyper-bridge," which swings above the Pacific, connecting Vladivostok and South Sakhalin. There is nothing on South Sakhalin, the real economic benefits are almost zero, but the opportunities for graft are great. The new planned "hyper-project" is a tunnel between Russia and Japan. The USSR built mega-projects that made no macroeconomic sense but fitted the hallucinations of the planned economy; the new hyper-projects make no macroeconomic sense but are vehicles for the enrichment of those whose loyalty the Kremlin needs to reward, quickly.

But it was power, rather than money, that was always Berezovsky's interest. The oil company the two oligarchs are fighting over was never more than a means to an end; he needed it to fund his control of television. He had been the first in Russia, in 1994, to understand that television could bring him that power. It was Berezovsky who introduced the "fabricated documentary" to Ostankino, inventing barely credible scandals about the President's political opponents, his presenters brandishing random pieces of paper at the camera that "proved" corruption. In 1999 it was Berezovsky's TV channel that created the new President, supporting his war in Chechnya and turning him from gray "moth" into macho leader. It was Berezovsky who invented the fake political parties, television puppet constructs, shells without any policy whose one point was to prop up the President. Russia's slide from representative democracy to a society of pure spectacle was given its great push by Berezovsky. He created the theater I would later work inside, and which, after his exile, cast him as the eternal bogeyman: his old Ostankino channel blaming him for everything from sponsoring terrorism to political assassinations. And Berezovsky plays up to the role of Übervillain, claiming, once his influence was almost gone, that he was sponsoring attempted revolutions in Ukraine and Russia.

On Shrove Sunday during the trial, Berezovsky posts a confession on his Facebook page:

> *I ask for your forgiveness, oh People of Russia . . . for destroying freedom of speech and democratic values. . . . I confess for bringing the President*

to power. I understand confession is not words but deeds, these will soon follow.

The Russian journalists covering the trial chortle in response. No one can believe a word he says. Berezovsky is not so much the opponent of the Kremlin's system as its progenitor turned absurd reflection. The shape-shifter spun to the point of tragicomedy.

"I found Mr. Berezovsky an unimpressive, and inherently unreliable, witness, who regarded truth as a transitory, flexible concept, which could be molded to suit his current purposes," says Justice Gloster in her final judgment. "I gained the impression that he was not necessarily being deliberately dishonest, but had deluded himself into believing his own version of events."

Berezovsky is sitting just in front of me and begins to shake and laugh as the judge speaks. It's a choking sort of laugh. In the hall outside the courtroom he paces up and down and then walks in circles for a while. He is still laughing when he goes outside to face the press.

In the following months he fades from view, for once refusing to give interviews.

The rumor is that he is destitute. The trial has cost him over $100 million. Six months later he sells a Warhol at Christie's, one of 120 silk-screen prints of *Red Lenin* showing the Soviet leader in suntouched yellow emerging from (or being submerged by) a canvas of blood red. It sells for $202,000.

Three days later Berezovsky is dead, hanging himself in the bathroom of his ex-wife's Ascot mansion. I had assumed the Ostankino channels would gloat. Instead the atmosphere is mournful. The President's press secretary sets the tone, announcing that the death of any person is a tragedy. Eduard Limonov, a former dissident émigré writer who transformed himself into the leader of the National Bolsheviks—a movement that started as an art project, became an anti-oligarch revolutionary party mixing Trotskyism and Fascism, and then transformed again to become a Kremlin ally—writes: "I had always admired him. He was great, like a Shakespeare character." Vladimir Zhirinovsky, the ultranationalist scarecrow used by the Kremlin to frighten voters, who normally spits and scowls when he speaks of Russia's enemies, sounds almost tender: "I'd seen him a few months ago in Israel. He was tired, disillusioned." An Ostankino channel shows black-and-white photos of Berezovsky as touching mood music is played. "After all this time," the presenter says, "and all the roles he's played, we never did find out who he really was." It is as if the vast charade of Russian politics has suddenly paused and all the actors are turning to the audience to applaud a fallen player, welcoming in his corpse.

But though the old master may be dead, the system he begat is growing, mutating, swelling now out of Moscow and flowing through many offshore, tax-free, beneficiary-disguised archipelagoes in Cyprus, the British Virgin Islands, and Monaco and from there into Mayfair, Belgravia, Sloane Street, White Hall, Central Park West. For the President's men and those who fear him, for the bully-bureaucrats and the gangsters-turned-oil-traders, for the real entrepreneurs and the Russians who just want to get out and live a normal life. For everyone the pattern is the same. Make, steal, siphon your money off in Russia. Stash it in New York, Paris, Geneva, and especially London. My Moscow has landed.

• • •

I have been working on a TV show. My nine years in Russia are a bit of a black hole in my résumé, and I'm back at the bottom of the pile again: officially a "producer" (the word has lost all meaning), but actually an assistant with no editorial control, on a glitzy, trashy, documentary entertainment series for an American-English cable channel. *Meet the Russians* is about the new, post-Soviet rich in London, and the ad promises to take the viewer "into a world of wealth he has never before witnessed."

There's the pop star married to the steel tycoon who has spent $2 million on her career, including albums, winning Mrs. World (the husband bought the rights to the competition the year before she won) and starring in a Hollywood B movie with Stephen Dorff (the husband financed the movie). She keeps a falcon in their home. The home is decorated to copy a seven-star Dubai hotel she once stayed in. She takes baths in champagne to keep her skin smooth.

There's the footballer's wife who has spent over a hundred grand on Louboutins ("I can't walk on anything less than 5-inch heels!") and thinks that English women are frumpy ("They don't even look like women!").

There's the ex-wife of the entrepreneur whose partner fell foul of the President and now can't go back to Russia; she poses for us in her $180,000 fur coat.

And as the nine-part series rolls out, we see how those who have been in England for a while learn their Ps and Qs, learn how to spend righteously, not vulgarly, learn about charity and the virtues of flat shoes. Become, and I seem to hear this word a lot as I work on the program, "classy."

The show rates well and feeds a double appetite. The local audience get to titter and feel pleasantly superior to the new rich they are selling parts of their country to: "Meet the most vulgar reality characters ever on TV," explains the *Daily Mail*. But beyond this there is a deeper comfort in the thought that though the new Russian rich might be wealthier than any English person could ever hope to be, though the *Sunday Times* rich list is topped no longer by the queen but by Abramovich, Usmanov, and Blavatnik, at the end of the day these global nouveaux all yearn to fit into "our way of doing things." Instinctively, out of habit, the editorial producers on *Meet the Russians* reach for some version of *Vanity Fair*, *My Fair Lady*, the myths the English grow up with. The Victorian compromise, the traditional marriage between new money and old class, is extrapolated to the era of globalization.

The new global rich, the myth goes, all yearn for our culture, law, schools. Civilization.

Except I'm not entirely sure that's what is happening at all.

• • •

Sergey is a character in *Meet the Russians*. He grew up in a Russian family in Estonia. In 1999, when he was thirteen, his parents took him on a holiday to London. He had never been abroad before. They took the ferry over and booked into the small, three-star Earls Court Hotel. Sergey was crazy about basketball, and he had never seen real black people before. They were all wearing the Nike Air Jordans that were his dream, and his head was already bursting with all of this, when his parents sat him down on the edge of the bed.

This was not a holiday, they explained. They were asking for asylum as Russians discriminated against in Estonia. This was his new life.

They moved to Kent. His father became an alcohol delivery driver. Worked hard. Bought a semi. On weekends Sergey would sneak up to London. First he organized underground raves in North London. As he turned eighteen, the Russian wave of money was just cresting: Abramovich was buying Chelsea, Lebedev the *Standard* and the *Independent*. The English were retreating, pulling out of their own post codes of aspiration, out of Mayfair and Belgravia and Knightsbridge, selling up and moving out to Oxfordshire or Tuscany or Norfolk, leaving behind the polished stucco squares and gated gardens to be inhabited by the new heroes of sudden wealth from Kazakhstan, Azerbaijan, India, Krasnoyarsk, Qatar, Donetsk.

Sergey has found himself a niche.

He's the artful dodger of this world. The Mr. Fixit. Need a Mayfair penthouse? A Warhol? A live flamingo for your party? Sergey's your man. He's got different business cards for all his different roles, but his main one is as "club promoter." But that just means he knows everyone in the golden triangle between New Bond Street in the east, Sloane Street in the West, and Berkeley Square at its tip.

When we first meet he's running nights at Baku, the Azeri place on Sloane Street, rumored to be owned by the Azeri president, Heydar Aliev's, daughter, where the dance floor is decorated with $50,000 bottles of wine guarded by bouncers. Then there is Kitsch on Upper Burlington, where two Russians, Sergey likes to boast, came in and dropped $200,000 in one evening after they signed some epic deal. Now we're having lunch in Selfridges, a few days after New Year's, when the English are still asleep, but the store is packed with Arabs, Chinese, Russians. They're the ones who bring in the profits.

"When my mum and dad asked for asylum here they probably thought I would become English. British. Whatever," says Sergey. "But in the world I work in, in Mayfair, Knightsbridge, Belgravia, I often end up speaking more Russian than English. The English aren't the ones with the real money any more. They still might rule the other side of Sloane Square, down in Chelsea, but in Mayfair they can't keep up. A good club night here brings in $180, 000. That's three times more than out there."

At the tip of London the city breaks through and out of England and up into a different space, which is neither Europe nor the Middle East nor Asia nor America but somewhere altogether offshore.

Sergey's core clientele are the Golden Youth. The kids of Russian (and Ukrainian and Kazakh and Azeri) bureaucrat-businessmen (the roles are hyphenated), sent away to be educated at the prettier boarding schools and then on to international business schools in Europe and America. Wellington and Stowe, with their porticos and playing fields, are favorites. The more patriotic the Russian elites become, the more they sing hymns to "Orthodoxy, Autocracy, Tsarism," the more they damn the West—the more they send their children to study in England.

In a previous age, when the English were the club you aspired to join, some new immigrants would change their names, from "Vinogradov" to "Grade," "Mironov" to "Mirren," "Brokhovich" to "Brook." But that wouldn't occur to the Golden Youth: why bother when the richest people in the city have non-English names now anyway? The parents of the Golden Youth send them to boarding schools not because they want them to become English, but because it's the status thing to do, along with having a home in St. Tropez or a bank account in Switzerland. But neither do the Golden Youth I meet peg themselves to Russia. They don't deny their roots. But their reference points run Hong Kong-Geneva-Fifth Avenue-London-South of France and from there to private yachts, private planes. Offshore. Having one nationality, whether American, Russian, or British, seems passé, a little twentieth century.

"So what are you?" I ask the daughter of a Russian pop star (childhood in a gated community in Moscow, boarding school in Switzerland, and now college and clubbing off Sloane Square). "Where do you feel you belong to?" I ask two sisters, who went to boarding school near Cambridge, and whose father from Orienburg has bought them a boutique in Mayfair where they sell gem-studded Uggs.

And they pause, think, and say: "We're sort of in-ter-na-tio-nal."

Sergey echoes this. "My clients are the internationals" (though large swathes of those at his parties are former Soviets).

But when you press to find out what "international" means, no one can quite answer.

Evenings start at Novikov on Berkeley Street. The same Novikov who created all the zeitgeist Forbes-and-girls restaurants in Moscow where Oliona used to do (maybe still does) her hunting. This is the first place to bear to his actual name, a name that has become a signifier for the New Moscow. And the New Moscow, it turns out, is now something to aspire to.

Past the bouncers outside and the girls smoking long, skinny cigarettes, past the tinted glass doors and the jade stone Novikov has put in near the entrance for good luck. Inside, Novikov opens up so anyone can see everyone in almost every corner at any moment, the same theatrical seating as in his Moscow places. But the London Novikov is so much bigger. There are three floors. One floor is "Asian," all black walls and plates. Another floor is "Italian," with off-white tiled floors and trees and classic paintings. Downstairs is the bar-cum-club, in the style of a library in an English country house, with wooden bookshelves and rows of hardcover books. It's a Moscow Novikov restaurant cubed: a series of quotes, of references wrapped in a tinted window void, shorn of their original memories and meanings (but so much colder and more distant than the accessible, colorful pastiche of somewhere like Las Vegas). This had always been the style and mood in the "elite," "VIP" places in Moscow, all along the Rublevka and in the Garden Ring, where the just-made rich exist in a great void where they can buy anything, but nothing means anything because all the old orders of meaning are gone. Here objects become unconnected to any binding force. Old Masters and English boarding schools and Fabergé eggs all floating, suspended in a culture of zero gravity.

But now it's not just Moscow anymore where this style resonates. Over in Bernie Arnaut's Bulgari Hotel, on the corner of Hyde Park, the most expensive hotel in London (rooms start at $1,200 a night; the penthouse is $26,000), the floors are black granite and the walls are black glass, with older men and younger women in the blackness hard, scowling, and sparkling. The lost-in-new-wealth world of Moscow rises and blends with the sudden global money from all the emerging, expanding new economies. And the Russians are the pace-setters, the trendsetters. Because they've been perfecting this for just a few years longer, because the learning curve was so much harder and faster when their Soviet world disappeared and they were all shot into cold space. They became post-Soviet a breath before the whole world went post-everything. Post-national and post-West and post-Bretton-Woods and post-whatever-else. The Yuri Gagarins of the culture of zero gravity.

Just south of Piccadilly, on St. James, England looks like the same old-boy country it always was: the Reform Club, Brooks, the members-only halls with their worn carpets, secret passwords, and centuries-old walls. But one simply doesn't need "in" here anymore. A partner from Novikov's, I'm told, is buying up a building on St. James for his own private London gentlemen's club. It'll be more discreet, more private, more exclusive. And Novikov itself is crowded every night, bringing in $1.3 million a week, full of Paris-raised Qataris and Monaco-registered Nigerians, American hedge fund managers and Golden Youth and Premier League Football agents, escorts from Brazil and Moldova and the Swiss "lawyers" with offices in Moscow and Hong Kong, complaining loudly over house music that their business is about to go to shit because the Swiss parliament now demands that foreigners with accounts in Swiss banks reveal their real identities.

"The point of a Swiss bank account is that it's fucking secret!" they shout at the bar in the style of an English country house library. "I'm going to lose all my Moscow business! It's the end of Switzerland!"

• • •

Skinners Hall, built in 1670, just off Cannon Street in the "heart of the City." The Great Dining Room, oak paneled and hung with tapestries and coats of arms, is lit with spotlights of acid pink and dark cobalt blue, which combined make a sort of neon dusk. Tonight there's an evening for the London Russian great and good who have sponsored the annual "Russia week": a week of ballet galas at the Coliseum and Slavic rock concerts in Trafalgar Square that celebrate the Russian influx.

The men are in black tie and the women are dressed uneasily in gowns that feel just off the rack. A quintet plays something classical. Then comes the Babushki, a trio of old women singing village songs to

Euro-beats who were the Russian entry at the Eurovision Song Contest. One of the Russian wives is putting on some sort of fashion show. There's no catwalk for the models, and they have to move in between the tables. The dresses are velvet, swooping, Italianate aristo Grace Kelly gowns: "timeless classics." But you can't make out the colors because of the pink and cobalt lighting.

"Look," whispers the fashion wife to me, "there's T. I last saw him in Monte Carlo. That man can never go back to Russia, he's such a crook. What is he here? A philanthropist? It's like he's had plastic surgery for his identity. Pulled on a new face."

"Is that A?" asks someone else. "The one who makes out she's an aristo? Ha. I remember her in Moscow. Fine aristo she was then. You know how she met her first husband, the billionaire? She was 'modeling.'"

Original identities become as obscure as the true ownership of funds flowing between the former Soviet Union and the West. Especially since the President has passed a law banning state officials and the heads of state companies (and now most of the companies are state companies) from having bank accounts or stocks and bonds abroad, even when the point of rising in the system is the privilege to lift money over there and migrate it over here. And so the Kremlin both regulates the status that confirms the privilege and keeps everyone scared. And as long as everyone is scared, they'll remain loyal. There might well be more FSB agents now in London than at any time in history, but their aim is less nuclear secrets and more the other Russians and whom you can hit up. A paranoia runs through every meeting and conversation.

"See B," a Russian high society writer leans in and says to me, "the one there in the pearls? With all the guys around her? She appeared from nowhere and opened her own networking agency. Everyone thinks she's FSB. Why else would she need to have everyone's contacts? Know who is here and who is not?"

And all this makes conversation difficult outside tiny circles of loyal friends. The usual openings—"What do you do?" or "What are your politics?"—lead to dead ends. A lot of the time, the only neutral thing that people seem to be able to talk about is Art.

• • •

"I spent a lot of time in London when I was studying. I loved the museums, Tate Modern especially. And I thought it would be great to create a space like that in the Russian context," says Dasha Zhu-kova, with the disarming simplicity only the really, truly rich can carry off: she's building a new modern art museum in Moscow as we speak. She is the daughter of one Russian tycoon, the longtime girl-friend of another, Roman Abramovich. I'm interviewing her before an event at Art Basel that she is sponsoring. (I'm taking up a bit of writing to paper over the gaps in television work.) Trying to set up a meeting has been complicated. Within a few hours the location switches from London to the south of France to Moscow to New York. We end up meeting in Los Angeles, where she grew up. I fly economy for a one-hour chat.

Her father made his money trading oil. There was also some story about his selling arms from Russia to the war in Yugoslavia, and he spent some time in an Italian prison on account of this (he was even-tually cleared of charges). The last time I saw Abramovich he was in an English courtroom timidly revealing the moves he had pulled to make his first money.

But all that hinterland seems to just fall away when I talk to Dasha.

She's beautiful in an unaggressive sort of way. She nods and listens. Her accent is unplaceable, wavering among tough Muscovite and breezy Valley Girl and hints of London. She was nine when she left Moscow, living with her Russian academic mother first in Texas and then LA. Whenever I try to steer the conversation to politics, she just ignores it. We just talk art. About the cool spaces in the gaps between

Donald Judd sculptures. About the honesty of 1960s modernism. About not knowing quite where to belong.

Identities are dissolved, reborn, in the clean, pure, simple lines of abstract art.

Whenever I meet a candidate for the TV show they tell me to come along to the Arts Club on Davies Street. It's the most "international" of the private members' places. There's a chandelier of shiny plastic bubbles as you climb up the staircase, and when you get up to the first floor you can soon spot the clusters of Russian wives. The men are still mainly in Moscow or Tyumen pumping crude and cash. The wives are here, worried about or resigned to whomever *he* is sleeping with out there (the stewardesses of private planes are always suspect), while they sit in London watching over the cash flows and keeping the bolt-holes ready, lunching in little groups in La Durée at Harrods; perfectly dressed in Hermes or something equally "classy" and restrained to the point of tautness, going for private showings at Fabergé and then meetings with a dealer at the Arts Club. The wealthier wives run galleries. In the surrounding streets, north from Piccadilly, up Albermarle and along Upper Burlington the new galleries belong to the post-Soviets: the Erarta, the St. Petersburg, Most 26.

Those who can afford it become patrons.

The former Moscow mayor's wife, who made part of her billions by winning construction contracts from the city government while her husband was mayor (she denies there's any connection), is the latest to arrive. Back home Mozhayev and his friends, the defenders of Moscow's historic architecture, blame the mayor and his wife for the "cultural genocide" of Moscow's buildings, swathes of the old city destroyed to make way for menacing imitations of Disney towers and Dubai hotels; Russian constructivist masterpieces, which admirers come across the world to see, left to decay. Now based in London, the mayor's wife has a foundation called Be Open, launching a Young Talent Award at Milan Design Week and devoting a new program at

London Design Week "to innovative projects that reach out to the sixth sense, or intuition."

I'm invited to a Russian party during the Frieze Art Fair. During the last financial crash many thought it meant the end for Frieze: the Wall Street men and City boys were broke. But it turned out a Russian (and a Ukrainian and an Armenian) will still trust London over Moscow or Kiev to secure their wealth. Your bank accounts might get seized, but no one can get to your family's Jeff Koons or seize your wife's Knightsbridge mansion. So Frieze didn't collapse; it swelled. (In Moscow itself the market for contemporary, Western art has been failing. Not because there is no money—there are more Russian billionaires every year—but because the new demand, issued from the Kremlin, is for the patriotic. So now you buy socialist realism for your Moscow place and Rothkos for your London and New York ones.)

The party is in one of the Nash stucco mansions on a crescent opposite Regents Park (these places can go for $50 million). The London Russians have banded together to show off art from their collections: Van Goghs are spread about casually on the walls of the stairwell and in little corners, right next to student works by wives and girlfriends who are taking courses at St. Martins College of Art and Design to pass the time in London. Most of the crowd is Russian. Around them swarm the English art dealers, with slightly worn elbows, looking to start a conversation about some trade. The big thing recently is Russian avant-garde: that little moment in the early twentieth century when Russia was not just in step with but defined the world, and which you buy to be both a patriot and global. And it so happens this is the easiest art to copy. Who can tell one pure black square apart from yet another? Much of Russian avant-garde art on the market is fake. Churned out in factories run by Russian crime syndicates in Israel and Germany, then confirmed by Western art historians. Without them the fakes would never make it to the market. They play the same role as the Swiss and English lawyers who act as "nominal beneficiaries" for money-laundering shell companies, lending their signatures to help make the simulated real, and like those lawyers, they are only too happy to look the other way, as are the dealers who then sell all the fakes to the more gullible new money.

The Russians swerve around the dealers and move to the VIP area on the third floor.

Down by the bar on the first floor roam the estate agents. Many are graduates from private schools. They look happy. Business is good: three-quarters of houses over $10 million in the golden triangle are sold to the new global rich.

The estate agents tell great tales. About the new oligarch exiled from Russia who misses his childhood dacha so much he asked an architect to fly to Moscow, then re-create the place, panel by panel, with the same 1980s wallpapers and settees in the English countryside. Sourcing the old Soviet wallpaper was tough; there's only one factory in Russia you can get it from. And then there's the tycoon who wanted a new house in Belgravia. That wasn't hard. But then he asked for six apartments, of equal size, in a ten-minute-walk circumference around the house. They were for his mistresses, so he could walk in any direction and arrive at one. And have you heard the one about the thief the police caught recently? Who put on an accent and would turn up at viewings for mansions saying he was a Russian oligarch and then steal jewels from the bedrooms as he went around? Actually he was a hood from Tottenham. But everyone fell for him, the accent was so good.

There's free champagne.

Some can remember the easy days when new Russians were still suckers. In the 1990s an agent in Geneva managed to sell the head of Russian Railways a property on the slope facing away from the lake for the price of a property facing the lake; that's twice the price. You don't really get dunces like that anymore. Now you rarely meet the owners. They send an English lawyer. The deeds are all in the name of some company in an offshore Crown dependency. The estate agents don't ask too many questions.

• • •

As I wait for William Browder to come in for his interview in *Meet the Russians*, I look at the newspaper cuttings that are all over the walls of his office on Golden Square: "One Man's Crusade against the Kremlin," "The Man who Took on Vladimir Putin." Browder used to be one of the President's more vocal supporters, back when he was the largest foreign investor in Russia. He'd come to the country in the 1990s, when most in Western finance said it was crazy to even try. He proved them all wrong. Then in 2006 he pissed off the wrong people in Russia and was banned from the country. Then things got worse: the documents for his old investment vehicles were taken in a raid by the police. Browder told a Russian lawyer, Sergey Magnitsky, who worked for a Moscow-based law firm called Firestone and Duncan, to follow the trail. It turned out the investment companies were being illegally signed over by the cops to petty criminals, who would then ask for tax rebates on the companies worth hundreds of millions of dollars, which were then granted by corrupt tax officials, signed off on by the same cops who had taken the documents in the first place, and wired to two banks owned by a convicted fraudster, an old friend of the aforementioned cops and tax officials. Officially the tax officials and cops only earned a few thousand a year, but they had property worth hundreds of thousands, drove Porsches, and went on shopping trips to Harrods in London. And this was happening year after year. The biggest tax fraud scheme in history. Magnitsky thought he had caught a few bad apples.

Magnitsky gave an interview to *Bloomberg Business Week*. Twelve days later he was arrested; he was tortured and eventually died in a Russian prison a year later. It hadn't been a case of a few bad apples. An anonymous letter by a whistle-blower to a Russian newspaper said the tax rebate mechanism was known as the "black till of the Kremlin," used systematically for everything from personal enrichment to financing covert wars or foreign elections.

"The day I found out about Sergey's death was the worst day of my life," says Browder when we start the interview. "He was killed to get at me." He is tall and balding, with glasses, direct but emotionally contained. (How many times, I wonder, must he have given the same interview?) He is American but based in London. "I have sworn to get justice. The Putin regime has blood on its hands. I used to be an investment banker, but now I'm a human rights activist."

We carry on shooting as we drive through Belgravia: "Your viewer probably thinks the sort of people who killed Magnitsky and stole that money are gangsters with gold chains. But they're officials who dress nicely and own nice houses and send their children to nice schools," continues Browder.

We arrive at Parliament. Browder is having a meeting with a member of Parliament in a corner office of Portcullis House overlooking the Thames. Since Magnitsky's death he has researched where the stolen money went. It all went abroad, via Moldova, Latvia, and Cyprus, and from there into bank accounts in Switzerland and property in Dubai and Manhattan. A Russian businessman who helped reveal these flows died of a sudden heart attack after a jog near his gated compound in Surrey. He was forty-four and had no history of illness. He had a lot of enemies. Two postmortems could not determine the cause of his death.

Browder takes out some files: lists of UK companies that helped launder bits of the Magnitsky money. (We do several takes to get a nice shot. Browder and the MP are used to it.)

"I've filed complaints with the authorities, but there's no response. Could you see what's happening?"

The MP says he will try. The English financial authorities are notoriously slow at clamping down on money laundered through the country. London is the perfect home for money launderers: terrific lawyers to defend your stolen assets; great bankers to move it; weak cops who don't ask where they came from.

A little later I'm invited back to Parliament for a presentation, "Why Europe Needs a Magnitsky Act." The US version of the act is Browder's great achievement, banning Russian human rights abusers and corrupt officials from entry into, investments in, and owning property in the United States. The White House and the business community all initially opposed the bill: human rights and finance, they argued, shouldn't mix. Browder pushed it through even though most said it would be impossible. But now no government in Europe is prepared to touch the act: it might stop the money coming in. Browder hopes to provoke a referendum.

There are only a couple of dozen people at the presentation, in a small room at the end of a long corridor in a quiet corner of Parliament. I see a couple of backbench MPs, a leftie journalist, a neo-con magazine editor. No one from government. Jamison Firestone is there, too; he looks to be in his mid-thirties though he is actually pushing fifty and just has that everlasting boyish thing. Firestone was the American lawyer for whom Sergey Magnitsky worked at Firestone and Duncan, the Moscow law firm Browder hired. Browder never really knew Magnitsky, had rarely seen him. It's all very different for Firestone. He seems to twist in pain every time he talks about his dead colleague. I see him regularly, pacing through every party and every conference and business meeting and lecture about Russia, calling out on the money launderers and murderers and repeating the name "Magnitsky! Magnitsky!" until it burns in everybody's ears. A canary in the mine of Mayfair calling that this is all wrong.

We meet a little later in a café in Maida Vale. As we speak Firestone's voice sometimes rises, and people look around at us, startled. When I glance up again later I spot them quietly listening in. There's a downpour outside with reports of flooding further down the Thames estuary. Firestone calls Magnitsky by his first name, Sergey.

"Sergey was the best lawyer I ever knew. I never saw him lose a case, never. We would have clients charged for taxes they didn't owe, and every time he would challenge the courts and win. He was an optimist. He only ever got emotional about classical music. Even when he was arrested. He called me from the car on the way to the police station and he was calm: he was sure it would all clear up."

After Sergey was arrested the police came for Firestone's other lawyers. He had to take one colleague down the fire escape of her home with the police at the front door, and then they took a night train across the Russian-Ukrainian border. Another flew straight to London.

"I had spent eighteen years in Russia but for my colleagues it was their whole life. We rented a three-bedroom apartment together. My colleagues would sit in their rooms crying. Their relatives were ill or suffering, but they couldn't go back to see them. But none of us could really say anything, since what was happening to Sergey was so much worse."

When Sergey had been in prison for nine months, nine months in which no one was allowed to visit him, his wife managed to get hold of his prison diary.

"I received it by e-mail," continues Firestone. "Just page after page of stoical, detailed description. Like a lawyer, just cataloguing everything calmly. How the sewage would flood the cell and they would live with it for days; how he would have to stand to write because there was no room there were so many prisoners; how each cell got worse because he wouldn't confess and incriminate others; how there was no glass in the windows in the cell in winter and it was freezing. In the summer over-crowded cells and prisoner transport trucks were like filthy never ending saunas; how he would not get treatment when the pain in his stomach was becoming unbearable. . . . What made it worse was the calm way he was cataloguing it all. I could hear his voice. Same as always."

Firestone's own voice is rising again. He never thought he would end up taking on the Kremlin.

"I had a wonderful life, my colleagues had wonderful lives. And to hold onto it, all we had to do was shut up and let this pass. But somebody was killed."

He tells me he still yearns to go back to Russia. He had Russian residency and was about to apply for a passport for a second citizenship, planned to spend his life there. He had first moved to Moscow in 1991, straight after he graduated from college. It was his father who had advised him he should learn Russian in high school; back in the 1980s he had already told Jamison the USSR would collapse one day and Russia was where the money would be. Firestone's father was a serial entrepreneur who had made and lost a fortune in California real estate, created the only Internet porn site to lose money, and then made $12 million by creating another site that helps kids with their homework. At the time Firestone went to Russia his father was in jail for selling fraudulent tax shelters.

"My dad liked to hang out with gangsters the way Frank Sinatra would like to hang out with gangsters. When he was released he came over to Russia and tried to get a protection racket involved in my first business: importing cars to Russia. He said everyone in Russia needs protection, but I didn't want the mafia in my business and he took a hit out to break the legs of my friend and law partner: 'If I have your legs broken you'll ignore it because you're strong. If you see your friend with broken legs you'll understand the cost of opposing me,' my dad told me. I resigned and then the protection racket my dad hired stole our cars and that was the end of his foray into Russia. My dad was always my moral compass: whatever he suggested I did the opposite."

Firestone had many moments in Russia when he had to think about his dad: all the times he was asked to "move some money"; the partner in his audit company who told him they should cheat on their firm's taxes. (Firestone had him thrown out of the building by guards with AK-47s and reported him to the police.) Then there was the time the Russian minister for development (the same one Benedict had worked for) asked Firestone what he thought needed to change in Russia to protect private property. The minister expected a polite answer, but Firestone told him publicly that while ministers and oligarchs were above the law, the country was fucked. Firestone was a board member and head of the small business committee of the American Chamber of Commerce at the time. One of his fellow board members from a Fortune 100 company told him off for being outspoken: "We like what you're saying Jamison—but could you say it quieter?"

"We were all making a lot of money," says Firestone, "but I could tell things were getting scummier."

But I can also hear the thrill in his voice when he talks about his Moscow adventures.

"I'll wear the lawyer's hat," says Firestone, "but I was a really good street fighter. I fired mafias twice on behalf of my clients. Mafia, like police, can only react to two responses: 'yes sir' or 'no sir' (which gets you killed). One time a client was raided and had his business database stolen by the mafia group that was meant to be protecting him: they'd crossed over to a rival. So we went to meet these guys in a hotel on Petrovka and I told them in Russian and in my nicest corporate voice:

"My client pays you 100,000 a month for a package of services that you say includes protection. We don't understand how you can also work with other clients protecting their right to steal from my client, who is also your client. I'm a lawyer, for example, and I could never defend both sides."

"That's why we're different from you lawyers," the mafia guys answered. *"You guys quarrel all the time. We work with everyone and ensure peace for all sides."*

"You're quite right. We didn't understand. And I'm sure it's our fault— but now that we understand the services you offer we don't need them anymore."

"We walked out of a room of shocked Mafiosi. The others were only paying them 30,000. Next week the racket came back with all the computers from the rivals."

Firestone still smiles when he relates this, playing out each line of the dialogue in Americanized, but nearly perfect, Russian. And he tells me of the time he had to hide out in a government hospital to hide from corrupt cops (they could grab him anywhere apart from a hospital full of ministers); and when his first office was raided by thugs working for his neighbor and his staff were handcuffed to the furniture and threatened at knifepoint; or when he had to fly to New York and buy up all the bugging equipment at the Spy store to give to the anti-fraud squad in Moscow so they would have the equipment with which to bust other bent cops trying to extort money from him.

"You know, one of the problems I have living in London is that if I actually tell the truth about my story people just assume I'm lying. They never call me back. I've learned to just talk pleasantries. Or if someone really wants the truth I tell them there's a condition: 'You give me your e-mail now before the conversation starts, and I will tell you my story and then send you some links and you can see me on the BBC or read some newspaper articles about me. And then maybe you might call me back. Because you won't call me back otherwise. It's just too weird. . . .'"

Russia as the place where you are forced into extremes, which then make you examine your every decision and what you're made of, where the choice between good and evil becomes distilled. Is this what makes it so addictive? Another incarnation of Moscow as Third Rome. We all end up becoming sucked into the city's myths, become expressions of the only story it knows how to tell. The same tragedy can happen in so many places, but in Russia it takes on that iconic intensity.

When I refocus on what Jamison is saying, his voice is rising again.

"London shocked me. The whole system is built around wanting that money to come here. We want their money. We want their trade. And now you've got former German chancellor Schroeder and Lord Mandelson and Lord So-and-So working for these Russian state companies, and you know I think they should just be honest and say 'some Kremlin company offered me 500,000 to sit on their board and

I don't do anything and I don't know anything about how the company is run but sometimes they ask me to open some doors.' And the argument I hear from everyone is 'well if the money doesn't go here it will go somewhere else': well here ain't going to be here if you take that attitude, here is going to be there. We used to have this self-centered idea that Western democracies were the end point of evolution, and we're dealing from a position of strength, and people are becoming like us. It's not that way. Because if you think this thing we have here isn't fragile you are kidding yourself. This," and here Jamison takes a breath and waves his hand around to denote Maida Vale, London, the whole of Western civilization, "this is fragile."

And I see Jamison pacing through Parliament and through every think tank meeting and dinner party in London agitating and crying out, full of his American fervor and that pain that seems to physically twist him when he talks about Sergey Magnitsky. And the pain is even greater because he feels the men who are responsible for killing Sergey are here too, enjoying their stucco mansions and Harrods, and they are utterly untouchable.

But what Jamison says causes no great revelation in the golden triangle. Rather it's assumed that everything everywhere is, well, terrible. And though most agree that yes, Mayfair and Belgravia and Knightsbridge might belong to a different order now, are part of the great offshore, and naturally we would never approve it if our own ministers did the same as that Russian (or Azeri or Nigerian) deputy prime minister who just bought that penthouse off St. James's with money made through self-dealing government contracts, but overall we'll be fine because we'll keep all that bad stuff up in the spare room of our culture and it won't change us. And Jamison, poor soul, had a terrible time, and he means well and in a way of course he's right, but let's not get carried away: the world has always been this way. Or others sigh and say well everything has changed here already anyway and there is no West anymore: for who are we to teach anyone how to behave?

And in the end the editorial producers cut the story about Sergey Magnitsky from *Meet the Russians*, including all those scenes we shot in Belgravia and Parliament, because try as they might they just can't make it fit with the overall master concept: it's meant to be a feel-good sort of show.

NOTHING IS TRUE AND EVERYTHING IS POSSIBLE

I am at the airport, getting ready to catch the Moscow flight. My daughter is with me. Her mother, my wife, is a Muscovite; we met during the almost decade I spent in Russia. My daughter was born while I still worked in Moscow. Now we all live together in London. When I travel to Russia it is less often on TV projects and more frequently as a father. I don't travel with a camera anymore. I find I do less of those sorts of TV projects, the ones where you push your way into people's lives, try to get as close to things as possible. For all our claims to capture the real, a factual director is always a manipulator, a miniature vizier, seducing, framing, spinning his subjects, asking one question but waiting for another slip up, always thinking how every action we're shooting relates not to its direct environment but to the final cut. And when we begin to edit, our subject's video representation takes on a life of its own, a hologram cross-faded, saturated, flipped, squeezed, and cut in different ways for US, UK, Internet, and promotional edits. So almost no person is ever happy with themselves on screen, even when we've done everything to make them "positive," because it's never the "him" or "her" they think they are. Yet here's the rub. Those holograms we have created then pursue us. The emotions our subjects once poured out to us stay with us. And we begin to live in a parallel reality of video ghosts. The parents of the dead models in their deep grief, the gold diggers, the soldier off to Chechnya, Jambik, the milkmaid, the terror victims, everyone I've ever filmed: they visit me from time to time.

"Come back!" my wife exclaims when she sees me with that distracted look. "Look at your daughter. The real world. We're here."

The airport is packed. I'm taking my daughter over for summer holidays, and she is looking forward to the trip. She has recently started school in London, and it can be tough for her. I have been away filming so often that her Russian is still better than her English. The other day she came home from school crying: "I can't understand what the other children are saying about me, what if it's something horrible?" Russia for her means adoring relatives. When we land at Domodedovo my in-laws will be there to greet her in a scene straight out of *Hello-Goodbye*. They will take her out to their small family dacha. The front of the dacha faces onto mild hills, with a little church peeking out on the horizon. The back porch runs into wild woods. She will spend the summer wandering among the hills and in the woods, listening to Russian fairy tales and imagining herself in them, stopping by little rivers, picking wild strawberries in the intense light loveliness of Russian summer, which is so short and thus so special.

I imagine how when I land my in-laws and I will talk about the weather. Will there be peat fires this year? Will the fires reach the dacha? We will think about the best way to drive out of town; the traffic has only gotten worse. Maybe they will recommend a concert I should attend at the conservatory, and we will negotiate our conversation through the pleasant byways of our relationship. As if everything is normal. As if there is no war. And at first glance the city will seem just as it ever was: the bulletproof Bentleys will still be triple parked across from the red-brick monastery; the flocks of cranes will still swing across a skyline changing in fast-forward. And everything will be fine until someone (a taxi driver, an old friend, someone in a bar) will casually mention, mantra-like:

"Russia is strong again, we've got up from our knees!"
"All the world fears us!"
"The West is out to get us!"

"There are traitors everywhere!"

And then I will switch on the television.

The weekly news roundup show is on. The well-dressed presenter walks across the well-made set and into shot, briskly summing up the week's events, all seemingly quite normal. Then suddenly he'll twirl around to camera 2, and before you know it he's talking about how the West is sunk in the slough of homosexuality, and only Holy Russia can save the world from Gay-Europa, and how among us all are the fifth columnists, the secret Western spies who dress themselves up as anti-corruption activists but are actually all CIA. (Who else would dare to criticize the President?) The West, he'll say, is sponsoring anti-Russian "fascists" in Ukraine, and all of them are out to get Russia and take away its oil; the American-sponsored fascists are crucifying Russian children on the squares of Ukrainian towns because the West is organizing a genocide against us Russians, and there are women crying on camera saying how they were threatened by roving gangs of Russia-haters, and of course only the President can make this right, and that's why Russia did the right thing to annex Crimea, why it's right to arm and send mercenaries to Ukraine, and this is just the beginning of the great new conflict between Russia and the West. When you go to check (through friends, news wires, anyone who isn't Ostankino) to see whether there really are fascists taking over Ukraine or whether there are children being crucified, you find it's all untrue, and the women who said they saw it all are actually hired extras dressed up as "eye-witnesses," and the whole line between fact and fiction at Ostankino has become irrelevant. But even when you know the whole justification for the President's war is fabricated, even when you fathom that the real reason is to create a story to keep the President all-powerful and help us all forget about the melting money, the lies are told so often that after a while you find yourself nodding because it's hard to get your head around the idea that they are lying quite so much and quite so brazenly—and at some level you feel that if Ostankino can lie so much and get away with it, doesn't that mean they have real power, the power to define what is true and what isn't? Wouldn't you do better just to nod anyway? And flipping over to another channel, there are the Night Wolves riding in caval-cades through Sevastopol to celebrate the annexation, the resurrection of the Empire, holding aloft icons of Mary the Mother of God and quoting Stalin and playing their great theme tune:

Russian speech rings like chain-mail in the ears of the foreigners,
And the white host rises from the coppice to the stars.

The Night Wolves are just one of the many stars of the new Os-tankino cast. There are the Cherubims, who dress in all black embla-zoned with skulls and crosses, calling to cleanse Russia of moral darkness; the neo-Nazis with MTV dancer bodies who film themselves beating up gay teenagers in the name of patriotism; the whip-wielding Cossacks at-tacking performance artists on the streets. And all of them are pushed to the center of the screen to appear on trashy talk shows and star in factual entertainment formats, keeping the TV spinning with oohs and aahs about gays and God, Satan and the CIA. Their emergence is not some bottom-up swell; only a tiny number of Russians go to church. Rather, the Kremlin has finally mastered the art of fusing reality TV and author-itarianism to keep the great, 140-million-strong population entertained, distracted, constantly exposed to geopolitical nightmares, which if re-peated enough times can become infectious. For when I talk to many of my old colleagues who are still working in the ranks of Russian media or in state corporations, they might laugh off all the Holy Russia stuff as so much PR (because everything is PR!), but their triumphant cynicism in turn means they can be made to feel there are conspiracies everywhere: because if nothing is true and all motives are corrupt and no one is to be trusted, doesn't it mean that some dark hand must be behind everything?

Flipping over onto another channel, there is the life trainer from the Rose of the World giving advice on how to deal with all your hang-ups (after the story with the models broke, he just changed the name of his organization and carried on regardless). How similarly Ostankino works to the Lifespring courses: repeating and endlessly playing out all of Russia's fears and panic attacks and fevers, not searching for some criticism or cure, but just stirring them so you're sucked in but never free, while the Kremlin ties the public to itself by first humiliating and bullying with werewolves in uniform and baron bureaucrats, and then lifts the country up with marvelous military conquests.

Later in the schedule come the shows with Duma deputies, some still spitting or beetroot-faced but more now with English suits, rimless glasses, and prim buns, their latest challenge to make up laws so flamboyant in their patriotic burlesque it will get them noticed. They conjure motions to "ban untraditional sex" or "ban English words"—and to sanction Russia's invasion of Ukraine. Glance through the careers of these new religious patriots, and you find they were recently committed democrats and liberals, pro-Western, preaching modernization, innovation, and commitment to Russia's European course, before which they were all good Communists. And though on the one hand their latest incarnations are just new acts in the Moscow political cabaret, something about their delivery is different from the common Russian political performer who gives his rants with a knowing wink and nod. Now the delivery is somewhat deadpan. Flat and hollow-eyed, as if they have been turned and twisted in so many ways they've spun right off the whirligig into something clinical. Because isn't some sort of madness implicit in the system? If at one end of the spectrum are the political technologists toying with reality, or Oliona transforming herself for every sugar daddy, or Vitaly acting out a fantasy of himself in movies he himself directs about his own life, then at the other is Boris Berezovsky, the progenitor of the system who became its absurd reflection, bankrupt, making no sense in an English courtroom, told that he "deludes himself into believing his own version of events."

And on every channel is the President, who as a made-for-TV projection has fitted every Russian archetype into himself, so now he seems to burst with all of Russia, cutting ever quicker between gangster-statesman-conqueror-biker-believer-emperor, one moment diplomatically rational and the next frothing with conspiracies. And on TV the President is chatting via live video-link to factory workers posing in overalls in front of a tank they've built, and the factory workers are promising the President that if protests against him continue, they will "come to Moscow and defend our stability." But then it turns out the workers don't actually exist; the whole thing is a piece of playacting organized by local political technologists (because everyone is a political technologist now), the TV spinning off to someplace where there is no reference point back to reality, where puppets talk to holograms when both are convinced they are real, where nothing is true and everything is possible. And the result of all this delirium is a curious sense of weightlessness.

But look underneath the Kremlin's whirligig, and don't you see the most precise, hard calculations? For if one part of the system is all about wild performance, another is about slow, patient co-optation. And the Kremlin has been co-opting the West for years: "The English likes to make fun of us," said a Kremlin tabloid after *Meet the Russians* was released, "but is it prepared to lose our investments?"

"*It was the first non-linear war,*" wrote Vladislav Surkov in a new short story, "Without Sky," published under his pseudonym and set in a dystopian future after the "fifth world war":

> In the primitive wars of the nineteenth and twentieth centuries it was common for just two sides to fight. Two countries. Two groups of allies. Now four coalitions collided. Not two against two, or three against one. No. All against all.

There is no mention of holy wars in Surkov's vision, none of the cabaret used to provoke and tease the West. But there is a darkling vision of globalization, in which instead of everyone rising together, interconnection means multiple contests between movements and corporations and city-states. Where the old alliances, the EUs and NATOs and "the West," have all worn out, and where the Kremlin can play the new, fluctuating lines of loyalty and interest, the flows of oil and money, splitting Europe from America, pitting one Western company against another and against both their governments so no one knows whose interests are what and where they're headed.

"A few provinces would join one side," Surkov continues. *"A few others a different one. One town or generation or gender would join yet another. Then they could switch sides, sometimes mid-battle. Their aims were quite different. Most understood the war to be part of a process. Not necessarily its most important part."*

The Kremlin switches messages at will to its advantage, climbing inside everything: European right-wing nationalists are seduced with an anti-EU message; the Far Left is co-opted with tales of fighting US hegemony; US religious conservatives are convinced by the Kremlin's fight against homosexuality. And the result is an array of voices, working away at global audiences from different angles, producing a cumulative echo chamber of Kremlin support, all broadcast on RT.

"We're minority shareholders in globalization," I hear from Russian corporate spooks and politicians. Which, remembering how the system tried to break Yana, might mean that the best way to imagine the Kremlin's vision of itself in the world is as a "corporate reider": the ultraviolent cousin of Western corporate raiders. For "reiding" is how most of the Russian elite made their first money, buying into a company and then using any means possible (arrests, guns, seizures, explosions, bribery, blackmail) to extract its advantages. The Kremlin is the great corporate reider inside globalization, convinced that it can see through all the old ways of the slow West to play at something more subversive. The twenty-first century's geopolitical avant-garde.

"Without Sky" was published on March 12, 2014. A few days later Russia annexed Crimea. Surkov helped to organize the annexation, with his whole theater of Night Wolves, Cossacks, staged referendums, scripted puppet politicians, and men with guns. As punishment, Surkov was one of the first Russian officials to be sanctioned by the West, banned from traveling to or investing in the United States and European Union.

"Won't this ban affect you?" a reporter asked Surkov as he passed through the Kremlin Palace. "Your tastes point to you being a very Western person." Surkov smiled and pointed to his head: "I can fit Europe in here." Later he announced: "I see the decision by the administration in Washington as an acknowledgment of my service to Russia. It's a big honor for me: like being nominated for the political equivalent of an Oscar. I don't have accounts abroad. The only things that interest me in the US are Tupac Shakur, Allen Ginsberg, and Jackson Pollock. I don't need a visa to access their work. I lose nothing."

My daughter and I are through passport control. We'll be boarding soon. She's choosing souvenirs in Duty Free, mementos of England for Russian relatives. I always feel so at home in airport lounges, when you're neither here nor there, where everyone is stateless. It used to be easy to spot the Russians in the lounge: either under- or overdressed. You'd never notice now, it's hard to tell whether passengers are going home or departing.

And as the flight is called and we move toward the plane, I wonder whether I will find any of the other Russia on this visit: sometimes when I visit Moscow the streets are filled with protests against the Kremlin. "Don't lie, don't steal" is the protesters' slogan, which might sound somewhat priggish and maybe matronly in English, but in Russian "ne vrat i ne vorovat," with its vibrating repeating Vs and rolling Rs, sounds like an angry Old Testament growl (maybe "thou shalt not lie, thou shalt not steal" is a better approximation), capturing in four words the connection between financial and intellectual corruption, where words never mean what they say they mean and figures on budgets are never what they are.

One time, on the boulevard ring at dusk, there was a protest leader on a stage addressing a crowd, holding up the old picture of Vladik Mamyshev-Monroe impersonating the President, and he was saying: "This is a portrait by our favorite artist Vladik and this is what we need to get rid of." And by that he meant not so much the President himself but the whole culture of simulation that eats up everything and which Vladik tried to describe: "One day we will reach into the cupboard, and reach for our clothes, and they will turn to dust in our hands because they have been eaten by maggots."

Vladik himself has died. He was found floating in a pool in Bali. Death by heart attack. Right at the end an oligarch acquaintance had made him an offer to come over to the Kremlin side and star in a series of paintings in which he would dress up as the new protest leaders engaged in sodomy. Vladik had refused.

I've noticed something new when wandering around the protests and talking to the new Moscow dissidents. If once upon a time they used the word "the West" in general, and the word "London" in particular, to represent the beacon of what they aimed toward, now the words "London" and the "West" can be said with a light disgust, as the place that shelters and rewards and reinforces the very forces that oppress them. And so, in the classic Third Rome twist, the Russian liberal can become the last true liberal on Earth, the only one still believing in the ideas preached by Benedict and the international development consultants.

I hope I'll be able to find Mozhayev, still searching for his Old Moscow, wandering and talking with a bottle of port in his pocket (he's abandoned vodka). He never did emigrate, of course. I've heard he's even managed to save a few buildings recently. But he could do nothing for Pechatnikov house 3, which was destroyed, and now only Mozhayev's elegy of it survives. "This place was known as 'the heart of Moscow,'" wrote Mozhayev in an essay I came across.

The yard was an odd sort of shape, leaning on the slope. There was a broken bench in the middle where I would like to sit. It was best to come here in the evening, when the lights were coming on in the houses, and you could feel time stopping: the ivy crawling up the open brick work, the sheets hanging out in the yard to dry, the children's strollers by the open doors . . . they all seemed to belong to another time. Of course the sheets and strollers actually belonged to illegal migrants from Central Asia squatting in the houses, and many of the windows were boarded up and broken, and there was graffiti everywhere—but oddly the migrants gave the whole thing a sense of lived-in-ness. And there was one first-floor apartment, whose windows looked directly out onto the bench, which was pure Old Moscow, with a yellow low-hanging lampshade, and books stacked up to the ceiling where they seemed to be keeling over, and a big man with a big beard moving about with tea inside, and a cat that would fling itself repeatedly at the wood-framed windows.

We're flying now. My daughter has the window seat she likes best. She's bent right over, forehead pressed up against the cold glass, looking to glimpse the lights of cities between the clouds. The burning concentric rings of Moscow will soon be coming into view. One never really leaves places anymore. The whole "I went on a journey far away" yarn doesn't feel quite real. Movement between Moscow and London has become so casual (eight flights a day including budget airlines, with the weekend plane nicknamed "the school bus") that the two cities have become smudged in my mind. I walk into an underpass by Hyde Park Corner and emerge out on the Boulevard Ring and see many of the same faces I just saw off Piccadilly. Turn the corner of Prospekt Mira, and I am back walking along the Thames.

My daughter already finds these jump cuts between countries normal. Sometimes she likes to play a game in which she divides her face into the identities she gets to toy with: "This half of my face is Russian—and this half English. My cheek Jewish. My ear belongs to London and my mouth to Moscow, but I'm keeping my eyes for . . ." And then she starts to laugh. Already a child of the great Offshore? And what will it turn out to be like? *Almost Zero*? The Street-of-All-Fridays?

And before I know it this trip will be over and I'll be back in London, on my way to another of Grigory's Midsummer's Night parties, which he hosts in both Moscow and London now. It's at the Orangerie in Kensington Palace. I try to get a costume at the last minute, but by the time I call the stores, all the Midsummer's Night costumes in central London are already gone. I make myself a lame garland out of flowers plucked from some gardens near the subway. I'm running late, and for some reason I assume the entrance will be from the Knightsbridge end of the Palace, but then when I cross the park I'm told I have to go round to the other, Queensway, side. There's no clear path, it's getting dark, and I get lost. I'm scrambling through hedges and thorns, then turn off somewhere and find myself on the edge of Kensington Palace Gardens, which is the most expensive street in London, and the guards by the high gates are looking at me strangely. Then I'm back in the park, my trousers smeared with dirt, and hear the music and finally emerge by the right entrance. There's a spiked black rail and a bouncer and a woman dressed as the god Pan with a guest list on her iPad. Beyond the gate I can see elf-girls in high heels and Queens of the Night in shining gowns, all talking in many languages and all disappearing beyond the corner of the palace to the party proper, which I can hear but can't quite see. I say my name, but I'm told it isn't on the guest list, and I'm late, and they won't let me in. I try texting Grigory, but of course he must be busy with his guests and doesn't answer. And I lean over the rail as far as I can go, with the blunt tips digging into my stomach, one hand holding my garland to my head, craning my neck to see if I can somehow catch a glimpse of him.

ACKNOWLEDGMENTS

This book wouldn't have been attempted without Paul Copeland, and it couldn't have been completed without his generous help. He has taught me new meanings in friendship. I am always indebted to my parents, with this book more than ever, and to Aunt Sasha for being our guardian angel. I would like to thank Daniel Soar and Mary-Kay Wilmers at the *London Review of Books*, who gave me a chance; Tunku Varadarajan and Tina Brown for giving me some more; my agent and publishers; and Ben Judah, for the last-minute read-through. Also my producers at TNT: both for letting me make some exciting projects and for showing grace and kindness when I failed.

EXTRA READING

The biography of Surkov was informed by Zoya Svetova's "Who Is Mr. Surkov?" in *New Times Magazine* (December 26, 2011).

Alena Ledeneva's *Can Russia Modernise?* (Cambridge University Press, 2013) provides context for the battles among various Russian security agencies and "reiding."

Yana Yakovleva published her book of prison letters, Неэлектронные Письма (Праксис, 2008).

A detailed account of architectural destruction in Moscow can be found in "Moscow Heritage at Crisis Point," updated edition (SAVE Europe's Heritage, Moscow Architectural Preservation Society, 2009).

Vitaly Djomochka's latest novel is Газовый Кризис 2 (Gas Crisis 2) (Зебра Е, 2010).

Credit: Natasha Belauskine

Peter Pomerantsev is an award-winning contributor to the *London Review of Books*. His writing has been published in the *Financial Times, NewYorker.com, Wall Street Journal, Foreign Policy, Daily Beast, Newsweek,* and *Atlantic Monthly*. He has also worked as a consultant for the EU and for think tanks on projects covering the former Soviet Union. He lives in London.

PublicAffairs is a publishing house founded in 1997. It is a tribute to the standards, values, and flair of three persons who have served as mentors to countless reporters, writers, editors, and book people of all kinds, including me.

I. F. STONE, proprietor of *I. F. Stone's Weekly*, combined a commitment to the First Amendment with entrepreneurial zeal and reporting skill and became one of the great independent journalists in American history. At the age of eighty, Izzy published *The Trial of Socrates*, which was a national bestseller. He wrote the book after he taught himself ancient Greek.

BENJAMIN C. BRADLEE was for nearly thirty years the charismatic editorial leader of *The Washington Post*. It was Ben who gave the *Post* the range and courage to pursue such historic issues as Watergate. He supported his reporters with a tenacity that made them fearless and it is no accident that so many became authors of influential, best-selling books.

ROBERT L. BERNSTEIN, the chief executive of Random House for more than a quarter century, guided one of the nation's premier publishing houses. Bob was personally responsible for many books of political dissent and argument that challenged tyranny around the globe. He is also the founder and longtime chair of Human Rights Watch, one of the most respected human rights organizations in the world.

•   •   •

For fifty years, the banner of Public Affairs Press was carried by its owner Morris B. Schnapper, who published Gandhi, Nasser, Toynbee, Truman, and about 1,500 other authors. In 1983, Schnapper was described by *The Washington Post* as "a redoubtable gadfly." His legacy will endure in the books to come.

Peter Osnos, *Founder and Editor-at-Large*